# WHO'S YOUR DADDY?

# WHO'S YOUR
# DADDY?

## LIFE IS A CHOICE

TANIA HOYT JENSEN

Palmetto Publishing Group
Charleston, SC

*Who's Your Daddy?*
Copyright © 2018 by Tania Hoyt Jensen

First Edition

Printed in the United States

ISBN-13: 978-1-64111-093-8
ISBN-10: 1-64111-093-7

# DEDICATION

This book is in loving memory of my parents, Richard and Phyllis Hoyt, who were the most amazing parents and an amazing team. Their lives inspired me growing up, as it still continues to amaze and inspire me to this day. My father always said that life is a choice. We can choose to let life pull us down or we can choose to rise above. I hope you find the Hoyt's story as heart wrenching and as fascinating as I always have.

Also dedicated to:
Amanda, my beautiful daughter
Michelle, my beautiful little sister
Philip, my older brother
Terri, my best friend
Sami, Evyn & Perry, my nieces and nephew
Auntie Tootsie, Auntie Dotty, and Aunty Lolly

Grammar and Punctuation Editor: Kelly Wylie
Content Editor: Vanessa Brookman
Special Thanks to Ric Drasin and Inna Tuler for the Title
Special Thanks to Dennis Merritt Jones, my father's friend,
for his guidance on publishing.
Special Thanks to my cousin, Ellie Foster who helped me fill in
information about my paternal grandmother, Julia Mahoney.
Special Thanks to my husband, John Jensen, for allowing me to
slow down enough to write this book.
Special thanks to Kelly Wylie, who encouraged me to dig deeper,
add more details, and to expand on each topic. Thank you as well
for your time and energy in assisting me in my new endeavor.
Special thanks to Vanessa Brookman, who also utilized her free time
and energy to assist me in my new endeavor.

# TABLE OF CONTENTS

# CHAPTER 1

# DOOMED

It was a cold, dark day on November 15, 1929 in College Point, Long Island, New York, when Charles Edward Hoyt Jr. and Julia Mahoney gave birth to a baby boy who they named Charles (Charlie) Joseph Hoyt, a boy who was doomed from the start. The economy was in the midst of a depression, as were Charles and Julia, who already discovered that their marriage was on shaky ground.

Charles Hoyt Sr. was born December 10, 1898 in New York. Charles ranked as a 3rd Class Fireman in the US Navy from 1918-1920 until he was Dishonorably Discharged, reason unknown. While in the Army, Charles took up boxing. Boxing was how he entertained himself while enlisted and was how he proved himself and his manhood. Soon after his discharge, Charles married a 19-year-old gal named Elise E Schlathaus. He chose to lie on the marriage certificate stating he was 23 years old, when in fact he was 26 years old. She had no idea at the time that he lied to her about his age. Charles and Elise were married in 1925 and divorced shortly thereafter.

When Charles, a 30-year-old Irish man, standing no taller than 5'8", met Julia Mahoney, a 22-year-oldsassy, seductive young lady, sparks flew. The two were married by 1928. Charles was a fair skinned, good looking man, with blond hair and blue eyes, what he lacked in height, he made up for in attitude. He drove a meat truck by profession.

Julia Mahoney was born April 13, 1906 in New York City. Julia was one of four kids: James, Julia, Arthur, and Thomas. Julia's father, James Mahoney, died in 1913 when she was only seven years old. Her mother, Harriet then married a man who was much younger than she. Julia and her three brothers were not happy with their step-father; he treated all of the kids poorly and they hated him. In 1918 the great flu pandemic swept over all of the Mahoney kids. After the Flu, Julia's younger brother, Arthur, contracted Polio and his legs were never the same again. Julia took great care of her little brother as he struggled to use his legs in his youth. Julia was a beautiful, fair skinned, blue eyed, Irish gal with short, dark hair, and was ready to break free.

Like Charles, Julia also had a prior marriage, which was uncommon at the time, to a man by the name of Edward P. Kaufman. The two were married on September 4, 1926 in a Boro Hall, Corona, Queens, New York. Shortly thereafter, the two divorced. A woman had it rough if she wanted a divorce, she needed to find another man to support her. Julia met Charles Edward Hoyt. They met at a local pub, and would soon settle into a small apartment in College Point, Long Island.

***

Charles Joseph (Charlie) Hoyt was a growing and energetic Irish boy, trying to make it in a rough neighborhood on 123rd Street in Long Island, New York. The streets were filled with bi-level and tri-level apartment buildings and low income families. Their building was in the middle of the block, the street split, going around the building, then merged back together and continued on. Their building looked different from the rest; it was an all brick building and stood about five stories high. Buildings small and tall surrounded the area. The "backyards" were more like alley ways and only concrete front sidewalks lined the streets. When you stepped outside the front door of the building, there was a small porch, which included a few steps to get to the street level, and BAM, there you were, on the sidewalk. If you looked up into the sky, there were electrical wires all overhead. There was a wire coming from each apartment building which all came together at one junction, a wooden pole at the end of the block. The pole was actually tilted slightly from all of the overloading of wires. There was only one tree on the entire block.

Charlie was used to his Mom and Dad arguing all of the time. Mom was always mad because Dad was always out and about, gallivanting around town. Julia and young Charlie never knew when Dad would come stumbling in the door. Julia went from an asshole step-father, to another asshole husband. Some people find it hard to break the pattern when that is all they know. Sometimes Charles wouldn't make it home for dinner and when he did finally stumble in, he would be drunk. Charlie heard his Mom crying often, and watched her drink more and more drowning her sorrows. Julia was sinking into the doom of depression: her father died when she was a kid, her step-father was an asshole, her first marriage failed miserably, and her second marriage wasn't looking so great either. Julia was having a hard time remaining hopeful.

In January of 1933, Julia's brother Arthur married a woman named Eleanor; Charles and Julia were witnesses to this marriage. Arthur and Eleanor Mahoney would share living quarters with Charles, Julia and Charlie, until the newlyweds could stand on their own two feet. Of course, this living arrangement took off some financial strain for the Hoyt's and gave Charlie a break from his miserable parents. Eleanor observed Julia absconding through periodic spells of not speaking to anyone, nor would she look Eleanor in the eyes. Eleanor thought Julia was angry with her for some reason, little did she know the inner turmoil Julia was going through. Julia was not angry with Eleanor. Julia was troubled by her own thoughts, by her deepening depression, some days were worse than others, and on occasion she was very sociable. By 1934 Arthur and Eleanor were pregnant with a baby girl and would move out to work on their own family unit.

Julia and Arthur Mahoney, 1933

The Hoyts went to church every Sunday. Church was a great way to ask for forgiveness and sweep away all of their sins from the week. Charlie would put on his Sunday best and accompany his parents to the church where all his Irish friends would be with their families. Charlie was confirmed as a Christian as a young boy.

Charlie was a cute Irish kid; fair skin, piercing blue eyes, and blond, curly hair. He had several friends in the neighborhood he called his pals, but Blackie was his best friend. He lived in the same building as Charlie. Blackie was just a bit taller than Charlie, and had dark wavy hair. There was also Don who was the same height as Charlie and had red hair and freckles across his nose. And finally there was Sambo, taller than the rest and had dark hair. All four of the boys were fair skinned; it was a predominantly Irish neighborhood. The four of them palled around day in and day out.

Charlie Joseph Hoyt, 1938

Charles Sr. kept up with his boxing after leaving the army. Instead of going to the gym to keep up on his boxing skills, he had a son to practice on. Why did he need to go to the gym? Isn't that what a son was for? Sure it is! That is how you toughen up your boys; by playing rough. He was not raising a sissy boy. Charles repeatedly "played rough" with Charlie, using him as his sparring partner and his own personal punching bag.

On a typical day after supper and after his Dad and tossed back a few drinks:

Charles: "Hey Charlie, (he'd say in his thick Long Island accent), come on over here and learns to fight like a man."

Charlie would only briefly hesitate. He knew there would be consequences either way. If he didn't endure the beating now, he would endure a beating later for disobeying.

Charles: Already annoyed, "Come on Charlie! What's wrong? You scared you little punk?"

Charlie: "No. I'm not scared."

Charles: "Then what the hell is your problem? Get your ass over here and put 'em up!"

Charlie would obey and dreadfully cross the room to stand in front of his father. Charlie instinctively put his fists up attempting to protect his face from his father's blows, unsuccessfully of course. Charlie's little fists couldn't possibly defend him against a grown man's fists, the fists of his father. Charlie was just a child. Charlie endured the blows until his father was satisfied with their sparring. Eventually, Charlie learned how to bob and weave to avoid the blows however this seemingly made Charles Sr. even angrier. Charles Sr. retaliated, the next punch more unyielding than the last. Charlie dreamed about responding with a punch so great that it would knock his father on his ass and he would not dare ever lay a hand on him again, but this was just a fantasy. Charlie was afraid to throw his own blows in fear that his father would retaliate with an even fiercer vengeance. He learned to defend himself instead by taking a punch.

Following a sparring session with his father, Charlie would be questioned by his pals when they would meet at the pole to walk to school. "Gee Charlie, What the hell happened to you?" Charlie most often was decorated with a bruised eye or cheek bone, or maybe a busted and swollen lip, there was always a mark. Charlie would squash their questions by responding, "Nothing happened. I'm fine. Don't worry about it." After a while, they all knew what was happening and the questions ended. Not like it was abnormal to see him bruised, nor was it unusual to see any of the neighborhood kids with an occasional bruise from a smack down by their fathers.

Charlie's best friend, Blackie, was always concerned, but a guy can't show any signs of emotion around his buddies or he would be teased and called a sissy.

Blackie: "Hey Charlie, what happened to your face? You run into a doorknob or your Dad's fist again?" He would say as he laughed.

Charlie: "Shut the fuck up, Blackie! I'm fine!" He would shout as he looked away into the distance with a stone cold look on his face. Charlie learned to be tough at a young age; if he didn't talk about it, it didn't happen. He didn't want to talk about it anyway. Boys don't talk about their feelings. Charlie had to prove that he was not a wuss to the kids at school. He could take a beating, and he did. This was his life. Charlie learned to keep it all inside. He learned how to act tough. As he learned to be a tough guy on the outside, inside he was a wreck. He began to wear a face of stone. In fact, Charlie earned the nick name "Stoneface", from his pals

❋ ❋ ❋

Julia was always drunk and she was always depressed. There was always an argument with her husband, a fight, tears and trauma. Julia spent a lot of her time frequenting the bars while Charles was out driving his meat truck and/or out gallivanting around town doing who knows what. She could only imagine what he was doing, and that depressed her even more. Getting lost in the bottle seemed like a good resolution.

Charlie was often left alone while both his mother and father were out getting drunk and screwing around on each other. Charlie had free reign of himself; he took to the streets quite often to hang out with his friends, often finding many ways to cause a ruckus. Most often, Charlie had to find his own dinner too, or rather steal his dinner. No one was home to take care of him, so he did what he had to do to take care of himself.

When Charles Sr. was not using little Charlie as a punching bag, he was out driving his truck, or hitting up the pub on the corner. Charles Sr. would have extra marital affairs on a regular basis. There was also another disturbing aspect of this double life, his extra marital affairs were not always consensual, nor was it always with an adult.

One particular night it seemed just like any other dysfunctional night at first…

From Charlie's point of view:

It was a Friday night, December 4, 1937. My mom was passed out drunk and my dad was out of the house doing whatever he did on the nights he came home late; typical. I had just turned eight years old in November. Even at such a young age, I had to take care of my mom. I was too young to carry her to bed yet, so I would cover her with a blanket where she laid passed out on the couch, in a chair, on the floor, or wrapped around the toilet bowl. After I "tucked" my mother in, I went to bed. My dad wasn't home yet.

I had no idea how long I was asleep, but I awoke startled from some kind of loud noise. I then heard my dad come crashing into the apartment, out of breath and cursing up a storm. I lay as still as possible trying not to even breathe. I didn't want my Dad to come in my room and take his rage out on me. I did not know what time it was because I was afraid to move a muscle to look at the clock on the nightstand. I heard the clock ticking, or was that my heart I heard beating out of my chest? I heard Dad crashing around for a couple of minutes and then there was silence. Whew! He must have passed out. I fell back asleep. Not more than a couple of hours went by and another rude awakening.

There was a forceful knock at the door! BAM BAM BAM, followed by a man shouting, "Open the door! It's the police!"

Charles was panic stricken, thrashing about the apartment attempting to either hide or flee, not sure which. Julia answered the door in her robe and the police men entered the apartment. The Police struggled with Charles for several minutes as my father cursed them and struggled in their grip. The police finally detained him, had him face down on the floor with a knee in his back to keep him from fleeing. I watched as the police cuffed my dad and read him his rights. They arrested him. As it turns out, my Dad was a pedophile; he attempted to rape a young girl in the bushes near Grand Central Parkway.

The Long Island Daily Press reported on Saturday, December 4, 1937:

*"MAN ARRESTED AS ATTACKER"*

*A College Point truck driver, father of a 7-year-old son, was arrested last night on a charge of attempting to attack a 10-year-old Flushing girl in Cunningham Park, Hollis.*

*The prisoner is Charles Hoyt, 39, of 123rd street, who drives a meat truck.*

*Hoyt, arraigned today before Magistrate Gustav Wieboldt in Ridgewood felony court, pleaded not guilty and was held on no bail for a hearing on Wednesday.*

*He was seized at his home at 8 pm after Detectives Andrew McElligott and Theodore Burger of the Jamaica Squad questioned the child.*

*She told police that the man who tried to attack her had picked her up at 61st Avenue and 159th Street, Flushing.*

*Patrolman James J. Ryan of Mounted Troop F making his rounds at the park in the vicinity of 210th Street and Grand Central Parkway came upon the child and a man in the underbrush.*

*At the approach of the officer, the man fled, dodging six shots fired by Ryan.*

Another publication from the Long Island Daily Press dated January 7, 1938 read:

*"HOYT GETS JAIL TERM ON MORALS CHARGE"*

*Convicted of impairing the morals of a 10-year-old Flushing girl, Charles Hoyt, 39, who gave his address as 11-41 123rd St., College Point, was sentenced in Special Sessions Yesterday to a "substantial term" in the penitentiary. Court officials said the sentence means Hoyt will serve the maximum of three years for the offense.*

Well, that was that. Charlie and his mother, Julia, would be on their own for the next three years fending for themselves. Gee, this should be fun. Charlie had already been "on his own" so to speak just another day. At least he would not have to endure his father's blows for a while.

Julia was humiliated to say the least; her husband, a convicted pedophile. Julia and Charlie would have to find a new place to live. Julia's younger brother, Arthur, had a friend named George. Julia and George began seeing each other. Julia and Charlie moved into George's apartment around 1939/40. When George and Julia didn't work out, Julia and Charlie moved into a dingy apartment building in Manhattan. The building was brick and was sky high. In fact, all of the apartment buildings surrounding the area were sky high. Their apartment was on the corner of 28th Street and 3rd Avenue. There was a lot more action in this area compared to where he came from. Manhattan wasn't very far from College Point, Charlie and his pals were still able to get together and cause a raucous.

On their own and struggling, Julia would hit the local bars in order to bring in some extra money to support the two of them and in hopes of meeting a new fella. Women typically did not support themselves in this era; very few were independent. She made a buck here and there by getting drunk and dancing on table tops provocatively. The more provocative, the more cash she would collect. Charlie was forced to accompany her many a time.

Julia: "Come on Charlie, Mommy's got to go make some money."

Charlie: "Aw Mom, why can't I just stay home?"

Julia: "Because you are too damn young, that's why!"

Julia would hide Charlie under the table at the bars as she proceeded to make some money. These occurrences continued on a regular basis, Julia did not know how else to make money to support them.

Julia could not make ends meet with her table dancing career, so little Charlie was forced to take to the streets if he wanted to eat. They were hungry; Charlie was hungry. Charlie stole his food.

Charlie's pals were all going through their own rough experiences with their families. Whether that would be alcoholism, verbal abuse, physical abuse, financial struggles and hunger, someone was going through "something" that challenged them to have what one may call "a normal childhood." The kids in the neighborhoods formed their own gangs. Charlie, Blackie, Sambo and Don were tight and ran together on the streets, protecting each other from harm, all the while, possibly causing harm. They played both innocently together and caused a ruckus together. The four of them were also hungry together and learned to steal their food together. They stole cigarettes when they wanted to smoke, snag a bottle of booze from their parents and get drunk, and already knew where they could get their hands on various drugs. They found ways to get what they wanted, when they wanted it.

By nine years old, Charlie was smoking cigarettes. It was easy enough for the kids to smoke; they would steal cigarettes from their parents or steal "loosies" from the corner drug store. Cigarettes were sold loose, out of the pack, and would be placed in a cup on the counter at the liquor stores for a penny each. A penny is a penny, and when you don't have a penny, you do what you have to do, steal it. All they had to do is have one kid distract the cashier, while another stole what they were after.

Typically, Blackie would distract the guy at the register by asking him, "Yo, where do you keep your condoms?"

Charlie would swiftly swipe the cup of "loosies" off of the counter, spin around on his heels and step out the door. Blackie would join him outside and the two would join their pals around the corner.

Julia, too depressed and drunk to take care of herself, let alone her son. Clearly, she did not care about life any longer. She would go through bouts of long silence, too depressed to speak. Seeing his mother smile at this point in their lives was a rarity.

As with other neighborhoods in N.Y., electrical poles lined the streets, each with metal foot pegs for the electric company to be able to climb them. The kids used these poles as their jungle gym. It sure was fun to climb up and jump out towards the street sign that was next to the pole and try and touch it. Charlie would meet his pals by the pole on the corner every day before school so they could walk to school together and then again after supper. The pole was their central meeting point.

Going to school was the worst and Charlie found himself in many fights. He was teased and ridiculed for having pervert of a father. People do not take to that kindly. Kids would call his mother a slut; he would fight to shut them up. Charlie had to fight to protect himself and to prove he was nothing like his father. He vowed never to be like his father, ever. Charlie was filled with constant humiliation; his father was a convicted pedophile and an abuser to both he and his mother. Charlie hated him. His mother was too depressed to participate in Charlie's life.

One day…

Blackie: "Hey Charlie…what the fuck is with your dad?"

Charlie: "Shut the fuck up! I don't want to talk about it."

Blackie: "He's a fucking pervert Charlie? Your dad's a perv?"

Charlie grabbed Blackie by his collar and pushed him back up against a wall. Charlie was about to lose it, with fire in his eyes, he spoke intensely and deliberately, "Fuck you Blackie! I am nothing like him and never will be! Don't you ever mention him again or I will beat the fuck out of you!"

Blackie, attempting to smooth this over as he realizes how much he upset his friend, spoke calmly looking Charlie right in the eyes, "Easy does it Charlie! I know you ain't nothing like your old man. I've got your back, man. It's cool." Charlie felt like a jerk now and carefully let go. They continued on in silence.

Stoneface Charlie reached into his pocket pulling out a pack of cigarettes, flipped open the top, and pointed the pack in Blackie's direction. Blackie helped himself and pulled out a smoke and placed it between his lips. Charlie pulled one out, lit each of their cigarettes with one match, and buried both the pack of matches and the pack of cigarettes deep in his pocket as they proceeded down the sidewalk.

Blackie, Sambo and Don did have Charlie's back and defended him when it was necessary, as they all did for one another in times of trouble. In time, no one fucked with Charlie any longer unless they wanted a beating from each one of his friends.

Julia's depression and alcoholism continued to grow. Every day was a struggle. At nine years old, Charlie walked into the apartment to find the oven door wide open. It was normal when it was cold to heat up the apartment by turning on the oven and leaving it open a crack. But was it normal to find your mother's upper body in the oven while her lower body lay ass up on the floor beside it? No, not so normal. Julia managed to get her body half way in the oven, head first. The apartment was filled with gas fumes and the air was thick. Charlie ran to his mother.

Charlie acted swiftly pulling his mother's limp, drunk body out of the oven. He laid her carefully on the floor near a window. He then proceeded to open all of the windows to let the gas escape and fresh oxygen in. Charlie worked diligently to wake up his passed out mother by shaking her and yelling in her face, "Mom! Mom, wake up! Damnit, please wake up!" This went on for a couple of minutes, but felt like an eternity, she would eventually come to. Charlie held his mother in his arms as the fog wore off and she wept. He released her and slumped back, he was terrified as she lay sobbing. Unfortunately, this became a regular occurrence between him and his mother for the next several years.

Charlie was smitten with a cute, dark haired little Irish girl from his neighborhood. She was tough like the rest of them and would run with Charlie and his gang often. Her name was Mary Theresa Shally, born February 7, 1929; she was several months older than Charlie. They would hang out together, corralling the streets, until they were ready to go home and deal with their families. Home was not where Charlie looked forward to being. Charlie liked hanging with Mary; she helped to take his mind off of his undesirable life. Distractions were life-saving. Although, Mary's family had heard about Charlie and his pedophile father, and they were not pleased that their daughter was socializing with him. They thought he was no good, and definitely wasn't good for their daughter. But Mary liked Charlie. She liked him a lot.

Three years had passed and Charles Sr. had completed serving his prison sentence. When he went in to prison, World War II broke out. When he got out, Charles Sr. re-enlisted in the US Army in 1942, serving in the Navy, leaving Julia and Charlie to fend for themselves yet again, both a blessing and a curse.

Charles Edward Hoyt, pictured top right, 1942

Stereotypically, the Irish are known to drink heavily. Alcohol was a great way to warm up your insides during the cold winters on the East Coast. Julia was a kind woman, but depression and being forced to be a single female raising a child, was not a common occurrence during the mid-1900's. Julia drank for many reasons: she was Irish, to stay warm, and to drown her sorrows. Julia's alcoholism and depression continued to pull her further down into a dark hole. Charlie was becoming accustomed to carrying his mother to bed from wherever it was that she had passed out. Charlie was becoming very strong physically and emotionally, he learned to harden his heart.

It was a cold, wintery day in January, 1945. Living between such tall buildings made it even colder. When the sun could no longer make its way through and between the buildings, it was bitter cold, and if the wind blew, the cold hand of winter would slap you in the face. Charlie was fourteen years old now and had been hanging with his best girl, Mary. He left Mary at the normal parting hour and strutted swiftly down the street headed to his apartment. As he entered the apartment building, he wondered what he would find on the other side of the door tonight. He climbed up the stairway to his floor and as he climbed upward, he could already smell the aroma of gas. Shit. He ran up the stairs and down the long hallway towards his apartment. The smell was becoming stronger as he approached his front door. "Shit, Mom! Not again!" Charlie turned the knob and bolted through the door leaving it wide open for ventilation. There she was, head in the oven again. He darted over to the oven to pull his mother out. The gas fumes were overwhelming; thicker than usual. Charlie turned off the gas and carefully picked up his mother and placed her near the window as usual. When he laid her down, he noticed something was different. Julia was not breathing and her lips were blue.

Charlie: "Damn it Mom, no!"

He immediately began his typical routine of trying to wake his mother up, but this time with urgency he had never felt before. "Mom, please wake up!"

As he cursed and shook her, tried to get her to respond, he checked her pulse. No pulse.

"No Mom. Please don't leave me here alone. Wake up!"

Charlie tilted her head back and attempted CPR.

After several attempts, he realized that he was too late. Julia was not just passed out this time. Who knows how long she had been like this. This time she had finally done it. Julia Mahoney was dead. Charlie bowed his head and sat in silence for a moment before he gently kissed his mother on her forehead.

"Good bye mother."

He refused to cry. Crying was for pussies, that's what his Dad always said. Men did not cry. Charlie gently slid his arms under his mother's dead body and picked her up off of the floor. He then took the longest walk of his life back to his mother's bedroom. Each step he took was with trepidation.

When he stepped into the back bedroom, Charlie found another dead body; that of his mother's boyfriend, Henry Henigman, who apparently passed out and never knew what hit him. The gaseous fumes engulfed the entire apartment and peacefully took his life as he lay passed out in Julia's bed.

Charlie laid his mother on the bed perpendicular to Henry, ever so carefully placing her on her back with her head and upper torso on the bed, and her feet on the ground. She was wearing her underwear and her bathrobe. Charlie made sure the bathrobe covered her undergarments. Charlie took another long look at his mother before he ran out of the apartment never to return. He left the front door open as he ran back down the stairs and out of the building. The fumes escaped the apartment and filled the halls. A resident in the building smelled the gas and called the police. When the police arrived at the residence, the door was still open. They entered the apartment to find Julia and Henry deceased in the back bedroom.

Charlie would accompany his Grandmother Hoyt to the coroner's office to identify his mother's body. Because Julia's husband was serving in World War II, and Charlie was the next of kin, he would have to do the deed.

Charlie and his grandmother were taken to a table where her dead body lay. His grandmother and he stood rigid as the coroner unzipped the body bag. When the bag was opened to expose her pale, grey face, he replied in the stone cold manner in which he had conditioned himself to do, "Yeah, that's her".

As he had done so many times before, he turned off his emotions and left the morgue with his grandmother. Charlie did not want to feel this pain, so he would not, and that was that. No time for sorrow. He would shove his feelings deep down inside. He wondered what would become of him now. Damnit Mom. As he left the building disturbed at the thought of what he was going to do with his life now, he pushed the thoughts aside and walked the streets alongside his grandmother.

Charlie took long, deep drags on his cigarette. He had to come up with a plan. He had to get out of this shithole. He had to get a new life, because this life was bullshit. He was going to make something of himself someday! Charlie made a promise to himself that he was going to get the hell out of this place and as far away from this life as possible!

Julia's brother, Arthur, arranged for the burial and paid for Julia's services. Charlie would stay with his grandmother Hoyt until his father was discharged from his service in World War II.

Charlie took up boxing; imagine that! He did not want to waste those great skills he learned while his dad "sparred" with him. He would train and would soon take on amateur fights in both welter weight and feather weight. Boxing would pass the time as well as teach him how to protect himself on the streets and quite possibly to protect himself from his father. Charlie loved boxing actually; punching the bag helped him with his aggression and the speed bag took skill and focus. He could not focus on much else, but he and that speed bag were one. He would imagine that the bag was his father's head. Additionally, boxers were tough, and Charlie wanted to be tough.

Stoneface Charlie and his pals continued on their self-destructive path on the streets. Blackie, Charlie, Don and Sambo would all partake in doing dope, and when I say "dope" I do not mean marijuana, I mean the heavy stuff, heroine. Blackie took up dealing the dope. Heroine was easy to get on the streets of New York and it was cheap. Getting lit was better than reality. Slamming dope became a way of life for them eventually.

In July of 1945, Charles was (this time) honorably discharged from the US Army and received the Bronze Star for bravery. When Charles got home, he didn't know what to do with Charlie nor did he want him around; he had a new gal, Stella, and Charlie was in the way. Charlie couldn't stand his step mom, Stella, so when they dropped him off and enlisted him in the US Navy at age 16, Charlie was like, "Yeah, well, fuck you too! Who needs you anyway?!" They enlisted him under "Charles Colby Hoyt". Charlie's father lied to get rid of him; lied to the Army about the age of his son. Identification was not required during this era; the government took the parents' word that he was 18 years old.

Charlie didn't make it but a year in the Navy and went AWOL. Charlie was caught and went to prison, he was convicted as an adult, although he still only 17 years old. Charlie's father would not vouch for him; he had no intentions of admitting that he lied about his son's age.

Charlie Hoyt, Enlisted at age 16 as Charles Colby Hoyt, 1945

Charlie spent a year in prison. One afternoon when the guards weren't around, Charlie was in his cell minding his own business when a few men walked in. Charlie had no time to react as they approached swiftly. Charlie had no way of fighting off three grown men; he was just a boy. As rapidly as they crept into his cell, was also how rapidly they came at him. Two of them grabbed each of Charlie's arms and bent his torso over the prison cell sink. The third man yanked Charlie's pants off and let them drop around his ankles. Charlie yelled out and a sock was shoved in his mouth. He wiggled and squirmed trying to break free from their tightening grip. He heard the man behind him unzip his pants. He proceeded to rape Charlie. There was no one there to answer his silent screams. Charlie was helpless. When they were finished, they left his cell and didn't look back. The men never bothered him again. I guess they were the welcoming committee.

# CHAPTER 2

## DICK

Upon release from prison, Charlie went back to Mary's open arms. Charlie and Mary were still smitten on each other. She loved to party, as did he, loved the bad boy and Charlie was a bad boy indeed. Mary had her own family dysfunctions. Mary's family was still not receptive to their relationship. Charlie's dad and step mom could care less about Charlie's relationships. Mary and Charlie had each other to lean on. The more Charlie was with Mary, the less he was at home, which was a win-win for both Charlie, his dad and Stella.

Mary Shally was the oldest of five siblings: John, Patsy, Cathleen, Peggy and Billy. Both of her parents died before Mary was 18 years of age. Mary's father was part of the IRA (Irish Republican Army) and was assassinated by the British Army. Mary's mother, Margaret Magilicutti, died in a car "accident" shortly thereafter; she was run off the road. It was presumed that her "accident" was also the work of the British Army. Mary was in college when her parents passed away. She had to quit school to go home, get a job, and raise her siblings.

Charlie and Mary tied the knot on August 28, 1948; she was 19 years old, he was 18. Charlie's buddy Don was his best man. His buddy Blackie was away in prison for dealing drugs. Sambo was also in and out of prison for robberies and other random offences.

Don, Mary, Charlie (gal next to Charlie, name unknown), 1948

Charlie and Blackie messing around, 1949

Charlie Hoyt, 1949

Sambo, 1948

Blackie, 1949

Don, 1949

Mary and Dick, 1950

By 1950, Charlie did not want to be "Charlie" any longer, nor Charles Jr., he did not want the name of his father in any form. He wanted nothing to do with his father. Charlie went to the court house and legally changed his name; Richard was the name he chose. His new name would be Richard Hoyt. No middle name, no middle initial, just Richard Hoyt. Richard's friends would call him Dick, for short.

At some point, Dick picked up singing; he loved to sing and he was good at it. Dick also had a fascination for acting. He wanted to be an actor, to be anyone else but himself, it was a great escape. He decided to put some serious work in on his voice and his acting skills. Dick's idol was Frank Sinatra; he would hear him on the radio and sing along, imitating his sounds. Dick began taking acting, voice and dance lessons. In theater, it was helpful, and one may have a better chance at the role if they were a triple threat; actor, singer and dancer. He would prove to be pretty good at all of it. Dick sang and danced his way into local theater productions and Summer Stock Theater, which was an intensive summer long theater showcase. Dick loved the theater and aspired to be on Broadway. He was eager to work and eager to escape reality. He would do what every typical starving actor would do, wait tables at various restaurants and flip burgers at the White Castle.

Dick's father, Charles, married Stella in 1947. The couple had a son and named him Douglas Charles Hoyt, born February 16, 1950. Dick was 21 years old by this time and was worried about the life his half-brother Douglas would have, but it wasn't his problem and there was nothing he could do to save his little brother. Dick was already married and out of the house. He would never really know his half-brother Douglas very well.

Dick was a talented individual; he had many creative outlets. He had an artistic hand; Dick loved to paint, finding peace while he poured his heart out on the canvas. Dick's paintings were dark, reflecting his feeling in his life at the time. He painted clowns, sad clowns. Dick allowed his art to speak volumes about the dark place he was living in, without actually speaking a word.

Dick and Mary were drinkers. Ah heck, weren't the Irish ALL drinkers? Both Dick and Mary came from a long line of alcoholics; the Irish drank alcohol like it was water. In fact, I would take a wild stab in the dark and say they drank more alcohol than they did water. Dick and Mary were no different, the two drank together before they were married and would continue on the same path after they were married. It is what they knew, it was normal for them.

Dick desired and pursued his acting and singing career avidly. He was moved by the theater and was begging for the attention he never received as a child. Dick suppressed his dysfunctional childhood by temporarily "being" someone else when he was on the stage. Dick longed for the opportunity to attain the praise and approval of others, it fed his crushed ego. To hear someone say, "Great job, Dick!", was what he fantasized about. He was in need of a pat on the back, something he never had growing up. We all need a good pat on the back.

Top L: Dick, Sambo   Bottom L: (sambo's girlfriend, name unknown) and Mary, 1959

Dick landed many roles. The theater was his passion, the stage was his world. He landed roles in *Show Boat*, *Pirates of Penzance*, *Kismet*, *Can-Can* and performed in various Summer Stock Theater productions, which would bring in money to support Mary and him. He also landed a job as the Ring Master with the Neptune Music Circus. Dick could sing, he could act, and he could dance and therefore, he worked. The more Dick could work, the more able he was to pick himself up out of the dark hole he sometimes fell into. Keeping himself busy was a distraction from his troubled upbringing.

Dick and Mary's marriage was beginning to suffer greatly. They had been trying to conceive a child with no luck. It was beginning to put a strain on their marriage. Mary wanted so badly to have a baby with Dick; she loved him, he was her one true love. Mary was unable to become pregnant.

Broadway: Show Boat, Charlie pictured right (sailor), 1959

Dick began auditioning for television and movie rolls in addition to his work in the theater. He was ready for more. Dick was hungry for work; auditioning for any and all roles he could get his hands on. Dick wanted to be a star! He landed a featured role in a movie, *Song of the Loon*, which happened to be a gay film. It was an acting job and he took it. Beggars can't be choosers, right? The movie was being filmed was being filmed in Nebraska. Dick and Mary's marriage was struggling anyway, so he took the job. He spent the next year living in Nebraska. Mary stayed in New York.

Although Dick was acting, playing a gay man was difficult. Imagine what that may or may not do to a straight man's ego, a straight man who was previously raped in prison. Dick, along with some of the other actors and crew members would go out and hit up the bars after a long day of shooting. In order to shake off the day and to regain and his masculinity, Dick would flirt with the ladies. The ladies just loved him, Dick was handsome and charming. While Dick was on the road, he would have an affair, a year-long affair with a woman he met at the bar. When the movie was finished shooting, his affair was also finished. Dick went back home to New York, home to Mary, she would never know.

When Dick returned home, he returned to Summer-Stock Theatre. The Summer Stock would travel all summer long, from city to city. Dick was on the road frequently, embedding additional stress on the marriage.

Dick had a lot of female attention, not only was he handsome and charming, he was talented. Ladies loved a man that could sing, and Dick was eating up all of the attention. He landed a role in a Shakespeare circuit which performed in many cities, each city, quite possibly a new fling.

Mary had a horrible knot in her stomach each time Dick left. It was breaking her heart not to have trust in his faithfulness. When Dick was gone, Mary worried. When she worried, she would drink more than usual to calm her nerves.

Between their drinking, their lack of conceiving and Dick's plausible infidelity, the couple decided to seek the guidance of a psychiatrist by the name of Dr. Cort Robertson. Dick would also seek private therapy from Dr. Robertson as well, to begin the long process of overcoming his troubled childhood and upbringing, or lack thereof.

Dick did not want to be the kind of person his father was, nor depressed and suicidal like his mother for that matter. Dick found himself depressed often. He felt he was not worthy of being a father. Is it probable that is why Mary could not conceive? Maybe he was not meant to be a father. He had no idea how to be a father, let alone a good one. He was not taught him how to be a decent human. Dick had been flying by the seat of his pants from as far back as he can remember; life was rough from the get go he knew nothing else. Dick was in anguish about his marriage and distress about fatherhood. Dick became engrossed in therapy determined to come out of the dark. Dr. Robertson became a mentor to Dick. Dick's therapy and recovery would be a long road. He was grateful for Cort and held him in high regard. Dick's life was in Cort's hands so to speak.

Even with the guidance of their psychiatrist, Dick and Mary continued to struggle in their marriage. While doing a Shakespeare circuit in Boston, Mary was convinced that Dick was having an affair with a woman in the show. Mary had a friend up in Boston who she asked to check up on him. Mary's friend eventually told her that this other woman was pregnant with Dick's child. The news was devastating to Mary! Although upset and furious with Dick, she loved him, they were childhood sweethearts. And wouldn't you know it, after all the years of trying, Mary had also become pregnant, it was late 1959. They had been married more than eleven years already. Who knows if the woman in Boston was actually pregnant and if Dick had any knowledge, but Mary would give this a shot. She was not about to walk away now, her dream of becoming pregnant had finally come true.

Mary and Dick had a baby boy on September 13, 1960; naming him Philip Cortlan Hoyt. Philip was given the middle name, "Cortlan" after Cort, the couple's psychiatrist, and Dick's mentor.

Dick was still apprehensive about being a father. Was he ready? He was 31 years old, it was not that he was too young to be a father; it was the fear of what may be in his gene pool. Disturbed by the thought of what genes may have been passed on to himself, and what he may have been passed on to his son. He was afraid he would be a horrible father like his own father. He had no good role models and was tormented in his head by his perplexed life.

Dick came to terms with his worst fears when their baby, Philip, was a mere three weeks old; Dick let his frustration with the baby go too far and he lost his temper. Dick confessed to Mary that he had "battered" their three-week-old son. Dick sunk into a depression, he could not forgive himself, he knew what he was capable of doing to his child, could have done to his child. Being unable to control of his anger scared him to the point of wanting to run away. When Philip was a year and a half, Dick knew he could not move past it and he threw in the towel. Mary and Dick split in 1961; they had been married for 13 years. Dick left his child behind and he did not look back.

In 1961 Dick Hoyt moved to Birmingham, Alabama and landed the role of Will Parker in the Broadway production of *Oklahoma*. While in Alabama working on the show, Dick was also able to pick up work as a radio disc jockey. He found he loved being on the radio! He would practice his radio voice and work on speaking clearly, focusing on proper pronunciation and articulation. Dick developed a great, deep, radio voice!

Dick once again, fell in love, with an adorable, dark haired, cutie named Nancy Hardenberg. Nancy was his leading lady who played Ado Annie, in the show. The two became very cozy, so cozy that they got married. (Yes, the same year Dick divorced Mary, he married Nancy.)

Dick and Nancy were a hit in *Oklahoma*! The Birmingham Post reported:

"Doing some show stopping of their own was the comedy team of Nancy and Dick Hoyt as Ado Annie and Will Parker. Their "All or Nothing"," I Can't Say No", and "Kansas City" were exceptional crowd pleasers. The two are "show-stoppers".

Dick and Nancy Hoyt, 1961

The production of Oklahoma would run for a year. When the show ended, so did their marriage.

In 1963 Richard Hoyt decided to leave Birmingham and head for Hollywood to pursue his dream of becoming a star. He also wanted to escape and start anew in California. Dick arrived in Hollywood, and pounded the pavement looking for work, taking all kinds of odd jobs. He bussed and waited tables, parked cars at a beach club, and then some. You name it, he did it.

Dick was able to retain an acting agent in Los Angeles; he had already earned his S.A.G. card while still in New York. Since Dick loved to sing, he pursued local piano bars and lounges for gigs. He was happiest performing. Performing was still a great distraction from real life. When he noticed he had a fan club, he felt good about himself. Dick was a ladies man in New York and he did not leave that behind, the ladies loved him in California as well. They fell in love with his voice, his good looks and his charm.

Dick heard about a local piano bar in Santa Monica called *The Horn*, where all the local talent (anyone who wanted to be someone) frequented this bar in hopes of being signed by an agency and a record deal. Dick earned a spot next to the piano man and would be amongst many other talented performers hand-picked to perform at *The Horn*.

Dick Hoyt, 1963

# CHAPTER 3

# THE PRINCESS

Phyllis Evelyn Iritano was born on a late winter day on March 1, 1936 in east Boston, Massachusetts. Born into a large Italian family, Phyllis was the youngest of six children; she was the baby, the princess. Ana and Joseph Iritano married when Ana was 14 years old and Joseph was 31 years old; it was an arranged marriage. The couple had six children: Katherine (Katie) born in 1923, Grace (Tootsie) in 1926, Dorothy (Dotty) in 1928, Salamander (Sam) in 1930, Lorraine (Lolly) in 1931, and lastly Phyllis in 1936.

Phyllis, the "princess", was given this nick-name by her older siblings. Not only was she five years younger than Lorraine, she was the only child in the family born in a hospital. All of the other five children were born at home with a mid-wife. The youngest siblings, Lorraine and Phyllis, were the only children who were privileged enough to attended private catholic school. The Iritano's were a good Catholic family. Phyllis received her confirmation at age eleven and was confirmed as Rose, after her godmother who was also her Aunt Rose.

Phyllis and her typically large Italian family lived in a tenement building which had only three bedrooms to accommodate the entire family. There was one master bedroom and two rooms for the 6 kids to share. Ma and Pa had the master bedroom, Sam and Uncle Tony, Uncle Tony was Pa's brother who lived with them, shared a room. The final bedroom was shared by the five girls. Katie and Grace shared a double bed on one side of the room. A dresser was placed in the middle of the room. A second bed was placed on the other side of the dresser, in which the three youngest girls shared. Ma had some clever organizational skills; she was able to make the bed, a little wider by placing two chairs at either end of the bed and then placing an ironing board on either end of the chairs for a comfy extension.

Phyllis Evelyn Rose Iritano, 1947

Their maternal grandmother, grandma Fiantaca, lived on the second floor. Across the hall from their grandmother was their cousin's apartment. The Iritano family lived on the third floor. The families were very close knit. Cousin Salve on her mother's side had a piano. Phyllis would frequent Cousin Salve's place to hear him play. She was fascinated and was often mesmerized by her cousin's talent. Phyllis wanted to learn how to play and Cousin Salve would graciously accord her regular lessons. Musical talent ran in the family. Pa played the clarinet until the depression, until he was forced to place his clarinet in hawk.

There was always music on while they were growing up. Pa loved to listen to music on the radio. Lolly and Phyllis picked up singing, Pa loved to listen while they practiced. Phyllis and Lolly, in return, would love to witness their father beaming with pride as they sang.

Phyllis proved to be an excellent pianist, so exceptional that her mother and father invested in a piano for her. Ma and Pa were unable to buy the piano outright, so they financed it. The piano shop just so happened to be down the street and on the way to the furrier where Grace worked. She was the designated family member who would drop off the monthly payment for the financed piano. Grace did this every month until the piano was paid off a year later. Phyllis' piano lessons became more frequent and she took on more challenging projects. She was so exceptional; she was being trained as a concert pianist.

In the year 1949, Lorraine, at age 19, contracted Tuberculosis. Lorraine was sent to live away from the family in quarantine at *Mattapan Sanatorium*. She would be in quarantine for twenty-one long months, until the disease subsided. During this nearly two-year stint in quarantine, Ma would visit with Lorraine daily, Monday through Friday, Ma never skipped a visit. It took Ma an hour and a half to get to the sanatorium each way, which included a bus ride, three subway changes and then a long walk. She always brought a fresh, clean pair of pajamas, a bed jacket and a home cooked meal. Whatever the family was eating, so was Lorraine. Lorraine was very grateful to her mother for showing her such love. The family never verbally said the words, "I Love you", but they knew they were loved because love was shown.

The sanatorium would not release Lolly from the hospital until they knew she would be sleeping in her own bed and not sharing a bed with her sisters. Ma and Pa did not have the money to afford the luxury of a larger home.

Sam had completed one year of college when he was drafted into the military. He served in the Korean War and was stationed in Alaska for four years. He had a G.I. Bill to use when he was ready to purchase a home for himself. Sam proved to be a very selfless son and brother, turning over his G.I. Bill to Ma and Pa who were then able to purchase their own home on Marion Street in Boston.

Katie was already married and out of the house. Sam had a room, Tootsie and Lolly shared a room, each having their own beds, and Phyllis and Dottie shared the couch bed. Remember the television show, *The Walton's?* The end of each episode the family would call out "goodnight Louise, goodnight John boy." Well, the Iritano's had a goodnight ritual as well, although instead of calling out goodnight to each other, they would call out "Bony knock knees!" (Bony knock knees? I guess this was an inside joke, and you had to be there!)

After Lolly's 21-month stay at the sanatorium, she wanted so much to give back, (or pay it forward) she became an employee at the *Mattapan Sanatorium*, where she spent so much time.

The Iritano Kids, 1951
Top: Tootsie and Sam, Middle: Lolly and Phyllis,
bottom: Katie and Dotty

Phyllis was a silly little girl and loved to make Ma laugh. She would put on a fake, Jewish accent when it was windy outside (this was the only time she could pull this off!) and say to her mother, "Vhat a Vind!", all-inclusive with dramatic arm and hand gestures that went along with her thick, dramatic accent. Ma would laugh and then laugh some more. Phyllis would get her every time.

As mentioned, Phyllis attended a Catholic school through high school taught by nuns during a time when kids were "disciplined" with a swat to the back of the hands with a wooden ruler. Phyllis made sure to never cross the nun's. She was a good girl and played by the rules.

Phyllis' life was as normal as normal could get. She was sweet and petite; a very thin little girl. She didn't run around on the streets nor did she have boyfriends. In fact, she didn't even have her first date until she was in her early twenties. She was a good Italian, Catholic girl.

Phyllis was an intelligent young lady; she did very well in school. She kept busy singing and playing the piano. Phyllis was able to further her training on the piano at the Catholic school with the nuns. When she graduated high school, she was on the honor roll. In her year book, she was called out by the nuns as a "delightful" person, "a golden voice with a golden personality to match." Her ambition was to "one day sing with Eddie Fisher."

Dinner time at the Iritano house was plentiful; full house, full table, full of food. There was capacious Italian energy and there was constant chatter at the Iritano dinner table. Like most girls, we want what we don't have. Phyllis wanted blond hair and blue eyes. She thought that is what she needed to be beautiful and to be a star; all the movie stars had blond hair and blue eyes. Pa would tell her if she ate her carrots, her eyes would turn blue and if she ate her tomatoes, her hair would turn blond. Well, she listened to her Pa and she ate those warm carrots and squishy tomatoes time after time, and wouldn't you know it, her eyes never turned blue and the hair, it never turn blond. Not funny Pa, not funny at all!

Phyllis' sister Katie used to ride the street car five days a week to and from work. She worked as a "stitcher" in a factory, stitching together garments and such. When she rode the street car, Katie would sit in the front of the car for an easy exit. This made for frequent conversation with the street car driver, Nick. Nick Cappezzuto fancied her and would brighten up every time Katie stepped on to his street car. Their conversations were frequent and fluent. Nick felt confident enough on one particular evening to ask Katie for her phone number and a date. Katie and Nick would marry in 1949. Katie and Nick would have three children: Eddie born in 1949, Karen born in 1956, and Steven born in 1957.

Grace, aka Tootsie, was an independent woman. She was small and frail on the outside, but a pistol on the inside. If Tootsie had something to say, she would say it. Some people have a hard time with those of us who have no filters on our mouths. She was a tough cookie. She was still working at the furrier, the same place she was working when she would stop in to pay down Phyllis's piano long ago. Tootsie would work in the furrier for her entire career.

Dotty was a hairdresser in Boston. Her older brother, Sam, had a best friend in high school named Pat Candeliere; Dotty was 16 at the time. As adults, Sam and a group of his buddies joined the Y and would go dancing on Saturday nights. Sam had his own pad and would invite his sister, Dotty, to come over now and again. Dotty would stay over, get up in the morning just to make the coffee and set the table for the guys, then go back to bed. Pat was frequently at Sam's house as well, so Dot and Pat's friendship continued. She was under the impression that he just thought of her as Sam's little sister and that's that; never thought anything of it. Pat eventually moved to New Jersey to teach elementary school for 5th and 6th graders. One day, Pat called Dot, and out of the blue, mentioned that his parents were going to drive up to New Jersey to see him, and asked if Dot wanted to come along and ride with his parents. "Eh…sure, why not", Dot thought. She said ok. While there visiting with him and his parents, Pat asked Dotty out for New Year's Eve. It was a love affair from that night forward! The two of them were married; Dotty was 32 years old at the time. She moved to New Jersey and built a life for herself there, the two would not have children. Pat was able to retire from teaching at age 55. He was not old enough to collect social security, so to pick up extra income, Dotty and Pat became very crafty. They invested money and time in handmade crafting and would sell their items at house parties and craft fares. The two were successful enough to make a living

Sam would meet and marry an Irish gal named Joan. You will never guess where the two of them met! It seems to be a common theme here. Yes; you guessed it, The Y. Sam would work in the insurance industry after he served in the Navy. He also served on the Board of Education after moving to Connecticut, and was eventually elected Chairman. Sam and Joan would have four children: Debbie, Diane, Steven and Bobby.

Lolly was out of the house and in college earning her "two year degree" in Business from 1952-55. She focused on medical terminology, intending to pay it forward from the time when she was ill and quarantined as a teenager with TB. She would work at the sanatorium doing medical billing for quite a while. While she was working in the medical field, she would continue to take college courses for fun. In order to pay for her tuition, Lolly worked at the university's she attended. Boston University and Harvard University were amongst some of those colleges. She never would get that college degree, but was continuously enrolling herself in college courses, enjoying the learning process.

For fun, Lolly and her big sister, Katie, would go out dancing at the "Over 25 Club". Lolly absolutely loved ballroom dancing and in 1960 she would get dressed up and put on her 3-inch heels to strut her stuff on the dance floor. Lolly met a man named Leo at this club. She struck up a friendship with and be his dance partner, purely platonic.

Phyllis and Lolly auditioned and booked a singing spot on a local Boston radio station; they were beyond thrilled! Lolly was 23-years-old at this time and Phyllis was 18. Phyllis had a beautiful voice, angelic if you will. She was a kind, gentle, soft spoken gal and her voice matched this sweet energy. She was a shy little girl who came alive when she sang! She hoped the radio station was just a stepping stone for many more singing jobs to come. She still felt she had to strengthen her craft, but Phyllis and Lolly were good enough to attain duets together on the show. Lolly loved to sing, but Phyllis actually wanted to make a career out of it. The radio show would run for an entire year and was called, *Young and Fancy Free*, in Boston, MA. The sisters would take several busses on Wednesday nights to get to the set. Tommi was the director of the chorus of which they sang in; her husband accompanied them on the piano. The group sang songs such as *Over the Rainbow*. Phyllis and Lolly performed a duet to *Anything You Can Do, I Can Do Better*. They were "famous" on the show because they were the only two siblings. Phyllis was always very eager and confident to perform, but Lolly found she was often nervous. They both enjoyed their time performing on the radio; but for Phyllis it was much more

✳ ✳ ✳

It was 1960; Phyllis was 23-years-old and was ready to take her career to the next level. Phyllis felt that Boston was no longer satisfying her desire to sing, it was not the place to be if she wanted to make a career with her voice. She believed Hollywood, California was where she needed to be if she wanted a career in the music industry. Her mind was made up, she would go to Hollywood. The family was not thrilled with her decision to move all the way across the United States by herself. They were very worried, she was young and she did not know anyone in Hollywood. The family rightfully worried, Phyllis however, was excited about the new opportunities that were sure to come her way! After all, anyone who wanted to make it in the entertainment industry went to Hollywood, CA. During this era, the Watts Riots were threatening Los Angeles and its citizens; 34 people killed, 1,032 people injured, a shocking 4,000 people were arrested, and 600 buildings damaged and/or completely destroyed. The family was not keen on Phyllis living in these parts.

Phyllis needed money to be able to move across the United States and she had none. All she had was her dream and her determination. Phyllis went to her sister, Lolly, and asked her for some money so she could chase her dream. Lolly gave her little sister the money, therefore Phyllis packed her bags!

Phyllis did have a cousin who lived out in California, Sam Iritano (yes, the same name as her very own brother). She would make sure to connect with him. Her cousin was the son of her father's twin brother. Cousin Sam was married to Lucille; they had a son named Richard, twins named Barbara and Mary, and finally Cindy, the baby of the family. The Iritano cousins lived in a tiny little town called Simi Valley, CA, about an hour's drive from Hollywood. This was the only comfort her family had, knowing that cousin Sam was in the same state as Phyllis.

Phyllis moved to Hollywood and would stay at the Young Women's Club of America (YWCA). She did not know how to drive. Many people back east did not drive; there was plenty of public transportation. She did a lot of walking since the public transportation in California was nothing like back home. Everything in California was different from back home; culture shock. There was an adjustment period getting accustomed to a new way of life, new streets to learn, a new freeway system, getting acclimated to the climate and the time change. She was about to embark on an entirely new way of life.

Phyllis would eventually land a job working for an insurance company. She was then able to leave the YWCA and rent her first apartment up the street for $25 a month. It was very exciting to be an independent woman! After Phyllis' first few paychecks, she was able to save enough money to purchase her first bedroom set with her hard earned money! Phyllis was feeling like an adult all right, proving to be a very strong, independent young lady out here on her own in California.

Phyllis soon learned the news that her father was suffering from lung cancer. You are never quite ready for the day you receive that dreaded call. That day would come sooner rather than later, he would pass away from the cancer. She flew back to Boston to see her father laid to rest and to support her mother and her siblings. But she wasn't planning on staying; she had a life to build in California and a dream to pursue. Phyllis returned home to Hollywood and went on with her independent life.

Phyllis was a speedy typist, and proved to be a very diligent worker. While she worked at the insurance company by day, she worked on her singing career by night. Phyllis did not feel her name would suffice in the entertainment industry, "Phyllis Iritano" sounded so… so blah, she wanted something catchy… something unique. She needed a stage name. She chose to use all of her initials to come up with her new stage name: **P**hyllis **E**velyn **R**ose **I**ritano, P E R I. Yes, that's it. Phyllis Peri. Phyllis also hated her nose, her Italian nose. The nose had to go as well if she wanted to work in the entertainment industry. Phyllis would get a nose job. Phyllis was also very flat chested, and if she wanted to make it in the business, she felt she also needed some boobs. So she bought herself a new perky silicon pair, size C! In the 60's in show business, a certain "look" was desired, she felt she must follow suit if she wanted to be somebody. Phyllis was stunning and confidently pleased with her new and improved self. Like *A Chorus Line*, "Tits and ass, bought myself a fancy pair, tightened up the derriere, did the nose with it, all that goes with it!" Yup, tits and ass was how this was going to come together.

Phyllis Peri, 1962

By 1962 Phyllis Peri began to frequent a popular piano bar in Santa Monica called *The Horn*. Word on the street was that anyone who wanted to be someone frequented this spot. Phyllis was hoping to get picked up by a talent agent and be signed with an agency.

At the age of 26, Phyllis obtained her driver's license. She also saved enough money to purchase her first car, a used, red, Volkswagen Karmann Ghia, convertible sports car. Santa Monica wasn't that far from her apartment. She used her Thomas Guide map book to find her way around. Phyllis would put on her best outfit several times a week after work and go to *The Horn* in hope of being discovered. She would make sure she was looking impeccable; inclusive with false eyelashes, black eyeliner to accent her big, brown eyes and a fall (fake hair attached to a headband). She slipped on her cool, cat eye sunglasses and walked down the sidewalks of Santa Monica headed for the club. Her high heels would make 'click clack' sounds on the pavement beneath her feet as she strutted her stuff. Phyllis was stunning, time for others to take notice!

Sam Iritano, Phyllis' cousin in California, was an amazing guitarist. Musical talent clearly ran in the Iritano genes. Sam made his living with his guitar, accompanying many artists in the studio. Now that she had a car and a driver's license, Phyllis would take the hour drive down to Simi Valley on the weekends to spend time with her cousin Sam, his wife, Lucille, and their family. During her visits, Phyllis and Sam would have little jam sessions, she would sing and he would accompany her. She was very interested in this instrument- the guitar. Phyllis bought one and Sam provided her with lessons. Phyllis would visit with Sam and Lucille often. Sam and Lucille were family and she was happy to have them around to remind her of the comforts of home. Phyllis and Lucille would become very close friends.

Towards the end of 1962 and after work one evening, Phyllis received a phone call from her sister Lolly who was in a bind, she was pregnant. She was pregnant and unmarried. Although she was a 32-year-old woman at the time, this kind of predicament was unacceptable. Lolly felt strongly that this was an embarrassment to her family; to her mother. It was shameful. A proper lady did not get pregnant until they were married. Lolly could not shame the family. Lolly asked if she could come to California and stay with her so she could have her baby in secrecy.

Lolly and Leo, who had previously met dancing at the *Over 25 Club* back in 1960, had only had a few friendly encounters. When her Pa passed away, Lolly was in mourning and would not go out dancing for a few months. When she was finally ready to go out dancing, she spotted Leo there with a red head; Lolly surprised herself, she was jealous. Leo happened to spot Lolly in the crowd and crossed the room to say hello, regardless of the fact he was with the red-haired woman. Leo would be so engrossed in conversation with Lolly; he never left her side that night. I guess the lady with the red hair was not so attached. Leo reminded Lolly of her father, a quiet, gentle man, also an intelligent man and she was keen on him leading a book discussion group. The two fell in love and conceived.

Naturally, Phyllis agreed to have Lolly stay with her. Lolly and Leo chose to give the baby up for adoption, they saw no other way around it. Lolly would not shame the family and she did not want to be forced to marry because she was pregnant. This was going to work. Lolly would be able to be pull this off. Leo would stay back east during Lolly's trip; they didn't want the family to question her traveling to California with a man. Still in college at the time of her pregnancy, she would put that on standby for now. Lolly flew to California. She was surprised to find that the apartment building on Curson Street that Phyllis lived in, was pink. A pink building; well isn't that a hoot? It was an interesting neighborhood in Los Angeles, very flamboyant. The Princess living in Los Angeles, it was surreal. Lolly was grateful for her little sister.

Lolly stayed with Phyllis until the baby was born and gave it up for adoption. Lolly's secret was safe with Phyllis and she knew it. Giving up this baby was the most difficult act she would ever encounter in her 32 years of living. Giving her baby to another family did not sit well with her; she was distraught. Lolly continued to stay with Phyllis and continued on her previous mission to pursue her college degree. Lolly had a hard time with this adoption and a hard time leaving California, the state where her child was born, therefore Lolly would stay in Los Angeles for now and enroll in classes at UCLA. She knew she could not be with her baby, but she would be near. As she did previously at other Universities, Lolly would work for UCLA in exchange for her tuition. She would also at times just audit classes. Lolly loved school and learning but Ma was upset that she would only audit classes. She did not understand the point of an audit. Her Ma wished she would pursue a degree.

Phyllis and Lolly used to frequent *The Horn* together at night. It was fun and exciting hanging out there. Lolly thoroughly enjoyed accompanying her little sister. Phyllis was always anxious for her turn to sing! The way it worked at was that all of the local talent hoping to be discovered would wait for an opportunity to sing at the Piano Bar. Apparently not just any-one could get in, this was not karaoke night. Phyllis would not only get in, she would also prove to have a voice that people wanted to listen to. Lolly was proud to be a part of this experience, it was an exciting time! Phyllis made a friend at *The Horn*, Jim Neighbors, who also performed at *The Horn* in hopes of being discovered. Jim and Phyllis were good friends and shared a table together, each awaiting their shot at fame. Many talent scouts fre-quented this club as it was the hot spot and the best talent performed here. When Lolly accompanied Phyllis to *The Horn*, she felt honored to have the opportunity to hear her sister sing as well as the opportunity to meet new friends; she was enjoying Los Angeles. Phyllis, Jim and Lolly would occa-sionally meet for lunch and/or coffee, their friendship would not be exclu-sive to *The Horn*. Jim was eventually discovered while performing at *The Horn*. He would go on to become a successful tenner and then a very suc-cessful actor. Jim starred on the Andy Griffith Show and then would move on to have his own sitcom television show called "Gomer Pile", amongst many other credits.

After her friend Jim was discovered, Phyllis met another young man one night at *The Horn*, he too an ambitious singer. The two of them eventually became singing partners and began to book local gigs singing together. He was tall, dark and handsome and much younger than Phyllis but they had the same goal in mind, to become "somebody", so they joined forces. His name was Rob Kaiser; for his stage name he chose to be called Beau Kazer. Phyllis was in her later twenties now and Beau was probably a wee nineteen years old. The two had no love interest, but were a cute singing duo, suiting up in corduroy, like the hippies that they were. Phyllis was gorgeous! She grew her hair long; it was thick, dark hair that flowed down her back, all the way to her bottom. Phyllis and Beau both played the guitar and both sang. Phyllis Peri was making a life for herself in Hollywood, California.

Phyllis Peri and Beau Kazer, 1969

Beau Kazer and Phyllis Peri, 1969

# CHAPTER 4

# LOVE AT FIRST SIGHT

Phyllis Peri always walked into *The Horn* looking her best; excited to sing! When she entered the club tonight, she noticed a new talent. A mysterious man, that she had not yet had the pleasure of meeting. This mystery man was a handsome fellow, dressed sharp and looking fine. He was fair skinned with blond hair and piercing crystal blue eyes. Phyllis noticed him staring at her, he would not take his eyes off of her. She had never been in the presence of any man who looked at her that way. She was flattered. She shyly looked away and walked over to her usual table to await her chance to sing with the pianist.

Although she was 28, Phyllis Peri had little experience with men; in fact she was a virgin. Phyllis was a proper young lady from a proper family, and a proper girl did not have sex prior to marriage. Phyllis was a classic beauty and a class act! She was flattered at the attention she was drawing now that she had a new nose and an enhanced set of breasts. Week after week, Phyllis found herself running into this mystery man at *The Horn*. When it was her turn to perform, he was so focused on her. Phyllis approached the piano, leaned over slightly to let the pianist to let him know which song to play. He played the introduction as Phyllis sang *Go Away Little Boy*, which was originally titled, "Go Away Little Girl". The song was written by Gerry Goffin and Carole King, one of Phyllis' idols. The song was recorded by Bobby Vee in 1962. When she performed, she came alive with passion. Richard had just heard the voice of an angel. Phyllis was equally impressed with his performance of *Wonder Why*. His big energy and his Frank Sinatra-like voice drew her in. *Wonder Why* was a song from the movie, *Rich, Young and Pretty*, starring Jane Powell and Vic Damone. *Wonder Why* reached number 21 on the music charts in 1951 and was nominated for an oscar for Best Song in 1952.

After weeks of silent flirting and exchanged glances, the mystery man approached her and introduced himself, "Hi. I'm Richard Hoyt, Dick for short.", as he gently reached for her hand and delicately kissed it while never taking his blue eyes off of her big brown eyes. The two had small talk at first and then time after time, their conversations began to deepen. Phyllis and Richard began to support each other in their performances every week…same time… same place.

Phyllis was fascinated by his charm and intrigued by his life's stories. It appears that this guy had it pretty bad. She was also very flattered at how much time and effort he put in to getting to know her. Richard was fascinated by her confidence, the strength in her performance, by her sweet nature and her radiating beauty. She was amazing; he had never met anyone like her. Richard was attracted to fair skinned, dark haired girls and she was right up his alley.

Dick had his own fan club for sure; the ladies loved him. Prior to meeting Phyllis, Dick would take a lady out for a coffee or a drink, depending on which way he was hoping the relationship would go, or not go. Dick asked Phyllis out for a drink. Although Phyllis did not drink, she accepted his invitation.

Word got around that Dick was keen on Phyllis and some of his lady fans were envious, some were jealous. Some were shaking their heads thinking she was just another fool in love and she better keep her guard up with this guy because he was a player. Most women did not think of Dick as a commitment kind of guy.

In 1963, Dick and Phyllis began dating officially. Phyllis found Richard to be charming, he made her laugh and he made her feel beautiful. Isn't that what every girl wants? They would walk down the streets and Richard would sing Frank Sinatra songs to Phyllis, "You make me feel so young, you make me feel there are songs to be sung". He never missed an opportunity to break out in song. "The best is yet to come and babe won't it be fine". Phyllis was flattered by all of his attention.

Dick Hoyt, 1963

Phyllis Peri, 1963

Lolly and Phyllis were still living together, Lolly's room was under the staircase and Phyllis had her room upstairs. Lolly did not see Dick very often because they typically came home from *The Horn* late at night, and Lolly was already in bed. Phyllis was still performing with her partner, Beau and began performing duets with Dick. Dick found himself falling head over heels in love with Phyllis. He had met a living angel.

After a performance one evening, and upon return to Phyllis' apartment, as they walked through the threshold, Dick leaned towards Phyllis and ever so delicately kissed her. He pulled back to admire her beauty and breathe in her innocence as he looked deep into her big brown eyes. Dick swept her off of her feet and carried her off to the bedroom. Phyllis worried about her sister, Lolly, downstairs. Dick put his finger to her lips and whispered, "Shhhh", and then kissed her passionately. Phyllis gave herself and her virginity to Dick on this beautiful evening, un-protected.

Phyllis skipped her period the next month, she was typically very regular. She feared the worst and went to the county doctor to see what was wrong. Phyllis was pregnant. This cannot be happening. Is it? She was beside herself. This just happened to her sister. How could this be the same predicament she now found herself in? Phyllis was pregnant and unmarried, just like her older sister Lolly. How on earth was she going to explain this to her family back east? Just as Lolly felt, this would be an embarrassment to the entire family, but especially for her mother. Times were far different in the 60's. Phyllis was raised to be proper and proper young ladies did not have sexual relations with men before marriage! She wanted a do-over! Lolly did not want to shame the family, nor did Phyllis. Abortion was on her mind, but was illegal. In order to have an abortion, one had to go to Tijuana, Mexico. Phyllis would not risk an abortion, nor did she really consider that to be an option. Phyllis could not tell anyone, except for Lolly, of course. The rest of the family must never find out. Considering they were on the other side of the United States, hiding her pregnancy would not be a problem, just as it had not been for Lolly. She knew her sister would not say a word because she had already been through the same predicament. Phyllis prepared herself for a talk with Lolly.

Lolly came home from work one evening to find Phyllis crying and pacing about.

Lolly asked Phyllis, "Are you alright? What is wrong?"

Phyllis blurted out through her tears, "You have to move out!"

Lolly was confused. She asked Phyllis, "Why?" Shaking her head and in shock, "I don't understand! WHY?"

Phyllis screamed through her tears, "Can't you see?"

Lolly, "See what?"

As Phyllis pointed towards her mid-section, "Can't you see? I'M PREGNANT!"

Phyllis was hysterical and ran out of the room crying, leaving Lolly standing there in complete shock and bewilderment. No. No, she couldn't see. She did not "see" that her little sister was pregnant. Phyllis was so petite, she didn't show. Lolly still did not understand why Phillis had asked her to leave. Did Dick have something to do with this? Was Dick moving in? Even if he was, he would share a bedroom with Phyllis, right? Lolly was hurt and perplexed.

Lolly moved out. She did not question Phyllis any further and respected her request to move out of the apartment on Curson St. They never discussed their feelings; they were not raised to. In fact, Phyllis and Lolly would not speak again for many years. And they would never again speak of this.

Respectable girls didn't live with men, but considering the situation she would have to make the exception and take it another step further. Dick moved in, into the pink, round building on Curson Street.

Phyllis' mother, Ana Iritano, was appalled when she learned of her youngest daughter moving in with a man! Little did she know it was due to her pregnancy. Dick was seven years Phyllis' senior, twice divorced, and a son back in New York, whom he had no relationship or contact with him. According to most people at this point, it was a sin to be living together as man and woman and not be married. But it was the 60's, and this was Los Angeles, things were done a little differently here than back in her hometown of Boston.

When Ma would call to speak with Phyllis, if Dick answered, "CLICK", was the sound the phone made when she hung up. Her mother was astonished that Phyllis, her princess, was living in sin with a man and refused to speak with Dick. Phyllis always knew the hang up was her Ma and would call her back. Her family was not thrilled about her relocation down to Hollywood to begin with, let alone that she was now living with a man, in sin. God forbid they know she was also pregnant!

Phyllis was not ready to marry Dick. Phyllis recognized that Dick was a party guy, a ladies man and was pretty unstable. She knew about his past, she knew he struggled with depression, and knew of his severe family dysfunction. She did not know if this was the man she was going to marry. Phyllis did not want to marry Dick just because she was pregnant; she was too independent for that. This was not how she imagined her life. This was not how she wanted to start a family.

Phyllis and Dick decided she would have the baby and give it up for adoption. Phyllis hid her pregnancy from the world which was easy considering she only gained 15 pounds, and life went on as usual. Phyllis continued to perform at *The Horn* with Dick and she also continued to perform with her singing partner, Beau. Beau would eventually land a reoccurring, starring role as "Brock Reynolds" on *Young and the Restless*. Life continued.

Someone, somehow, suspected that Phyllis was pregnant. "Someone" meaning a past lady friend of Dick's; a "fan" he had taken out for coffee that used to come to *The Horn* as an audience member on occasion. This woman had since married and was having trouble conceiving. She noticed something different about Phyllis. Although Phyllis took great measures to hide her pregnancy, this woman was suspicious. Since it was out of the norm to have a child out of wedlock, the woman decided to have a private investigator follow Phyllis and Dick to find out what their plans were for their baby. Upon learning Phyllis and Dick were to be giving their baby up for adoption, this woman and the investigator made sure that SHE was the one who would adopt it. Phyllis delivered a baby girl on May 4, 1964 at St John's Hospital in Santa Monica, "Baby Iritano" was the name on the birth certificate.

Dick continued to struggle with depression. His psychiatrist, Cort, was still back in New York but he was in contact by telephone. Eventually, (and for reasons unbeknownst to me) Cort moved to Los Angeles and built a practice there. Dick and Cort continued their intense therapy sessions, thanks to his Screen Actors Guild (SAG) insurance. Dick had guilt over giving up this baby for adoption, had guilt over the fact that he impregnated his virgin angel. Guilt over the same dilemma, was he ready to be a father? Dick didn't know if he would ever be capable of that and he absolutely did not want to be a bad father. He felt like a failure. He wasn't' able to fulfill his commitment of being a father to his son Philip, back in New York. He was still struggling with the horrors of his childhood. Life was rough for Dick as he had not yet let go of his past. Did he deserve to be a father?

Dick was in love with Phyllis and he was (they were) really struggling with the choice they had made to give their child up for adoption, but it was done and could not be reversed. They hoped they found the proper home for their child. Prior to delivering, they were contacted by the adoption agency that had a couple who were very interested in adopting their child. No one wants to give up their child to incompetent parents; but how can you know? How do you really know? What you see is not always what you get. They seemed to check out all right on paper. Phyllis and Dick hoped they did the right thing, and in their minds, they did. They wanted what was best for their child, and they felt adoption was best.

Dick was Irish, and a heavy drinker and a heavy smoker. Alcohol and depression are not the most recommended combination. Most hope it will dull the pain, alcohol only made the pain flourish. Phyllis did not smoke; she did not drink. Dick did leave his heroine abuse back in New York but would still smoke marijuana, do cocaine, and LSD; it's the 60's people, "sex, drugs, and rock 'n' roll." Phyllis did try marijuana once with Dick, but she didn't like it and never bothered to try it again.

Dick was having a particularly hard night one night; the guilt of giving up the baby was taking him deep down into a spiraling hole of darkness. He was drunk and he was out of control, crying and shaming himself for what had transpired with Phyllis. He did not feel his life was worth living. Phyllis would be better off without him. Shit, Dick actually figured HE would be better off without him, he would be better off dead. Dick was wasted. Intoxication has a way of pulling you down even further into the pits of self-pity. Distraught and out of options, Dick staggered purposefully to the bedroom, he was headed for the nightstand by the bed. He opened the drawer and retrieved his hand gun (kept for protection, although it was not going to protect him now.).

Dick continued to apologize to Phyllis as he held the gun in his hand, through his tears he turned around and said, "I am sorry I did this to you Phyllis. I am so sorry. We would both be better off if I was dead."

Wait, dead? What in the hell was he saying? He was just going to shoot his brains out in front of the woman he loved? Phyllis was not having any of that. In a drunken rage and with tears streaming down his face, Dick raised the gun to his head. Phyllis reacted without hesitation! She bolted towards Dick without a second thought. As he began to squeeze the trigger, Phyllis shoved the gunned arm in an upward swoop! The gun went off.

Deafening silence filled the room. Phyllis looked into Dick's eyes and the two of them fell to the floor. The bullet hit the wall. She saved him. Phyllis held him as he sobbed.

The next day, they had a serious conversation about the night before. No more, that's it, pull it together. Phyllis encouraged him to better his life, to choose a different path, to walk the higher road. Dick would continue with his professional guidance from Cort, except it was time to kick it up a notch. Dick obviously needed additional extensive therapy. Dick loved Phyllis more than he had ever loved any other woman. She was his living angel and this angel was ready to fly away. He could not let that happen.

A few years later, Dick's therapy had taught him to disconnect. Dick had to learn to start anew; to leave his past in his past and live in the present. Through his intensive therapy, Dick learned to put his life as "Charlie" in the past and keep it there, this was not his life, it was a past life. Therapy included referring to his parents not as "Mom and Dad" like the rest of the world, but began referring to them as Julia Mahoney and Charles Hoyt. When he spoke of them, it was as if it was just a story he was telling of a little boy he once knew. In order to move forward in his life, he had to disown his childhood. Charlie had to stay Charlie, and Dick needed to be Dick. Life was a choice and he chose to overcome.

Dick finally had his head back on his shoulders and it appeared that he now had it screwed on pretty tightly, he was feeling great! Their lives had evolved over the past few years, in a positive direction. Phyllis and Dick were in love and were ready to settle down to start their own family. Two years after they gave their baby up for adoption, Phyllis and Dick were married in a court of law in Los Angeles, California on October 8, 1966. Two people stood by their sides; Dick's best pal and fellow actor, Don Matheson, along with his girlfriend at the time, Deanna Lund.

Don Matheson and Dick were the same age, only a few months apart. They met while working together on set over several occasions and struck up a friendship. Don is best known for his role in the late 60's on the television series, *Land of the Giants*, and later *Falcon Crest* and *Dynasty*.

Richard (Dick) and Phyllis Hoyt
Los Angeles County Courthouse
Oct. 8, 1966, their wedding day.

Don Matheson pictured in front, Phyllis and Dick in back,
1966, Los Angeles County Courthouse

Three years after they married, Phyllis conceived. Richard was 40-years-old when their first child as a married couple was born; finally ready to be a father and have his own family, to give parenting another shot. It is amazing what years of therapy, perseverance and being 40-years-old can do for you. They had their first child as a married couple on September 24, 1969 and named her Tania Susan (that's me!). (And from here on out, when I am referring to my father, I will call him "Richard" or "Dad", but not "Dick". I am sure you can understand the reason for this. I just cannot call him "Dick".) Phyllis would also begin to call him "Richard".

When I was born, Tanya Tucker was a popular country recording artist. She pronounced it differently than how they wanted my name to be pronounced. They chose to spell my name, Tania with and "i" so it wouldn't be pronounced like "Tanya Tucker" with a "y". Tanya was pronounced with a hard "a" sound opposed to the softer "a" of which they hoped people would pronounce my name by exchanging the "y" for the "i", pronunciation (Tahn-ya). It did not make a difference, by the way, but good try Mom and Dad, good try.

Twenty months after Tania was born, Michelle Deanne was born May, 24th 1970. Mom was a huge *Beatles* fan and *Michelle My Bell* was a popular tune at the time, so there you have it.

Dad vowed to create a great family, one of which would be filled with love, care, support and stability. There would be food on the table always, no one would go hungry. There would be family outings; there would be hugs, kisses, and family sing-a-longs. They would say the words, "I love you", often. Dad was determined to have the family of which he always desired. He wanted the "perfect" family.

Avidly working as an actor at this time, Dad managed to support the family with his acting career. He was a SAG actor and had enough work to have both of us kids under the SAG insurance. Dad landed a small role in the movie "Support Your local Sherriff" with James Garner and could not be more thrilled. He was a huge fan of westerns and of James Garner! Dad also appeared in a couple episodes of *Gomer Pile* with Jim Neighbors, *Streets of San Francisco*, *Pushing up Daisies*, and too many other roles to mention. Dad made a career out of his bit roles for as long as he could.

Dick Hoyt, *Support Your Local Sherriff*, 1969

Phyllis delivered her babies so small that it never affected her work as a singer. While she was pregnant with Tania, Phyllis was still performing with Beau Kaiser. After Michelle was born, however, Phyllis had her hands full. Her singing career would be put off as she embarked on this journey called motherhood. Phyllis would keep her job at the insurance company but would retire from her singing career.

Richard hadn't made it as BIG into the movie business as he hoped and now that he had a family to take care of, he decided it was a good time to establish a backup plan and begin a new career. Richard wanted a career that would be more stable for his family and thought it was fitting to choose to pursue his new career in psychology; clinical psychology specifically. Hell, most of his adult life was spent in therapy, he was quite familiar with the effects and benefits of therapy and it was time to give back. He knew he wanted to help others overcome tough times, just as his mentor, Cort, had helped him to overcome his. Richard felt he would be a good psychologist, the kind of psychologist who had "Been there, done that". He would have a deep understanding of other human suffering, because he himself had experienced abundant suffering and was eventually able to overcome his past; learning to choose to be a better person.

He would attend college with the aspiration of acquiring his Ph.D., and continue with his acting career on the side to keep food on the table. Phyllis was very supportive of his decision. It would be a rough road financially, but they would come out on top in the end; they just knew it. Life was not an easy road, but if you make a goal and stick to it, amazing things can transpire. Richard enrolled in and began attending college. He was in his forties and he was about to prove that it is never too late to start anew!

# CHAPTER 5

# LEFT BEHIND

Philip, son of childhood sweethearts, Mary and Dick Hoyt, never knew his father growing up. He knew his father left him and his mother when he was too young to remember. He recalls talking to his father once on the telephone when he was around seven years old. Philip often wondered what he did to make his father leave, children often blames themselves. Why did he leave? He knew his father lived in California and that was about it.

Up until Philip was eight years old, it was just him and his mother, Mary. Child support laws were "different" during this era. Mary had filed for child support from Dick, however, Dick left the state and nothing would come of it. Dick was not pressured or pursued, after leaving the state, to pay child support, so he didn't. Mary was raising her son on her own.

Philip Hoyt, 1968

Philip saw his paternal grandfather a few times as a child. Why his grandfather wanted to see him is a mystery. Why Mary allowed the visits, is also a mystery; however, the visits were supervised as she knows well of his history, and always in a neutral place; like a busy parking lot. Mary would pull into the parking lot and park, while Philip would admire his grandfather's Cadillac as it pulled in. The visits were short as well as few and far between, which was best. Mary would never allow her son to be in the presence of Dick's convicted pedophile father alone at any time.

One morning Philip woke up, just like any other morning, or so he thought, and went out to the front room in hopes of finding his mother making breakfast. But no, instead he walked out into the front room to find "a big, fat slob" sleeping on his couch. What the hell? Who was this stranger and why is he sleeping on his couch?

Phillip looks at his mother, "Mom? Who the heck is THIS guy (he points towards the strange man on his couch) and why is he sleeping on our couch?"

Mary: "He's just a friend, Phil. He spent the night because he wasn't feeling well, that's all." She assured him gently as she turned Philip towards the kitchen leading him to the table where his breakfast was waiting.

The big, fat, slob, never left.

His name was John; John "Kataldo", and he was now a permanent fixture on their couch. Philip was not happy about this, not happy about this at all. Unbelievable, he thought. He did not understand.

Eventually, his mother would marry this man. Great; his step-dad was a big, fat slob.

Philip's step-dad, John, was a limousine driver. John would pick Philip up from school daily while his mom was working. Mary was a secretary for a well-known doctor in the Dialysis Unit of the hospital. Living the apartment life in Queens made for undesirable parking conditions. John would become peeved and pissed off waiting to find a parking space in front of their apartment building. The frustration and impatience accelerated each time he had to circle the block trying to locate a parking spot big enough to accommodate his limousine, cursing the world for his problem. Phil would have to endure his step-dad's hissy fits daily. That was fun.

John had a bright idea, a resolution for his parking crisis. Why didn't he think of this before? Why not let the kid wait down here with the car until a parking spot became available? The kid can wait it out in the driver's seat and park the car. Problem solved. He would teach the kid how to park a limo. John would pull up and double park in front of the building entrance, leave the kid, go upstairs, crack a beer and hit the couch. Perfect. Why did it take him so long to think of this? Philip was eight years old.

In front of their apartment building:

John: "Hey kid, you's (that's NY slang for "you") wanna learn how to drive?"

Philip: "Um yeah, sure."

John: "How about you park the car?"

Phillip: "Really? Yeah. Ok."

What eight year old little boy wouldn't want the chance to drive a real car? This was cool, Philip thought.

John: "Alright, all you gotta do is wait right here in the driver's seat and when you see someone pull out, you pull the limo in, got it?"

Phillip: "Yeah, I got it."

John proceeded to show Philip the basics of parking the car and went in to the building and out of Philip's sight. And so, Philip would wait. Sometimes hours would go by before Philip would see a parking spot free up. Why was no one questioning this? Not their business? After a while, Philip caught on; that lazy, manipulative jerk, Philip thought.

Philip was not a big fan of his step-dad. He didn't want to be home where his step-dad and his mom would be tossing back the beers and an occasional shot of liquor. Mary would be functional the next day; she never missed a day of work. Philip would stay away from his apartment as often as he could, only going home when he was good and ready to lay his head down to sleep. Philip found many ways to keep himself busy. Philip was drinking as well. When Philip was eleven years old, he had his first beer, courtesy of his Uncle John.

John, his step-dad, was a gambler; a heavy gambler. Dealings with bookies made for a crazy life. John always owed somebody something. Always trying to dodge paying back money because he would lose every penny borrowed. John was incapable of contributing to the household. They were always broke. Mom waited 8 years and this is what she chose?

By the time Philip was eleven, he knew cars pretty well, John showed him how to change a car battery. Word on the street was that car batteries were a hot item and "people" were willing to pay cash to have them, used or new. Cool. Philip thought of this as an opportunity; he was very familiar with cars so he chose to give it a shot and see what would happen. And the bonus, making cash for something he was good at; his first "job", so to speak. He was tired of being broke; tired of his step-dad draining them dry of all of their money. It was disheartening watching his mom struggle. Philip wanted to step up and make his own money so he could help his mother out.

Philip was out and about as usual, staying away from home. He was on his first mission as he scoped the streets for a good target. He waited to make sure the streets were clear of any witnesses. He targeted his first vehicle in a back alley. Philip popped the hood of someone's car and pulled his wrench out of his back pocket. All he had to do was unscrew a couple of screws and shimmy out the battery and BAM, the battery was now his. Easy peasy. He bolted away from the scene to come upon a different alleyway where he could absorb and asses what he just got away with. Phil snickered to himself in amazement and amusement. He did it. He pulled it off. Now, off to find "someone" to purchase his goods. Another generation of criminal entrepreneurship had been born.

Philip was becoming quite the business person at age eleven and was making a name for himself on the streets by stealing car batteries and selling them for $100 bucks. Within a few years, Philip upgraded from stealing car batteries to stealing cars, a promotion in his career if you will, as "people" were willing to pay good money for those stolen cars.

The Italian's happened to hear that Philip was a good car thief and therefore, naturally, another promotion was in order. Yup, the New York Italian Mafia wanted Philip to work for them and hired him to steal cars for them. Philip was now a hired car thief for the mafia and would be paid well.

Philip was moving up in the world; cool. He was pulling in a lot of money and he liked it. He liked it a lot! Every so often Philip handed his mother a wad of cash and told her to use it for the rent. He knew his step-father had gambled away their rent and hated to see his mother suffer. Mary would ask Philip where he got the money and he would simply say that he made some money on a "side job", she did not persist further.

Philip would win some and lose some. Every so often, he would get caught in the act and would be sent to juvenile hall. He did not let this dampen his spirit; he would choose to remain a car theft, even though he was caught, time and time again. He would do his time as a minor and upon release from the juvenile detention center, would go right back to his life of crime. As a juvenile, his sentences were not severe so Philip figured being caught every so often doing business, outweighed the number of times he actually got away with it. He could handle this, no big deal, Philip was finically rewarded well. His mother, Mary could not seem to control his activities and hated his disregard for the law. She begged for him to end this life of crime, but Philip figured, why should he discontinue doing something he was so good at and was rewarded so well for? Mary had to work all day; she could not keep tabs on him 24/7. Philip did what he wanted regardless of the consequences.

Philip was hanging out in the school yard kicking back smoking some reefer and cigarettes. A German Sheppard dog walked over to him and sat right down next to him. Philip giggled to himself a little and introduced himself to the dog, "Hey dog, what's up?"

Philip gently reached out to the dog and gave him a little rub on his head. Philip got up and walked away. The dog followed him. "Hey dog, go home."

The dog cocked his head at Philip which made him laugh; silly dog. He left the school yard and was on his way to pick up another pack of smokes at the liquor store, the dang dog followed him. "Listen dog, you gotta go home."

Again, the dog cocked his head at Philip. He laughs and gives the dog another good rub between the ears. Philip notices the dog does not have a collar around his neck. As Philip continues on his way to the corner store, the dog stayed in toe. Cute little guy, Philip thought. As Philip gets to the store, the dog attempts to follow him in. "Now dog, you can't come in here with me. Stay put." The dog obeyed. Philip buys his pack of smokes and expected the dog to be long gone, but as he exits the store, low and behold, there's the dog, right where he left him. He and the dog locked eyes and Philip couldn't help but laugh again. The dog would not leave Philip's side. He went back to hang out at the school yard again, he didn't want to go home yet. He figured the dog would find his way back home from the school yard.

Philip and the dog hung out all day long, the dog following him wherever he went. The dog never did left the schoolyard to find his way home. It was time to get home and Philip could not just leave the dog alone in the schoolyard. The dog followed Philip all the way home, so he figured, eh, I'll just keep her. He named her Akiva, which was the name of a character in a book that Philip liked, *Exodus*. Akiva was the name of a great Hebrew warrior.

By the time Philip was twelve years old, he began stealing Mary's cigarettes. When he had to walk the dog, he smoked. Mary began asking Philip to go down to the candy store and pick up a pack of True Blue Greens for her and a pack of Lucky Strikes for John. Mary had him put the cigarettes "on account", Philip would add another pack to the order, his own pack. He was never asked for identification when purchasing the cigarettes, because he said it was for his mother. This was typical for this era.

By the time Philip was sixteen years old, he had been in and out of jail for grand theft auto and other sorts of offenses and robberies, so many times that his mother was losing count, as was he! The courts and the judges were keeping count however and were through with seeing this kids' face in their courtrooms. Clearly something wasn't registering in Philip's head; why did he not understand that he cannot continue on this path? Juvenile detentions centers were obviously not harsh enough to scare Philip straight. Philip didn't care, he was doing a job and he was getting paid well. The amount of time he spent in jail was pale in comparison to the reward that was waiting for him when he got out, another job and another wad of cash. The judge had had enough of Philip. The prosecutors were pursuing the current sentence as an adult, which would put Philip in prison with grown men as a 16-year-old minor. Stealing cars was a felony and the judge had let him off lightly too many times already. The judge on this current case felt it was time for Philip to do his time in prison with the big dogs.

Mary was at a loss. Philip was out of control, he was angry and rebellious. He was angry that his father left him and never looked back, without explanation. And to top it off, he had to deal with his piece of shit step-dad who couldn't stop gambling all his money away and leaving his mother struggling to pay the rent as well as to put food on the table. The only way Philip knew how to express himself was to rebel. "Fuck everybody", that was his thought. He sure did hate to see his mom so upset though. He was sorry, but not sorry enough. Mary was desperate to save her son; desperate to stop her son from going to prison. Prison? Her boy in prison? No, she was not going to let that happen. Mary pleaded with the judge and came up with an alternative plan.

Mary placed a phone call to Philip's father, Dick in California. Mary knew he was remarried and had two young daughters, but hadn't talked to Dick in years. She had raised their son without any help from Dick. Dick walked away, literally-walked away from his child and from Mary after 13 years. Mary explained to Dick, in desperation, the situation and begged for Dick to intervene. Mary reminded Dick of his own situation in prison as a minor and asked for his empathy. She could not bear the thought of their 16-year-old son in prison. Mary could not fathom that the same thing that happened to Dick in prison would happen to her son. Rape. "Please Dick; please don't let this happen to our son!"

Mary begged for the judge in New York to give Philip's father in California, a man who was about to earn his PhD. in psychology, a chance to rehabilitate their son. Dick had empathy. After much deliberation and an agreement from Phyllis, Dick agreed to step in. The courts sympathized with Mary and would honor her request. The judge agreed to allow Philip to stay with his biological father in California for a term of one year, in exchange for a prison term. The intention was for Dick to rehabilitate his son free from a life of crime. They hoped Dick could knock some sense into Philp, so to speak. The judge and Dick spoke extensively.

Philip was beside himself and argued with his mother and the judge, "Fuck this", he said. "I'm not moving to California to stay with my father who left us 15 years ago. I don't even know that mother fucker!"

The judge gave Philip an ultimatum: he could choose to go to prison for several years or he could choose to go to California and stay with his father for one year. The choice was his to make. Philip was furious but saw no other way out. His mother was crying and he hated to see his mother cry.

"This is going to fucking suck" Philip said, but he agreed to go to California for one year to appease his mother and avoid prison. Mary was relieved and was grateful that Dick and Phyllis agreed to take Philip into their home. Mary hoped they could guide her son and get him on a new path. Philip had to live with his dad and his dad's family in Simi Valley, California for one year. Simi Valley? Where the fuck was Simi Valley?

# CHAPTER 6

# SHENANDOAH

When Michelle was born, Phyllis and Richard decided it was time to move from Curson Street; away from the flamboyant neighborhood into a more kid-friendly neighborhood. Within a couple of months of Michelle's birth, Phyllis, Richard, Tania and baby Michelle, moved into an apartment building in Los Angeles, on Shenandoah Street, where they managed the same building in exchange for rent. The financial struggle was real, as Richard was going to college and working part time in the entertainment industry, while Phyllis was working part time and managing the kids and the household. Their hands were full.

Phyllis, while working part time for the insurance company, also picked up typing jobs on the side for extra cash. She was a speedy typist. Phyllis would receive hand written documents that she was paid to transcribe into a typed document, from home. Copies were made by placing a sheet of carbon copy paper between two sheets of typing paper and inserting all three sheets together into the typewriter roller. The front sheet was the original; the back sheet was the carbon copy.

Phyllis and Richard were involved in a babysitting "co-op", which was a group of working and/or part-time working parents that provided day-care to each other's children on a rotational schedule. It was a convenience and a shared effort amongst those families that needed to work but could not afford private child care costs. This particular co-op was a collection of friends and psychology majors at the same university Richard attended. Collectively and for a graduate project, the co-op filmed a documentary about the babysitting co-op from a psychological standpoint and the value it had on the children and the parents involved. The film would make its way around to other co-ops and types of venues, and eventually makes its way into the school systems, unbeknownst to Phyllis and Richard.

Dad was in a television show that was going to be aired on night time television. It was on later than our bedtime, however, Mom made an exception. She would allow us stay up late this one night, to watch Dad in an episode of *Streets of San Francisco*.

In our little apartment, we had two white bunny rabbits that were part-time residents, in addition to our two kitty cats who were full-time residents, Algernon (a white long hair) and Beelzebub (a fat, black cat with white paws). Phyllis loved animals. Algernon was named after Algernon Ashton who was a creator of piano sheet music, and Beelzebub in Christianity means "little devil". The bunny rabbits were part of the co-op and all participants would take turns caring for the rabbits on a weekly basis.

Our apartment building was in a neighborhood that was parallel to several other apartment buildings, co-mingled with single family homes. It was a very eclectic neighborhood. Our apartment building was four stories high and was the fourth building from the corner. We lived in the very back of the building on the first floor. Our "front door" was actually a sliding glass door that led to the private, fenced in, back alley. Around the corner and in front of our apartment unit were all of the car ports and then a long driveway which ran alongside the building, leading to the street. Michelle and I used to play in the back alley and along that side driveway. Mom could watch us through the sliding glass door from nearly everywhere in the apartment.

One day, Mom was listening to and singing along with Gladys Night and the Pips, *Midnight Train to Georgia*, as she did the dishes. Music always filled our house. Michelle and I were playing in the back alley; I was probably three years old and she about a year old and barely walking. I was riding my tricycle around doing my thing when Mom came out of the house looking a little panicked as she searched our back porch; she asked me where Michelle was. Hm; I didn't know.

Meanwhile, at the apartment next door, Connie is preparing dinner for her family for. Connie's daughter also named Michelle, who was three years old, bursts into the apartment and runs towards her Mom, with her arms stiffly stretched out in front of her, holding a baby. What on earth? As she approached her mother in the kitchen, she exclaimed proudly, "Mom, I found a baby!"

Connie gasps, "Oh my goodness! Where on earth did you find this baby? We have to get her back to her Mommy!" Connie took the baby from Michelle's arms and asked her where she found her.

Meanwhile, Phyllis was anxiously looking around her patio for her baby! She ran around to the car ports and began her search there. I saw Mom begin to panic. As she rounded the corner, she nearly ran right into a woman who was holding her baby.

From that moment on, our family became friends. Connie and Phyllis would become great friends. Connie was an emergency room nurse at a hospital in Los Angeles. She had two girls, Michelle and Janine and an older son, Michael. Michelle and Janine happened to be the same age as Michelle and I. What a coincidence.

Since there were two Michelle's, we all decided to differentiate between the two by having a Big and a little, which was determined by age. Michelle next door was the oldest, therefore, Big Michelle. "Big" Michelle and I became best friends and Janine and "Little" Michelle became pals. We all played together on a daily basis and would be involved in all kinds of shenanigans around the neighborhood. There was a "mean old lady" around the corner who had a reputation for yelling at kids to get away from her property, "keep off the grass!" as they say. We kids thought we would teach her a lesson about being mean to kids by throwing pebbles at her windows. We were shocked when she opened her front door and yelled at us, "You kids better knock it off or I will call the police!"

The police? Uh oh! We did not want to go to jail, so we ran! We ran as fast as we could! I happened to be wearing wooden clogs that day. Well, as I ran in my wooden shoes, I slipped and fell onto the concrete sidewalk and skinned my knee! I was bleeding and stunned. I rolled over onto my rear end to check out my wounded knee, as I did so, I saw the old lady standing on the corner waving her fist in the air and yelling at us "rotten kids". We thought maybe the old lady was going to chase us, so as Little Michelle and Janine continued to book it back home, Big Michelle scooped me up into her arms, she held my back with one arm, and my knees with the other, like a groom carrying his bride over the threshold. Big Michelle ran with me in her arms all the way back home, which was almost an entire block long. I still have a scar on my knee from this event. We never bothered that mean old lady again. She scared us straight.

We lived just around the corner from a main-street lined with retail shops. One shop in particular we would frequent was the candy shop! We were all under five years of age and were permitted to walk to the candy store by ourselves. We loved the candy Dots on paper, wax lips, wax cigarettes and candy cigarettes (the candy of our day-oh the 1970's!). A candy cigarette was designed to look like a cigarette because smoking was considered a cool thing to do then. Movie stars smoked, cowboys smoked, tough guys smoked, and the classy ladies smoked; it was a social thing. As a kid, the candy cigarette was put up to your lips, just as a regular cigarette, the difference was, you would blow out a puff of fine white powdered sugar designed to look like "cigarette smoke". Smoking was promoted and glorified. Ah heck, Dad smoked.

Big Michelle and I were the leaders of the pack being we were the oldest. Little Michelle and Janine were three years old and would accompany us while we held their hands on our walk down the main street to the candy store. There was more "freedom" and "trust" back then to do the right thing. Supervision was minimal during this era. Our parents knew where we were going as we asked them for the candy money. One hand held my little sisters' hand, the other hand held my change. Loose "change" could get you a fist full of candy back then. We always made it there and back without a glitch. We were taught how to look both ways before we crossed the street. We knew what we were doing, we were five!

I broke this rule once and darted across our street to another apartment to play with one of my friends and Dad snagged me right away! Boy was he mad! He walked with fury across the street and took me back home with him. I was scolded harshly, meaning he yelled at me; we were not spanked. He was a psychology major, he didn't believe in spanking. Dad however was scary when he was angry and we would get a stern talking to, it was enough so that I did not want to make him angry again, so I followed his orders from that day forward; I looked both ways before I crossed the street and I still do!

Little Michelle was playing on the driveway one afternoon. Dad pulled his car out from the parking stalls and proceeded to back out of the long driveway. He did not see Michelle playing, but she saw the car approaching. As the car quickly approached Michelle on the driveway, her natural instinct took over, thankfully and she ducked just as the rear bumper approached her head. Michelle laid down on the concrete as Dad's car drove over her. When Dad finished backing out, he turned his attention forward, opposed to behind him at this point. When he did so, he noticed Michelle on the ground. Thank goodness Michelle happened to be positioned in the center of the car and it would pass right over her. She was unharmed. Not a single scratch. Whew! Luck was on their side that day.

One afternoon, Big Michelle and I were hanging out watching TV together in the Czarnetski's apartment; their building was next to ours on the left. I had my hair in two braids that day, Mom liked to braid our long hair. The braids hung over my shoulders and down the front of my chest. For some reason, Michelle got a wild hair up her tiny little rear end and wanted to give me a haircut. I told her no but she begged and urged. She promised to just trim the ends of the braid below the ponytail. I'm a sucker and trusted the word of a 5-year-old and told her it was ok to only trim the ends of my braids, specifying it was just to be the ends of my hair BELOW the ponytail rings. We agreed. No one was around; her dad was working in the back room. Michelle went to the kitchen drawer and pulled out the big scissors.

She sat down behind me, pulled a braid back and proceeded to cut my hair. I felt her tug firmly at my braid as she locked the scissors around my hair. "Uh oh", she said.

What do you mean, "Uh oh?" I asked, "What happened?"

She said, "Um, I accidentally cut your braid off."

Accidentally? How does that happen exactly? We freaked out a little, as I told her my mom was going to be mad that half of my hair was missing. Michelle ran to grab her dad, David, from the other room. David's eyes grew large and his brows rose high on his forehead when he saw my braid in Michelle's hand, no longer attached to my head. He concluded that he could not send me home with only one braid. He thought it best to even it out and cut off the other braid. So that's what he did; David grabbed the scissors from Michelle and proceeded to cut off my other braid. Even Steven. He then, with great trepidation, walked me over to my apartment and tapped on the sliding glass door. The slider was always open, and as my mother was cooking spaghetti sauce in the kitchen, she turned around when she heard the tapping on the glass door. As she did so, I exclaimed, "Look Mom, David cut my hair!" My Mom dropped the spaghetti spoon as she threw her hands to her face and gasped in shock. David calmly explained the situation. So, temporarily, I would look like a little Dutch boy. Mom took me to the beauty salon to get me a nice bowl cut. At this time, Mom thought it was only fair that my little sister, Michelle, get a matching haircut. Mom always dressed us alike. People often thought we were twins.

Around the same year our mom was cooking dinner in the small apartment kitchen, we were listening to the *Momma's and the Poppa's* on the record player, I asked Mom if she could play the "bada bada" song, which was *Monday, Monday*, my favorite. Why bada bada you ask? Listen to the song, it's the first thing they harmonize prior to the lyrics beginning. "Bada bada", That's how I referenced the song anyway. Michelle and I liked to watch my mom cook. On this particular day, we both wanted to watch from the stool but there was only one stool. As Mom stood over the stove cooking dinner, the pot of water for the pasta began to boil. Michelle and I began to fight over who was going to sit in the stool and watch Mom as she cooked. The stool was clearly the best view! As we both argued and pushed to gain the prized seat on the stool near Mom, Michelle bagan to fall, as if in slow motion. (I remember every detail.) As she bagan to fall, her natual instinct at three years old was to reach out and grab something to stabalize her and keep her from falling. She grabbed on to the handle of the pot of boiling water with her left hand. As the stool teetered and we both went falling to the ground, the pot of boiling water tilted fiercely as the boilng water poured over her right arm, her delicate little 3-year-old arm.

I will never forget what I saw that day; thick white peaks of skin an inch tall stood up all over her entire arm from the shoulder to the back of her hand. I remember there was screaming and panic! My Mom picked up Michelle, and with me in toe, ran next door to her dear nurse friend, Connie, for help! Connie utilized her nursing skills to give Michelle the immediate attention and care she needed as she also helped to keep her dear friend, my mom, from losing it. This portion of the senario was not in slow motion, it all happened so fast that it is a blur. There was no way Mom was going to sit around and wait for an ambulance. The next thing I remember, I was watching in fear and complete worry from the Czarnetski's window, with Big Michelle and Janine on either side of me, as my Mom backed out of the long driveway and rushed my little sister to the hospital. I would stay with Connie until Mom and Dad were able to come and get me.

Michelle was very badly burned, it was a third degree burn which covered her entire right arm. Michelle would undergo surgery to replace the damaged skin. The surgery would involve a skin graft; skin from her rear end would be removed and placed on her arm. She would remain in the hospital for a couple of months. Mom was under investigation by social services for this tragic mishap, but would prevail; it was an accident.

Ater two months, Mom finally insisted that Michelle come home when she noticed Michelle calling the nurses "Mom". Two months was a long time for a 3-year-old to be living in a hospital bed; it was too long. Phyllis and Richard were ready to take her home, ready to endure the process of rehabilitation, both physically and emotionally.

We immediately began family therapy. Michelle would also participate in private sessions. Mom and Dad wanted Michelle to recover emotionally from the physical tradegy as well as the mental one. Phyllis and Richard wanted her to be able to understand what happened and how we were all going to deal with this going forward, as Michelle was badly scarred. People can not seem to help themselves when they see something out of what they think is "ordinary". People stared awkwardly at Michelle's arm and asked questions. Michelle began to cover the arm out of embarassment and shame, and also developed a finger sucking habit as a soothing mechanism. Maybe the therapy was more beneficial for Mom and Dad.

Michelle would grow up trying to cover that arm. Along with the finger sucking habit, would come the "blankie" to cover her habit and her scarred arm. Michelle would suck on two of her fingers and then carry her favorite blankie around at all times draping it over her hand which would hide her scarred arm, hide it from the world. The finger sucking started out with just two fingers but Michelle would eventually manage to fit three fingers in that tiny little mouth of hers, which would ultimately change the shape of her mouth. As a long term result, Michelle developed severe buck teeth. Altough we both had buck teeth already, the finger sucking made her over-bite much more severe throughout the years.

Dad was now in graduate school working on his PhD in clinical psychology at the California School of Professional Psychology (CSPP) in Los Angeles. He had been able to get this far on school loans, but in addition to this, he took on an odd job as the school's Janitor to work off his student loans and to bring in some income to support his family. The janitor position at his graduate school would be a family affair. The four of us would go to Dad's school and put in our contribution, which was to help Dad clean the classrooms and cafeteria. Michelle and I had the job of emptying the classroom trash cans. There was a break room with a tash can too. Michelle and I would hang out a little longer in this room and raid the sugar cubes by the coffee pot. Not just a few sugar cubes, it was as many as we could shove in our faces before we had to leave the building and as many as we could fit in our little pockets to save for later. We loved sugar!

# CHAPTER 7

# WALLACE

We lived in Los Angeles until 1976 when we moved to a small town called Simi Valley about an hour outside of Los Angeles ,on Wallace Street. We were renting again, but this time it was a three bedroom house with our own backyard! We no longer had to play in the back alley. Mom had cousins in Simi Valley so it is safe to assume this is why they chose this sleepy little town. Not only was it familiar to Mom from all of her visits here, but it was considered a "safe" town to raise a family, opposed to Los Angeles. There was no freeway yet to get in to Simi Valley. One had to come in through the back roads of the San Fernando Valley, through the mountains, through Santa Susana Pass Road, to get into Simi Valley . This area was also the old stomping grounds of Charles Manson.

Connie and Mom remained friends, as did us kids. Simi Valley seemed so far away from Los Angeles as a child, an hour drive was an eternity. When we were making the drive back and forth from Simi Valley to Los Angeles, we would bring our pillows so we could rest our heads from the long boring drive, and maybe even take a nap. Seat belt laws were not yet implemented and we would sit in the "way back" as we called it. We started saying that when we were still in Los Angeles and our parents owned a red VW Bug. The "way back" was the tiny area in back of the Bug where one would normally store their luggage or groceries and such. Yup, we sat back there. No one considered the possibilty of an accident. Tight squeeze, but we liked it. We thought it was fun to ride in the way back. And when I stop to think about it now, it wasn't so "way back". The VW Bug is a very small car, nothing is "way back". But to a child, perspective is different. While we were "way" back there, we would wave at people through the back window and see how many people would wave back! We loved car games. If we weren't laying our heads down on our pillows through the long drive, we were playing the "wave at people" car games. We would keep track of how many "nice" people there were, and how many that were not so nice and refused to wave back.

Coming from an apartment building in Los Angeles, we were excited that we now had our own backyard. And, a big back yard it was! As I sit and wonder, if I went back today, how big would the backyard actually be? We had a swing set and a teather ball that would each get a lot of use. We were active children from an active generation. We played outdoors as much as we could and for as long as we could.

As a child, I used to get horrible ear aches that would wake me up at night crying in pain. Mom would sit with me in her rocking chair and try to soothe my little soul by holding me in her arms and rocking me gently as I cried in pain. I will never forget her gentle touch and soothing tones, even in the middle of the night, she never showed frustration for being woken up by me night after night. I suffered for a couple of years with ear aches. I would have surgery to put tubes in my ears and take out my adnoids. My parents gave me a twirling baton as a gift when I was in the hospital, and boy was I excited! I never had any formal baton twirling lessons, but a kid didn't need lessons. I was able to keep myself entertained trying tricks I learned from friends or from watching other people twirl on the TV.

Along with my ear issues, I was also burdened with some allergies. Mom had just about every allergy known to man. It was determined that I was allergic to dust, feathers, tumbleweed, and grass. Mom and I took monthly treks to the Children's Hospital in Los Angeles to get my allergy shots. I loathe needles, but I don't remember being as bothered by it as a kid as I am now. Mom suffered far worse than I did from her allergies but I don't recall her ever complaining. She always had a tissue in a pocket or tucked in her sleeve. If you borrowed a sweater of hers, you had to be careful reaching into the pockets or you may get a surprise…a used tissue.

Across the street was a Mormon family and next door was Bill the Barber. A few doors down from Bill the Barber were the Dunkles. Once in a while, I would accompany the kids across the street to their Mormon summer school. Was I Mormon? No, but they invited me, so I went. Mom and Dad saw no harm in it either, they were hippies, all about peace and love. I loved it because we did crafts and I happened to thoroughly enjoy arts and crafts. Mom and Dad were raised in the church, but chose not to raise Michelle and me with any religion whatsoever.

In the summer time, there was a local pool that my Mom took us to often at Rancho Park. There was a stream and a duck pond there as well where we could feed the ducks. When Michelle and I got back from the pool one summer afternoon, I noticed the kids from across the street were playing outside. I was still in my bathing suit when they came over and asked me to play with them at their house. As I followed the kids into their home, I was greeted by their mother who had shocked and disapproving look on her face. She stood there for a minute stunned with her jaw hanging open. She finally shouted at me, "Sinner!" She pointed and yelled at me, continuing to call me a sinner and told me I was "going to go to hell!" She could not believe that I enetered her home wearing a two-piece bathing suit. She said only sinners wear a two piece bathing suit. I didn't realize that. Why didn't my Mom ever tell me that? Wait, what is a sinner? Whatever it was, this woman was angry with me and it scared me. She ordered me out of her house. I turned and ran out the front door as fast as I could! I was crying by the time I entered my own house. I ran straight into my Mom's arms. After she soothed my little soul, she asked me why I ran into the house crying. After I gave her a play-by-play, I asked her what a sinner was, she explained it to me and assured me that I was not a sinner and expalined how some people have different beliefs. So I got over it and continued wearing two-piece bathing suits for the rest of my life. The Mormon's would move shortly thereafter. I would not hold it agaisnt them because it wasn't just the Mormon religion. All through elementary school, many other kids would tell me that I was going to hell for not going to church, I got used to it. Hell better get ready for me.

When they moved out, the Frenes's moved in: Anthony, Lisa, Sonya, Rudy (NiNi), Richie and Vincent (VJ). There were also the Dunkles down the street as mentioned, Angela and Shelley. They had an older brother and a younger brother too. The Hoyts, the Frenes' and the Dunkles were all pals, attending the same elementary school and living on the same street. Those were the days kids played outdoors at all times. We were only inside when we had to be. It was also the ear where we walked everywhere, rode bikes, skateboards, climbed tree's, drank hose water, hung out at the park and the local pool. We were a generation that loved the outdoors. I loved climbing trees! We had a great tree to climb right in our front yard and a smaller tree in the backyard that I climbed too.

Michelle was still very attached to her blankie. It became her obsession; she had to have it wherever she went, asleep or awake. Mom and Dad would not allow her to take her blankie to school however, so she had to find other ways to hide her arm during school hours. She began wearing long sleeve shirts. After some weaning time and putting her and the blankie on a schedule, Mom and Dad decided it was time to take away the blankie completely, Michelle was six years old. The blankie was a mess: dirty, stinky, tattered and torn. Michelle would not let Mom wash it, she liked it the way it was, dirty and stinky. Just like Linus from *Charlie Brown*. It was time to put it to rest. Mom and Dad had a blanket burrying ceremony for Michelle's raggedy old blankie, in our backyard. This was tough on Michelle, she had been attached to that stinky, old blankie for many years. She was now being forced to say goodbye to her beloved blankie forever. And that she did. The infamous "Blankie" was buried and put to rest forever in the backyard at Wallace Street.

There was a *Stop–and-Go* mini-mart on the main street just outside of our neighborhood. The neighborhood kids all walked there in groups to buy our candy. We could purchase five loose pieces of candy for a nickel. Candy bars were 25 cents a piece. Our parents trusted us for some odd reason and gave us freedom of choice and independence. As long as we traveled in pairs or groups, and looked both ways before we crossed any street, it was all good.

One afternoon, Sonya, Angela, Shelley, Michelle and I were on recess at Hollow Hills Elementary School and decided it was a great idea to all ditch school and walk to our local *Stop-and-Go* for some candy. We each had our lunch money that our parents gave us before school, candy seemed more important than lunch at the time. Someone apparently saw the four of us elementary kids strolling down the street durning school hours and called the school. The school called my mom. As we were inside the *Stop-and-Go*, Mom walked in. Busted! She took us all home. We were grounded for the weekend.

✳ ✳ ✳

Cartoons did not play all day and night long on the television like they do now. There was a limited time period in which cartoons and children's programs would run; early morning before school and a breif period of time after school, and of course on weekends, Saturday morning cartoons were the best! Threre were only 13 channels back then, two different receptions: UHF and VHF. *Sesame Street* was on in the mornings before school. We learned to count with Count Dracula. Learned our words with Bert and Ernie. Learned about the Cookie Monster and his lack of sharing. We learned to be kind from Big Bird and we learned to love with Snoffulufugus. *New Zoo Review* was one of my favorties which was on at six in the morning. I was up to watch it and sing along with Henrietta the Hippo and Freddy the Frog. *The Muppet Show* was a family favorite, we all got a good kick out of that show. Who didn't love Kermit the Frog and despise Miss Piggy? *The Mupet Show* was entertaining for the entire family. Good times, simpler times. Since I was getting a little older, Mom and Dad would let my bedtime curfew go a half an hour longer than Michelle's. Therefore, I would get to stay up and watch *Three's Company*! Jack (John Ritter) always made me laugh, he was so silly and I loved silly!

Dad continued working on his PhD. in clinical psychcology. Mom was taking care of us, working part time, and now attending Cal State University of Northridge (CSUN). It was her turn to earn her degree. As Dad was winding down on his educational mission, Mom was gearing up. She would embark on the journey of earning her Masters degree in psychology as well, focusing on marriage, family and child therapy.

While Mom was studying and training for her psychology career, Sonya, NiNi, Richie, Vj, Angela and Shelley along with Michelle and I, would participate in psychology "games" and research for Mom's phychology classes; play therapy. The games were generalized questions and  puzzles and other such skill tests that she would have us kids perform.  Phyllis would keep notes on timing as well as other observations including the accompanied reactions to such puzzles.  Her role was to observe and document.  There was no stress or pressure.  It was all fun and games to us.  We all gladly participated.

I didn't know when I was a kid that we were poor, it just was what it was. We may have been poor, but we were not hungry nor were we deprived of anything for that matter.  Everyone in the neighboorhood was in the same position we were.  In comparison from where we came from in Los Angeles, this was an upgrade.  I also don't recall any feelings of neglect as our parents worked and went to school.  We were a generation of what they called, "Latch Key Kids".  We wore ID bracelets, carried our own house keys, walked ourselves to and from school and occupied ourselves until our parents would return home in the evening.  Parents saw no problem with this, apparently neither did the law. We were happy kids, had plenty of friends in the neighborhood and enjoyed the outdoors.  We didn't need fancy expensive toys back then to have a good time, we used our imaginations. There were stay at home moms on our street, so we did have a safe place to run to if we needed to. We would usually  hang out with the Frenes' anyway, Alice, their mom, was always home.  We could count on Alice if we needed an adult.

There was a period of time in which we collected Blue Chip Stamps, which was a rewards program, when one collected the appropriate amount of stamps, they could pick out an item from any participating retail store. And as I recall, they were literally "stamps".  Mom collected the stamps, we would all grab a sheet, carefully tear each stamp off the sheet, lick them, then stick them in a paper booklet.  When the booklet was full, we went to the store and presented the booklet of stamps to the cashier who would take them in exchange for the item.

We lived on a lot of hot dogs, vieena sausages, mac 'n' cheese, fish sticks and *Swansen* "tv dinners".  My favorite tv dinner was the salsbury steak and hot apple and cinnamon desert, yum!  We loved tv dinner night and eating with TV trays.

We were kids and kids ate junk, and that was ok. I never knew a kid who ate "health food" when I was growing up. It was unheard of. But junk food back them may have been healthier than the junk foods of today and the "super size" craze. Our parents were eating the same kind of "junk", it was a family thing. Affordable, quick and easy meals. No one was malnutritioned and no one was over-weight. We never stopped moving until our heads hit our pillows at night. And that wasn't just our family, that was everyone's family so it seemed at the time.

We were an active family. There were frequent family bike rides, and frequent famliy trips to Zuma Beach or the local community pool at Rancho Park. Our lives were content, we were surrounded by love. Dad loved riding his 10-speed bike. He would ride his bike frequently for exercise and for fun. One day he rode in the rain. Why was he riding in the rain? Who knew? It is possible that it was not raining when he stepped out the door to begin his journey. The bicycle and the rain slicked sidewalks did not get along and the tires hydroplaned, flying over the handlebars. He broke his collar bone. He had to ride back home all broken up, as there was no such thing as cell phones. Mom took him to the hospital to get a cast.

Hugs, kisses and saying, "I love you" were normal in our household. Michelle and I shared a room, we had bunk beds. I slept on the top bunk and she on the bottom. There was enough room for us each to have our own rooms, but it didn't work out that way. Our house had a "spare" bedroom for out-of-town guests, meaning Uncle Jim.

Our parents "tucked" us into bed every night. Every single night. They would come into our room and give us each a kiss and tell us they loved us. The only time they refused to step across the threshold into our bedroom, was if it was a pig stye and we ignored our Mom's repeated requests to clean up our mess. Our punishment for not cleaning our room was that Mom and Dad would not actually enter the room to tuck us in. They flat out refused. This was always devastating to us. They would both stand at the doorway while Michelle and I got up from our beds, ashamedly strolled over to where they stood in the doorway, gave them goodnight kisses there, then shamefully walked back to our beds and tucked oursleves in. We would spend all day the next day cleaning our room to ensure that this wouldn't happen again. Of course, it would and the cycle would continue.

Not sure why, but Michelle and I apparently like to put things in our mouths and accidently swollow things. I was chewing on a Barbie shoe and whoopsie, I swollowed it. It was stuck in my throat for hours as I recall, annoying me. I remember standing on a kitchen chair helping my Mom at the sink with the dishes while the shoe was stuck in my throat, you know, just trying to act like it was normal to have a Barbie shoe stuck in your throat while washing dishes. I didn't panic. My parents didn't panic. I was eventually able to swollow the tiny shoe, and WALAH, down the hatch she goes.

Michelle somehow managed to swollow a few pennies. Yes, pennies, plural! I will never forget my Dad panicking over this a tad bit. He bent down, wrapped his hands around Michelle's little ankles and turned her upside down attempting to shake the pennies right out of her like a piggy bank. This turned out to be an unsuccessful attempt. Michelle survived, the pennies came out eventually, just as did that Barbie shoe.

Michelle was a curious little girl. Dad was a smoker, he smoked cigarettes. Michelle decided she wanted to try smoking also; she was six years old. I am pretty sure she had no idea how to light the cigarette, it would be a futile attempt. Dad's entire carton of Marlboros went missing one day. The carton was not hard to find as Michelle did not quite understand how to hide something very well yet. She "hid" it under her bed. There was no long oversized comforter hanging down to the ground in which to cover that carton of Marlboro Reds. She just placed it under her bed at the same end as her pillow. All one had to do was simply look in that direction and, low and behold, there was the missing carton of cigarettes. The red and white box of Marlboros stood out like a sore thumb. Dad was furoius with her for stealing his cigarettes and for punishment, he told her to go ahead and smoke one.

Dad and Mom took Michelle into their master bedroom and sat down in some chairs that were placed in a circle. Dad lit her a cigarette and handed it to her. He said, "So you want to smoke, do you? Here, smoke this, see how much you like it! Go ahead, smoke it!" Michelle was scared and crying, but she took that cigarette from Dad's hand and took a puff. As she did, she coughed dramatically as all the smoke came billowing out of her little lungs. That was all she smoked, that one puff, but Dad wanted her to taste it and know it was bad and not for kids. "Do as I say, not as I do." It sure did work, she didn't smoke again, at least not until she was a teenager.

One day Mom took us to the animal shelter. Michelle and I would each be able to pick out our own kitty cat to take home with us. I chose a grey kitty and Michelle chose a black kitty, they happened to be brothers from the same litter.

Tania with Arpegio and Michelle with Andante, 1976

I liked to play with the Frenes' across the street. The Frenes' became our dear friends. Lisa used to babysit us whenever my parents went out or had an event. I thought Lisa was one of the prettiest girls I ever saw. She had long legs and long dark hair. Sonya and Rudy were my age. Everyone called Rudy, "NiNi", that was his given nickname by Sonya. Rudy had a darker skin color than his siblings and jet black hair. His Tias and Primos (aunts and uncles), called him "Negro" which means "black" in Spanish. "Nini" was the closest that Sonya could come to pronouncing it, and it stuck. "Nini" would be his nickname by peers and at school as well. Richie was around Michelle's age, he really loved our cats, especially Arpegio, my cat. Then there was little Vincent, who we called VJ, short for Vincent Jr. Sonya was born with only one kidney and it was small, she would get ill quite often. Sonya and I became best friends. She would come over frequently and spend the night, which was funny because she lived directly across the street. Sometimes you have so much fun as a kid that you don't want it to end, and it did not have to. So a slumber party it was, and many of them throughout the years.

Pictured top L to R: Tania, Sonya, Nini and VJ in front, 1978

On one particular day, which started out as a typical afternoon, Sonya, Michelle, Richie, Nini and I were playing down the street from our houses. VJ didn't feel like playing with us, so he stayed in his front yard and did his own thing. As we were playing in the street, a German Sheppard dog came charging out of the neighbor's yard. The dog looked angry and was growling as it crept his was towards us. There was something not right here. What was wrong with that dog? What was that white stuff under its chin? The dog picked up its pace and began to charge after us. We freaked out and screamed! We continued to scream as we all ran. Our instinct was to run on top of the nearest thing, which was a car. The dog was viscious and foaming at the mouth as it jumped up at us while we hudled together. As we stood up on top of the car, afraid for our lives, we screamed frantically and held on tightly to each other towards the center of the car. As the seething, vicious dog continued in its efforts to get to us, VJ, scared and confused, saw the entire thing unflold from down the street and alerted everyone in his household.

Lisa just got home from school. She attended the high school around the corner, Royal High, the same one I would attend in the future. When VJ told her what was going on down the street, she did not hesitate. Lisa bolted out her front door and down the sidewalk to save us. She ran towards us as fast as her long legs would allow, altough it all seemed to be in slow motion. I will never forget her courageous act on this day. As she charged down the street to save us, the dog changed its focus from us, to her as she approached the car that we were trapped on top of. The dog stopped her dead in her tracks as it opened its jaws, turned its head to the side, and clamped its jaw and those sharp teeth around her bare thigh; she was wearing shorts. The dog refused let go, would not let up. She was in agonizing pain and could not get the dog to release its grip despite her efforts to break free.

Lisa screamed at us to run! "Run! Run! RUN! Go on! Get out of here!" We did as we were instructed to do, we ran. We ran as fast as we could to the Frenes' house. Lisa continued to scream in agony as the dog stayed attached to her thigh. As she screamed, the neighbor, Mr. Thor, came out from behind the fence with a shovel and hit the dog over the head. The dog finally let go of Lisa's leg. Lisa ran limping towards home. Her leg had one giant bite mark which wrapped around each side of her thigh. The teeth marks were deep and there was white foam still on her leg around the punchture wounds from the dog's sharp teeth. Alice, Lisa's mom, got her into the station wagon and rushed her to the hospital. Lisa risked her own safety to save the four of us kids. It turned out the dog had rabies. Lisa would have to get a series of shots, 10 in all, and in the tummy no less, and many stiches. She was my hero that day. Although the wounds on her leg would heal, the event would scar her emotionally forever.

I walked down the street to play with my friend one day. Her older brother let me in. I asked if she was home, he said she wasn't. In fact, I don't think anyone was home. Next thing I knew, he grabbed me by the shoulders and came at me as if he was going to kiss me. Ew! I pulled myslef away in shock and disbelief. Gross. He grabbed me again, with a tighter grip this time. I yanked backwards wildly and protested, trying to get out of his grip. I broke free and ran behind their couch so I had something between him and me. He ran behind the couch to get me as I ran out from behind it to get away. As I got to the center of the room, he caught me and pushed me down to the floor, sat on top of me and pinned my shoulders down with his knees. He bent over to press his lips against mine. I turned my head to the side. What on earth was happening? I was scared. I didn't even yell because no one was around to hear me! As I struggled, I somehow managed to wiggle my way out from under him! I ran to the door which was still open but the screen door was shut. I frantically opened it and burst through it to the outside world! I ran as fast as I could! I did not look back. As I ran, I heard his footsteps slapping down on the concrete behind me. He was chasing me! I felt like I was in the middle of a strange nightmare! It is amazing what adreneline and determination can do. I had enough of a head start that I was able to out-run him and his long legs, he was twice my size. I heard his steps slow down before I reached my house. I continued to run all the way to the safety of my house where my mom was. It felt like my house was such a long way away, but in fact, it was only halfway down the block. I burst through the front door and shut it abruptly behind me. Mom must have thought I was just running in from an outside adventure. Yes, I guess you can call it that. I went directly to my room. I have no idea why I never told my mom, or anyone for that matter. I never put myself in that position again, I kept my distance. After this traumatic episode, I would become defensive and defiant towards anyone who figuratively tried to hold me down or tell me what to do! I shoved the incident deep down and I rebelled. I held that secret deep down inside of me, never to tell a single soul, until I was forty-six years old and again now.

The next day, I was playing with Nini and Richie. Richie said something to set me off. I said, "Come on! Let's fight!" I put my fists up by my face and he punched me in the nose. I ran into the house crying. I got what I asked for.

As I have told you before, we were animal lovers. We had hamsters at one point. We started out with two then they multiplied into eight hamsters. I guess Mom and Dad didn't think about getting same sex hamsters. We also had two ducks, Lucky and Ducky were their names. We bought a little kid pool for them to splash around in. I don't believe that lasted long, they were messy and hard to take care of. We eventually took Lucky and Ducky to Rancho Park to live in the duck pond and make lots of new duck friends. In addition, we still had three cats: Bealzabub (who we had in Los Angeles), Arpegio and Andante'. At one point, our parents had a friend that could not care for their cat any longer for some unkown reason to me, so our Mom took the cat into our home. We now had 8 hamsters and 4 cats. Little Girl was her name and she was a beautiful, long hair, black with white under her little chinny chin chin and down her chest. Little girl was scared to be in a new home, she hid behind the refrigerator for a long time and that broke my heart. I was determined to get her to come out and be my friend. I would sit by the frig patiently calling to the kitty to come out and see me, that it was okay, I would be her friend. Little Girl would eventually come out of hiding and put her trust in me.

Michelle and I were playing in the backyard one day near the plastic baby pool that Lucky and Ducky used to crusie around in. When I looked up at her at her, she was covered in ants from head to toe! Ahhhh! We screamed. She frantically tried to brush them off of her arms and legs but there were just too many! I called for our Mom. Mom ran out to investigate the screaming. When she saw the ants crawling all over Michelle's body, she also noticed they were on her head and stuck in her hair. Mom grabbed the hose and washed all of the ants off of my little sister, it took a while. There must have been a thousand ants that covered her! I have no idea how a thousand ants casually marched up my little sister's body, all the way to the top of her head before either of us noticed! I'm pretty sure Michelle still has ant issues to this day, who could blame her?

I find butterflies to be one of the most beautiful creatures. As a child, I used to somehow have the focus and ability to actually catch butterlies in my backyard. I was sneaky and stealthy like a cat, apparently. I also used to pick up caterpillars at Rancho Park so I could have my own butterflies. I was facinated by the furry little critters. I would collect them at the park near the wash. I carried them home carefully in the palm of my hand and put them in a jar when I got home. I poked some holes in the jar's lid, pulled some grass from my backyard, stuck in a good stick and in the jar the caterpillar would go. I would then bring the jar to my room and wait patiently for the catapiller to form its cacoon and for a beautiful butterfly to emerge. When the butterfly finally made its appearance, I would let the butterfly fly free. Mom must have loved butterflies too, as she had a pair of turquise butterfly earrings from the 60's that I always admired. Maybe someday she would let me wear those turquoise butterfly earrings.

Uncle Jim was our weekend guest, every weekend. Uncle Jim, who wasn't actually our uncle, was our parents best friend, Jim Symanski. Jim lived in Culver City and had been friends with Mom and Dad before we were born. They met in Los Angeles. We loved Uncle Jim and looked forward to him staying with us on the weekends. He used to pride himself on the fact that he looked like William Shattner. We sat down as a family to watch Star Trek on television, Jim would join us. He taught me how to separate my fingers like Spock did while he said, "Live long and prosper." Uncle Jim also taught me how to make a silly face by crossing my lips in the opposite direction of each other . Dad and Uncle Jim were always making silly faces, I wanted to join in.

Jim was a single guy. I don't recall if Jim was ever married, if so, he was divorced before I ever met him. Jim woked as a Culver City/Los Angeles

Taxi Cab driver. He proudly shared stories of the famous passengers who rode in his cab. He was particularly proud of giving Ray Bradbury a lift more than once. Uncle Jim's smile would beam bright when he told the story of their conversations in his cab, he thought Mr. Bradbury was a nice guy.

*Pic 'n' Save* was a retail store we frequented, it was an inexpesive place to buy fun stuff. No one ever admitted that they actually shopped at *Pic 'n' Save*, so if I saw someone from school there, it was quite embarrassing. I loved note pads, pencils and pens; I was a collector of stuff. I really wanted this turquise colored note pad but it had bad words on it. It was a square note pad with a turquiose plastic cover that read, "Bitch, Btich, Bitch". I expressed my disappintment out loud and Mom surprised me by saying that it was alright that I have it. Mom explained to me that the context of those words in such a way meant, "Complain, Complain, Complain". Sounded like a legit explanation to me. I grabbed the notepad for Mom to purchase for me. Michelle also picked out a fun notepad for herself, lacking the foul language of course, and we proceeded to the register. As we walked up to the cash register to pay for our goods, the shelves at the register had many small, ceramic, animal figurines. I saw a frog figurine on that shelf that I wanted. I just loved frogs! Instead of asking Mom if she would purchase it for me, I took it off the shelf and casually held it in the palm of my hand. No one noticed. When we got home, I took the little frog from my hand and began to admire it. Mom noticed me holding something and when she noticed it and did not recognize it, she asked me where I got it. When I told her, that I took it from *Pic 'n' Save*, she was pretty mad at me. She put me in the car a drove us back to *Pic 'n' Save* where she would present me to the manager of the store. Mom had me apologize for stealing the tiny ceramic frog firguine, as I handed it back to the manager. I wondered, why didn't she just pay the manager and let me keep it? She was not about to reward me for stealing.

Mom's niece, Karen, had just recently married Kenny Mason. Karen was the daughter of Mom's oldest sister, Katie. Karen and Kenny, who lived in Boston, had planned a trip to California after they were married for their honeymoon and stopped in to visit with us. Karen was a beautiful

Italian girl with olive skin, short, dark hair and big brown eyes. Michelle and I were always very shy at first. When Mom and Dad had visitors, we would hide and giggle. Eventually we would come out of our shells and participate in the moment. I thought my cousin Karen was the prettiest girl I had ever laid eyes on!

Grandma would come out next for a visit. Visits were few and far between. It was expensive to fly a family of four out to Boston. The previous visit from Grandma was when we lived on Shennandoah Street in Los Angeles. We always talked to Grandma on the telephone at the end of Mom's conversations with her. Mom would pass the phone around to Michelle and I so we could chat with Grandma. She always sent us a big box of presents during Christmas from her and all the aunts and our uncle. We looked forward to those Christmas packages, there was always something homemade by grandma especially for us. She was a tiny woman with super long gray hair that she kept in a bun on top of her head and a rounding of her upper back, she had osteoperosis. When her hair was not in that bun, it would flow down past her bottom.

We would eat very well when Grandma came to visit! She and Mom would be in the kitchen all day preparing homemade raviolli. Italians sure do know how to cook and how to eat. Mom called her "Ma", so did Dad. He hadn't had anyone to call "Ma" in decades, and he longed for her acceptance.

I do not recall how we were told or what we were told, but I found out I had an older brother, a half-brother from my Dad's first marriage, his name was Phillip. I am sure this involved a family meeting. Family meetings were becoming a "thing" in our household. So Philip was my Dad's son from a previous marriage and he was coming to live with us. Yippie! I had no idea what was going on, all I knew was that I was going to have a big brother!

# CHAPTER 8

# TOO LITTLE, TOO LATE

Philip packed a bag and his German Sheppard dog, Akiva, hopped on an airplane and flew to California. He would insert a cassette tape into his *Walkman* radio and listen to Led Zeppelin the entire flight. He would have to endure an entire year with his "Dad", his dad's wife, Phyllis, and their two children Tania, who was about to turn eight years old and Michelle, who was six. He was happy at least, when he demanded to be able to bring his dog with him to California; that his Dad agreed. At least he had his buddy to endure this with. And this had to be better than jail, right?

Philip arrived at Los Angeles International Airport (LAX). He, his dog, and his dad embarked on their hour long drive back to Simi Valley, where Philip was to live for the next year, per court order. As they dropped down Simi Valley, from the top of the mountain range that Los Angeles County from Ventura County, Philip thought to himself, "What the fuck kind of place is this? Holy shit, there are orange groves everywhere! What kind of hunky dory, sleepy little town did I just enter? This is the sticks, literally, there are sticks everywhere! I can't fucking do this shit! What the fuck am I supposed to do out here in the sticks? This is bullshit. This is not like home, NOT like home at all." His mind wandered for the entire hour long drive from the airport as his dad tried making small talk, it was all so uncomfortable.

He thought to himself, "Awkward. What was he even talking about? Shut the fuck up asshole." He didn't care to hear his dad speak. He wondered how the hell he would be able to do this for an entire year. Shit. Would this be better than jail? He was beginning to have his doubts.

Richard wanted to make sure Philip felt at home. He also wanted to build a relationship with the son he left behind. Better late than never, right? The only way Richard knew how to reach Philip was to relate to him. If you can't beat them, join them. Yeah, that's a great idea. One day Richard thought it would be cool to show Philip his saved, old stash (or was it new?) of LSD; sort of a father-son bonding moment, if you will. They didn't take the LSD, well Philip didn't anyway; he just looked at it with him. He wasn't going to trip with his dad. Philip would however, take that drink his dad offered him and that doobie too; he saw no problem there. Philip loved his reefer. Although, he'd quickly come to find out that getting high with his dad was a nightmare. Richard would want to talk about his feelings and his past and Philip could give a shit. He didn't want to hear about his dad's feelings.

Philip was agonizing over this drastic lifestyle shift, from non-stop New York to this "Mayberry" like town. "Damn, there is nothing to do in this boring place! What am I supposed to do here for fun?"

People were not out on the streets after dark, you could hear a pin drop at night in this small town. There was no action, anywhere, other than the bowling alley, the movie theater and the drive-in. There was no place to just hang outside other than Rancho Park! Seriously, what kind of place was this? He was not digging it.

Philip was enrolled at the high school on our end of town, Royal High; our town had two high schools. He made no real friends. Well, he made a few friends of the female persuasion and found out who to hang out with when he wanted to get high. That's about it. He wasn't going to be here long, no need to get attached. The few girls he met were only to keep him busy. Clearly he wasn't looking for relationships to flourish; he was just biding his time. Philip would frequent the house of these two chicks who were sisters. He met them at the high school. They were fascinated by his thick New York accent. They liked the bad boy image he portrayed. Philip would get it on with both of them, they didn't mind sharing. There was another girl he was messing around with as well. He thought it was fun to keep trading off. Teenagers in the 70's: sex, drugs, and rock and roll. Philip wore a tough outer shell and made no friends other than the girls he was sleeping with. And that's the way he wanted it.

Dad allowed him to paint his room so he felt more comfortable. Philip chose to paint it all black and then painted a constellation system on top of the black background on one wall. I thought it was trippy and cool all at the same time. It was a very dark room.

Philip had never been a part of a "family" before, we were very happy to have a big brother! Michelle and I always wanted to play with him and sit on his lap. Although he thought that was cute, he had no time or interest in playing with a couple of kids. It was foreign and uncomfortable for Philip to be a part of a family. But he did his best. He did not know just how long he could keep doing his best. This was not his lifestyle. This was out of his comfort zone. Who the fuck were these people?

His dog Akiva was greeted by four cats in the household, Beelzebub, Arpegio, Andante', and Little Girl . The cats were not thrilled to have a dog living in their house. Akiva got too close to Andante' one day and, SLASH, a sharp kitty cat claw right across the poor dog's nose. Akiva learned to stay clear of the angry cats. Phyllis was always worried about having the dog in the house around the cats, but it somehow seemed to work out.

Durnig Philip's stay, Dad graduated and received his PhD. in clinical psychology, he was now a doctor! Philip was able to be a part of that, not sure if he was thrilled about it, but picutes show a smile on his face and his body language was relaxed. Looking back, Dad must have rented him a suit. He was looking sharp at the graduation ceremony. Dressing up tends to make a person feel good.

Uncle Doug came for a visit on Wallace Street. Doug was Richard's half brother, 20 years his junior. Doug and his girlfriend happened to be driving across the country from New York to California like any hippie in the 70's, in their hippie van. Douglas knew his brother lived in California and looked him up. Richard was long gone before Douglas was born, so as you can imagine, they didn't know each other very well. Uncle Doug was a good looking blond with a tough attitude. He was a bit taller than Richard, both were slim in build. Uncle Doug liked to tickle Michelle and I, almost to death so it seemed! The hurt tickle that makes you laugh but yet hurts! You would be begging for him to stop but he would not! I wonder if one could be litterally tickled to death! Yeah, it was like that. He was an aggessive tickler. The hurt tickle was only for Michelle and I. Lucky for Philip, Uncle Doug would bypass him, unless Doug wanted a punch in the nose. Uncle Doug didn't stay long, he was just passing through.

Philip could no longer take this "family" crap! He planned his escape. Waiting patiently until everyone was asleep one night; Philip gathered all of the cash he could find around the house. He then found Dad's car keys to his light brown, 1968 AMC Rambler. He snuck quietly out of the house, quietly into the car, sparked up the engine and took off. One year? Nope. One year was not possible for Philip. Six months and Philip was over it. Stealing cars was his thing, so this was a piece of cake, especially because he didn't have to hot wire this one, he had the keys. He had to leave his dog behind as his plan was on a whim and he did not want to put his dog in danger, nor worry about how he was going to feed him and care for him while on the run.

Philip was able to get as far as Texas until he ran out of gas and out of money. He ditched the car on the side of the road and hitch hiked his way all the way back to Queens, New York. He called his mom. He made it back to New York, yes, but his Mom told him not to come home or he would be arrested because the police had already been there looking for him. Richard had pressed charges and there was a warrant out for Philip's arrest. The police eventually caught up with him and he would be forced to serve his time. Not only did Philip have to serve for yet another grand theft auto, but also for breaking his parole in the first place.

# CHAPTER 9

# ALL YOU NEED IS LOVE

I was heart-broken that Philip was gone. I was also upset to learn that the $20 of birthday money that Uncle Jim gave me was gone too. Apparently he needed the money more than I did. I did not so much want my money back as much I wanted my "new" brother back. I got attached quickly. We would give Akiva away to a man who lived on a real farm. Mom was not a dog person.

After Phillip left, we had another live in "visitor" for a bit, Dad's patient, Nancy. Nancy was suicidal and had attempted suicide several times. She had been in and out of the hospital just as many times and "they" wanted to commit her to a mental hospital. If you do your research, mental hospitals back then were not a place to heal and grow, they were places of torture and supression, patient housing not healing. Dad did not want to see this happen. Did not want to see his patient be commited. Dad felt it was necessary to put her on 24 hour watch though, at our house. Mom must have agreed to it because she would live with us in our "spare bedroom".

Nancy's most recent suicde attempt involved a deep slashing of her wrists. I vividly recall the scar on her left wrist, I remember it was a long deep cut. Nancy was pretty, with long blond hair and blue eyes. The door to her room was cracked open one day and I had a view of her sitting on the edge of the bed. She was leaning forward and had a small hair comb in her right hand as she manipulated the comb to scratch inside the deep wound on her left wrist. Back and forth the comb's motion, with the comb insterted in the wound. I was disturbed by this. I do not know exactly how long she lived with us, but I do recall that after she moved out, Dad was no longer her psychologist, she needed a psychiatrist who would be able prescribe her medication, along with intense therapy. Dad's degree did not allow him to precribe medications. A few years later, Dad had heard some disheartening news, Nancy had finally succeded in ending her life. Dad was crushed that he was unable to save her. He grieved for Nancy, Dad was not afraid to cry. He had learned in therapy that it was ok to cry, to let it out. Supressing your feelings will not provide comfort, but more pain. Mom would let him grieve and support his feelings. Phyllis and Richard were turning into an amazing team; supporting each other's educational journey, their journey as a married couple, as well as their journey to be successful independent individulas.

During this time there was a well-known pediatric psychoanalyst named Dr. Benjamin Spock. Dr. Spock wrote a book in 1946 entitled, "The Common Sense Book of Baby and Child Care" which became a bestseller. By 1998 the book had sold more than fifty million copies and was the second bestseller, the only book that sold more copies was the Bible. Dr. Spock's idea's were considered by many to be out of the norm but would bring about great change, he was the first pediatrician to study the psychoanalysis of children and family dynamics. Dr. Spock influenced parents to be more open, more flexible, more forgiving, and more affectionate. He encouraged parents to treat their children as individuals. During the 1960's and 1970's, the popularity of his philosophy declined and his collegues criticized him for relying on anecdotal evidence rather than research. However, Mom and Dad would follow Dr. Spocks idea's on parenting, "you be you" became their philosophy, forgiving and affectionate they would vow to be.

Dad got a job as the staff psychologist at Southern California Edison (SCE) in Rosemead. Rosemead was a long way from Simi Valley. Approximately a two-hour drive without traffic because the freeway in Simi Valley had not yet been constructed. Sometimes he would stay in Rosemead in a hotel during the week and come home on Friday nights because he had long hours. Appointments were scheduled prior to employees normal working hours, lunch hours and after work hours which was a heavy schedule. Michelle and I were excited on Friday nights when he walked through those doors. Not only to see Dad of course, but also because he always had a small gift, toy or treat for us when he came home. We looked forward to this samll gesture from him. And when Sonya from across the street would spend the night, he would bring a gift for her as well. He was awesome like that, never allowing anyone to feel left out. Michelle and I called Sonya our adopted sister and our parents always went along with it.

As you could have guessed, since our parents were fan's of the arts, they raised us with an appreciation for the arts as well. We were enrolled in dance classes when in Los Angeles and Mom continued this for us when we moved to Simi. There was a little dance studio in town inside a warehouse type building called *Dance Unlimited*. Miss Karen was the owner and our dance teacher. We took tap, jazz and ballet. I made a friend in tap class, her name was Stephanie Broad.

We were also involved in a performing group in town called *Bill Edward's On Stage Kids*. This was a performing group who put on song and dance shows in town at the local high schools, at retirement homes. We would also go Christmas caroling and give gifts to those in need. We had a live pianist and drummer that we practiced and performed with, Miss Julia, was our choreographer who put together our group numbers, as we sang our old time melodies, *"That's Entertainment! The World is a stage, the stage is a world of entertainment!"* (Julia and I would reconnect in the future on a professional level as well as a personal one.) We made a friend in the program, little Debbie Cohen. Debbie had two older brother's, the oldest brother Eric was our drummer. I thought Debbie was a great performer, she was small and mighty, she also performed solo's in the shows. She was an outgoing girl, like myself, a huge personality, and an abundance of confidence. Debbie was between the ages of Michelle and I and her other brother Mike was a year older than me, we would all attend the same high school in the future.

Michelle and I received guitars for Christmas. Of course, Mom would traverse us to Cousin Sam's on the weekends for lessons. Family lessons, of course, but we each had our own time with Cousin Sam. While Michelle and I would switch off playing *Barbies* with our older cousin, Cindy, the other would partake in her guitar lesson. Mom would chat and visit with Lucille until it was her turn, then both Michelle and I played with *Barbie*

*Dolls* with our cousin and listened to her record collection of her favorite band, *Chicago*. Good times, great memories.

Dad loved to write; plays as well as novels. None of which were ever published, however. But that did not lead him astray, he would not abandon his love for writing, he perservered. His philiosophy, *"If at first you don't succeed, try, try again."* Home computers, self-publishing and blogging we unheard of.

Dad kept himself busy at all times. If he wasn't busy writing his own play or book, he was starring in one or reading one. Dad and Mom were both avid readers. They believed a book was a wonderful place to use your imagination and a great way to keep your mind in shape, so to speak. I also wrote my own tiny children's books when I was in elementary school, inspired by my Dad's writing. They were litterally "tiny" books, maybe 4 or 5 inches tall. I was always enthralled with small things. I included an illustrated cover as well as illustrations inside my book. One was called "The Lonely Bunny". It was about a bunny who was lonely because he had no friends. In the end of course, he has plenty of friends. There was always a happy ending in the books I wrote.

Mom signed me up for a book club at our local library which required me to read a certain amount of books in a certain amount of time. I wanted to earn a book from the library and be able to get my face painted like a clown when I reached my goal. Reading is a great "time out" at the end of a long day, for a child or an adult. I enjoyed the challenge. I succeded in my goal and was able to chose a book for free! I chose *The Hobit*. I was also very excited to have my face painted! Our parents never forced us to do anything, and Michelle chose not to participate and that was alright with them. Even as children, Mom and Dad belived that our life was our choice.

We rode bikes as a family on the weekends, all four of us. Dad had to teach Mom how to ride a bike, and I will never forget it as long as I live. I was so confused by this, why didn't Mom know how to ride a bike? Who on earth doesn't know how to ride a bike, I thought. She also didn't swim. She didn't even drive a car until her later 20's when she moved to California. We utilized small, circular, metal clips to place around our ankles to keep the bell botton jeans from getting caught in the spokes of the bicycle. I absolutely loved my orange sparkly banana seat bicycle that I got for Christmas that year. There were tassles that hung from the handle grips. Michelle's bike had a yellow sparkly banana seat and tassles. Both bikes were also equipt with a little white basket that was attached to the front handlebars. Our parents made sure we always had the same things as not to create any, "Why does she have that and I don't?" Until we got older, then it was an age priviledge. I was the oldest therefore I got it first. Our parents tried to be very fair. I always appreciated that, not sure Michelle did.

Mom and Dad both had crazy schedules, but I do not recall ever feeling abandoned or lonely or neglected in anyway. Somehow they made it work and were able to provide a stable and very loving home. *The Beatles* said, "All you need is love. Love is all you need." I tend to agree.

While Mom was at CSUN, she took some ballet classes and would practice her ballet in the garage at a ballet bar that Dad put together for her. I always wanted to practice with her. I wanted to wear a leotard and leg warmers like she did. Mom let me practice with her. She would give Michelle and I, and sometimes Sonya too, dance lessons in the garage. The garage was our mulit-task room. Mom taught us how to do *The Hustle* while Dad played with his remote control toy race car track that Mom got him for Christmas. We did macrame' with Mom and other arts and crafts. The garage was a place to play, discover, learn and be together as a family.

Not sure exactly when Dad got into Buddhism, I just remember us buying him buddha figurines for birthdays and Christmas'. Dad said you were supposed to rub the Buddha's belly for good luck, that's about all I knew about Buddha as a child. Dad never shared his belief about Buddha or why he was interested with us kids. I assume this was a personal journey. I now know that Buddha is about overcoming the past, past suffering. I know Dad felt he suffered through a lot of his life. Buddhism practices acknowledgement of the suffering and then a release of the suffering. The concept is to leave the suffering in the past and allow room for peace.

Buddhism believes in Four Noble Truths: The first truth identifies the presence of suffering. The second seeks to determine the cause. The third is to seek the truth and end the suffering, which is called Nirvana. The fourth truth is the method for attaining the end of suffering, The Noble

Eigthfold Path. Buddism acknowledges that suffering exists and that there is a cause for the suffering. The belief that if there is a beginnig of the suffering, that there is also an end to the suffering. Dad attempted through Buddhism, to deal with his situation at hand, then to seek out a way to rectify his suffering. Buddhism also believes in Karma, whether good or bad, and Buddhism believes in reincarnation. This belief is a relavant point for me further down the road.

Dad joined a Moorpark theater actors group called *The Horizon Players*, which would later evolve into *Moorpark Players*. Moorpark is a little town next to Simi. The first stage production I saw Dad perform in was *Damn Yankees* and is still one of my favorite memories. Dad was cast as the Devil. Dad performed in *Damn Yankees* previously in 1964 when he first arrived in California, "Shoeless Joe" was the charater he played then. Dad rehearsed at night and on weekends. Sometimes when Mom had night classes at CSUN, Michelle and I would sit in the theater and watch Dad rehearse. It was totally groovy. I loved it! I thoroughly enjoyed watching Dad rehearse. He also performed in a production of *The Sound of Music* and played the role of Captain Von Trapp. I remember crying everytime Dad went over the hills to escape at the end of the play, both during his rehearsals and during shows. I always felt like my dad was "leaving". I was, and still am an overly empathetic individual.

Dad loved to perform and loved being the center of attention. He always pulled a silly stunt and at the end of each production during the bows. As he walked on stage from behind the wing, he would smile and wave at the audience and then suddenly trip on nothing and fall down into a forward roll and then pop right back into a standing position; he would pull a "Dick Van Dyke", if you will, that's what we called it anyway. Dad was a silly man and pulled these tricks at home as well. It made him feel good when the audience laughed at his little stunts. He felt just as good when his family laughed at his silly stunts. He was always "on", much like myself. Dad and I are cut from the same cloth.

# CHAPTER 10

# VERDA

In 1980, both of my parents were doing well professionally and were able to save up and borrow enough money to put a down payment on the purchase of their first home. We would no longer be renting the house we'd been in for some four plus years, the house on Wallace Street, where we had made many friends, and shared many experiences. We would be leaving our best friends, the Frenes Family. It was bittersweet to be leaving our neighborhood and our elementary school, Hollow Hills, the elementary school I attended from First through Fifth grade. We would now be attending Justin Elementary. The 2.4 mile difference from our former neighbors seemed a lot further than it actually was. Luckily for me, because of my dance classes, I already had a good friend who attended Justin Elementary, Stephanie Broad, which would make the transition easier.

Our friendship with Sonya Frenes would outlast just being neighbors, she would come spend weekends with us many a time through Junior High School. Sonya would be diagnosed with kidney failure at the ripe age of 14 and would have to endure the brutality of dialysis. She was home-schooled on and off from Junior High to High school, I didn't get to see her much during these hard times. After her treatments, her little arms would be covered in enormous welts from the dialysis treatments. I did not understand why my childhood friend had to be burdened with this ailment. I did not (and still do not) understand why any child must suffer so.

Sonya and Tania, 1981

On North Verda Court, we were in the culdesac. The neighborhood was an improvement from the neighborhood we came from. "Movin' on up" as George and Weezy Jefferson said. More than half of the neighborhood was filled with kids our age! Simi was an affordable place to raise a family. We would have time to get to know the neighborhood kids before school started too. All of the neighborhood kids would play in the safety of the culdesac.

There were the Oddones down the street: Gina, Vince and Lia. Lia and I ended up becoming besties. Gina was Lia's gorgeous older sister; she was already driving so she didn't partake in our kid games on the block. Vince was the middle child, Lia's rough and tough older brother. The Napolis lived on the corner next to the Oddones. Tawnya Napoli, who was an only child was cousins with the Kellers who lived around the corner on Cochran Street, Scott and Dawn. Scott was a grade below me and Dawn was Michelle's grade. Don McLean, who was the tallest guy I knew, played a good game of basketball, and lived across the street from the Kellers. Don was the best basketball player in town. Rumor had it that Don was going to make it to the pros. The Martins were a housefull of rambunctious boys who lived across from the Oddones, Eddie, Pat and Chris. The

Szolecks were also in the culdesac: Jill and Joyce. Jill would become our babysitter. Joyce was our age and was the gymnast on the block. Joyce would coach us and inspire us to begin gymnastics lessons at *Imagymnation*, the gymnastics studio that she belonged to. Next to the Szolecks was little Jenny, the youngest of all of us kids on the block. Jenny's mom, Cathy, was a single mother who eventually began dating a Simi Valley police officer named Bob. Next to Jenny was the Dugars, who moved in later, Ron, Rick, and Rod. By the time they moved in, they were already past the "playing" stage. Ron, the oldest, was the hot guy on the block, even Mom thought he was handsome. Rick was the long haired brother out causing a ruckus, and Rod the youngest and the tallest brother, he was our age but was a tough guy busy doing other stuff. Michelle Miller, an only child and was diagonally across from us. Michelle Miller and my little sister Michelle would become friends, they were the same age. Next to the Millers, were the Roes, Glen and Shannon. Their family was really into CB radio communication, their parents' cars both had tall antennas all over the hood and roof. Prior to our moving into the neighborhood, Shannon had a very unfortunate accident while she was riding her bike when she was twelve years old, she had a stroke. The stroke did not stop her from joining in our culdesac fun. Directly next door to us were the Childres', Kim, an only child and Kathy her mother. Kim's step-father was a bit older than her mother as I recall, he passed a few years after we moved to the block. Kathy was plagued with brain tumors and would have to endure countless brain surgeries, however she took a lickin' and kept on tickin'.

I always loved when Kathy would take her cats for a walk around the block. All four of her felines would follow her around the block and back home. This always fascinated me. Her cat had a litter of kittens and we ended up with one of them. We named the cat Big Foot because it had six toes on his little paws. We would soon get another cat and name him Snowy. I am sure you can guess by his name that he was all white. This would now make a total of five cats in our household.

All of the kids on the block would go to a different Junior High and High School than Michelle and I. The boundary lines for which school you would attend was changed when we moved there. While everyone else on the block went to Sequioa Junior High and Simi High School, Michelle and I would go to Hillside Junior High and Royal High School.

We would all get together in the culdesac and play games after school and on weekends; hide and seek, ding dong ditch, flag football, street races, you name it. We were outside as much as possible in the 80's, it was "like totally bitchen!" Atari , the first gaming console was introduced, however we only played Atari now and again and it was only when there was a rainy day schedule or mornings before we went outside to play.

Michelle and I were strong, must be in the Irish genes beause Dad was always a physically strong man. He was able to put his arms out staight out by his shoulders, bend at the elbows and make a fist on each side, he then let Michelle and I hang on each arm as he would walk us around like he was the strongest man in the world! We thought this was so fun! My point being, buff arms run in our genes, Michelle and I both had more strength than your average girl. Scott Keller called Michelle and I the "boy arm sisters" and would say, "Hoyt me! Hoyt me!" Get it? "Hurt" vs. "Hoyt". Silly boy!

We would often compete in what we called "street races". We all lined up like track stars and raced down the street to see who was the fastest! Michelle was fast, she had strong thighs and was able to win most all the street races, even beating the boys! Except for Scott Keller, Michelle could not beat Scott Keller.

We also played ding dong ditch which we thought was such a crack up! Daytime games included hand ball, kick ball, tag football, bike riding, skateboards, rollerskates, you name it, we were outdoors doing it. There was a roller rink, *Holiday Roller Rink*, on Los Angeles Avenue, where we would all hang out and work on our roller skating skills.

One summer day, a bunch of us kids on the block went down to *Edwards Cinnema* in Larwin Square to see a movie. Like many, we would always go the to the *Thrifty's Drug Store* to buy our goodies because the cost of the same snacks inside the theatre were so much more expensive. We would stash all we could in our pockets and sneak it into the theatre on our person. I finished my can of cola and as I tried to delicately put it on the floor at my feet, I dropped it! There was a silence in the theatre, at least in my head, and it seemed you could have heard the CLANG of that can meet the floor a mile away. Wait, it gets worse, the can then proceeded to tip over, and roll all the way from the last row where we were seated to the very front of the movie house, it seemed like it would never stop rolling. Just my luck, a theatre employee happened to be in the theatre at the time. He was furious with me for sneaking it in and he kicked me out, just me. I would have to wait out front for the others until the movie let out. But Vince, who had gone with us, must have felt bad for me, he gathered the whole group of kids, they would all leave the theater too and join me outside. We all went home together. Kids can be cruel, but they can also be very loyal. I don't believe I ever acknowledged how much I appreciated Vince for his act of kindness. (Thank you, Vince, for showing me your heart that day.)

Hanging out in the Mann's Theater parking lot was also a cool thing to do. A giant pink shopping center, known as the "Pepto Bis-mall" was built with mulitle retail shops including a new movie theater with six screens. The town was excited! Prior to this, our only theater was Edwards Cinnema in Larwin Square which only had two screens; we saw *Star Wars* here. We also had a drive-in movie theater in Simi, inclusive with the old fashioned speaker boxes that you would hang on your slightly opened window; we would see *Grease* at the drive-in. When we got a little older, when we went to the drive-in with our friends, a couple of people would hide in the trunk of the car so we could get in cheaper. Those were the good ol' days.

Most often we would sit down as a family and watch night time tv shows and movies together. Our family did things together more often than not. That is the way Dad wanted it. He loved being a part of his family, having his own family. *Rocky* was a family favorite movie. Who didn't love *Rocky*? Dad loved it for obvious reasons; he could relate as he was from a rough neighborhood in New York like Rocky was from a rough neighborhood in Philladelphia, and he loved to box too. Here is where we notice Dad's excess energy, as he would sit in his spot on the loveseat, he never stopped moving. His movement was subtle, but nevertheless, he was fidgeting. He rubbed the arm of the couch almost obsessively and instinctively. I know, you are thinking, "Yeah, so?" But here it is, Dad would rub the arm of the couch so often and so roughly that he litterally rubbed holes into the fabric, exposing the stuffing of the couch. Mom would purchase covers for the arms of the couch. When he wore out the cover, she would buy another. Finally, they would end up having the love seat reappolstered, and the process would continue. Dad was always moving, even when he was sitting still. I understand that, I have the same energy. We do not stop moving until the head hits the pillow. Which is fascinating, because Dad was able to nap. He loved his naps. However, I always laughed because I did not consider his naps to be a real nap. He would grab the kitchen timer, close his bedroom door, set the timer for 5 minutes, and "nap". I would giggle, "What was the point", I thought. Later I would come to understand that Dad would need to lay down and re-group, although I did not comprehend that concept as a youngster.

Mom was pretty open to a lot of things with us, we were allowed to watch *Saturday Night Fever* because there was dancing in it, but we were not allowed to own the Prince record which had the song *Erotic City* on it. Every time *Erotic City* came on the radio, she would be disgusted. Michelle and I would giggle at her disgust as if the lyrics were no big deal. She found the song far too vulgar for her liking. Mom forbade us to purchase this record and bring it into her home. Michelle and I would obey her wishes. We didn't want to make Mom upset as she would not forbid for us to do things very often.

Televised music videos were about to explode the music industry and MTV, a new channel exclusively for music videos, was totally bitchen, music videos all day long. *Michael Jackson*, of which I was a huge fan, always had the best choreography in his video's. I would record his music video's on a VHS tape and learn all of the choreography in our family room in front of our projector television set that Dad was so proud to own. Who didn't want to dance like Michael Jackson? Mom never seemed to be annoyed with me for using her VHS tapes to record the music videos of the dances I wanted to learn. In fact, I think she enjoyed it, she was my biggest fan when it came to dancing.

Music always filled our house. I worked on my homework while I listened to my favorite records. I could not focus in silence, believe it or not, I needed the distraction of the music to help me focus on my tedious homework. I also had an alarm clock radio that I listened to at bedtime to put me to sleep, and I woke up to the radio playing my favorite "Nu Wave" tunes on KROQ.

Dad loved to play their old reel-to-reel recordings of their own songs. Michelle and I loved to hear Mom and Dad sing. My favorite song of Mom's was her most up-beat song, *Other Side of the Tracks*, which was a song from the 1962 Broadway production of "Little Me", a musical written by Neil Simon. My favorite song of Dad's was his updeat song, *Wonder Why.* I did not know any of this information at the time, I just always thought these were my mom and dad's songs; I had no idea the songs had been previously recorded by other artists.

If you were at my house often, you may have caught Mom and Dad having conversations in song. If their conversation included verbiage that also happened to be a line from a song they knew, it would be sung as part of the converstation; our own real-life musicals, if you will. If Mom happened to happnened to mention "New York" in conversation, Dad would break out in song with "*New York, New York, a helluva town. The Bronx is up but the Batterey's down*", or as good ol' Frank Sinatra sang, "*If I can make it there, I'll make it anywhere. It's up to you New York, New York*", accompanying his songs with some Broadway-like dance moves. If someone metioned the word "memory" in conversation, Mom would break out with Barbara Streisand's "*Memories, like the corners of my mind, misty water-colored memories, of the way we were*", or from Mom's favorite broadway show, *Cats*, "*Memory, all alone in the moonlight…*" You get the gist of it, I'm sure.

Dad had learned a little tap sequence from one of the Broadway productions he was in back in the day, and taught it to me in the kitchen. It was choreograpy to a song that went something like this: "*East side, West side, all around the town*", which included a few "step shuffle ball changes" inclusive with a double jump heel click at the end, of which I always thought was so cute. I also thought it was cute that Dad was teaching ME tap in our kitchen, as I was the one who was a tap dancer. Dad was a man of many talents. He and I would bust out that tap dance together at any given moment from that day forward. He would begin the song and dance and I would jump right in.

I would often catch Dad coming home from the office and embracing

Mom in a giant, loving hug. Hugs are healing. Dad did not have any hugs as a child and longed for them as an adult. I would also catch Dad kissing Mom, and would gross out. No one wants to see their parents make out! Ew! So totally gross. Next thing you knew, Dad was swaying with her side to side in the kitchen, in a slow dance. He would then feel the need to break out in song. Who knew? As they swayed, he began singing one of his many favorite Frank Sinatra tunes, *"You make me feel so young, you make me feel so spring has sprung"*, as he danced with Mom around the kitchen like *Fred Atsaire* and *Ginger Rogers*. *"And every time I see you grin, I'm such a happy, individual."* Dad was still madly in love with Mom. I was priveledged enough to be abe to see that kind of love. *All you need is love, Love is all you need.* Love is all Dad needed.

Our garage and front yard was used to produce talent shows, theater productions and sing-a-longs. We put together muscial shows and the neighborhood kids would audition for their roles. *Grease* was our big pro-ductin number, our garage play, if you will. Lia was the prettiest girl in the neighborhood, she played Sandy. Scott Keller was the cutest guy in the neighborhood, who also happened to have black hair, he played Danny. He was also the only guy in the neighborhood who was willing to participate! Dawn Keller played the role of Rizzo. Tawnya played the "brusha, brusha, brusha" girl, Jan. Michelle played the role of Marti and I played Frenchie, the beauty school drop out, which would turn out to be ironic (I would drop out of beauty school myself in 1992). We walked the neighborhood door-to-door to sell tickets to our parents and other neighborhood kids, for a nickel per ticket. Mom and Dad had folding chairs in the garge that we would set up for the audience. Vince, Eddie, Pat and Chris were all too cool to be in our play, but they did ride their bikes over for show time, sit on them in our driveway, and watch our production from the comfort of their bike seat. Dad was in the background as the DJ. When the time was right, he would place the needle on the record and let the record play until the song ended, then pick the needle back up and standby for the next que. Dad was always proud to help us out with our garage plays. The neighborhood kids, I beleive, enjoyed their taste of the arts. Mom and Dad were once again influential in bringing the *Arts* to the neighborhood.

In addtion to *Grease* we put on random prductions, we would sing and dance to our favorite songs from artists like the Go-Go's, Pat Benetar, Air Supply, Rick Springfield and any other song from that era. The music would be played on cassette tapes through our boombox as we sang along with the artist. We always choreograhed an accompanying dance. The front yard was also used to perform our gymnastics tricks. Us girls loved to practice cartwheels, round-offs, back bends, and walk-overs! Joyce was our inspiration as well as our spotter. Our house was always open to the neighborhood kids and our many shennanigans. When we were done with our activity, all of the kids would come inside and get a *Hostess* snack from our "goodie drawer", we had plenty to share.

When we were not producing shows, we were being educated in theater, immersing us into theater culture. Mom and Dad were at least 10-15 years older than all of our friends' parents, so were exposed to different things.

Dad got his feelings hurt at the bank when the teller said, "It is so nice that you have your grandchildren so often." He explained that we were his children, not his grandchildren; she was quite embarrassed and apologized. It is almost as bad as if someone said to a woman, "When are you due?" and she is not even pregnant. His white hair made him look "old". He was older and wiser.

We grew up watching Gene Kelly tap dance his heart out, Fred Astaire dance with such elegance, Gregory Hines tap dance his feet off and Baryshnikov pirouette endlessly. We absolutley loved *Two on the Town*, with Frank Sinatra and Gene Kelly! Michelle and I also watched many "Road Shows" with Bing Crosby and Bob Hope on Sunday morings before we would go out and play. When we weren't watching the arts on television, Mom and Dad were taking us to broadway productions at the Pantages Theater, Shubert Theater, the Shrine theater and others. One of my favorite shows we saw was *A Chorus line*. I was obsessed! Mom bought me a *Chorus Line* record of which I would listen to and learn every word to every song. We saw Chorus Line twice because Mom too was obsessed. Dad would not be joining us for the second outing. We also saw *Cats* a couple of times. Mom was again obsessed, as was I. *Cats* was her favorite production. I enjoyed seeing my mom so excited about this production. Mom and Dad would take us to other broadway productions including *42nd Street*, *Don Quiote* and many more. It was always fun to go to the theater; we got to dress up! We put on our best dresses and our fancy shoes when going to the theater. It always felt good to dress up.

✳ ✳ ✳

Possibly because of their energy, hummingbirds always fascinated me. Mom happened to often be around when I spotted one in our backyard. Seeing a hummingbird always made me stop, focus and watch it in amazement. Such a beautiful, tiny little creature. There was not much that could get me to stop and focus, but the hummingbird always manageed to capture my attention. Mom and I would stare at the hummingbird together, without uttering a word, until it flew away.

As mentioned, Dad loved to box, he kept it up for fitness and to vent, I am sure. He had a speed bag in the garage. He was so good at hitting that bag, which took so much focus and control. He kept a very steady rhythm while he punched the small bag. Watching Dad hit it was like watching a beautiful dance, he had grace and flow, he had such focus when he was boxing. He was really good at it and I loved to watch him pratice, as did Michelle. He really wanted a heavy bag so Mom, Michelle and I went all the way to the San Fernando Valley to *Big 5* to purchase this heavy bag. We kept it a serect and would give it to him for Christmas. Mom wanted to surprise him, and surprised he was! He used that bag often. Michelle and I would accompany him in the garage and he would teach us some of his boxing skills. It was fun to put on his big gloves and hit the bags. There was definitely an art to boxing. Dad never missed a boxing match on television, ever.

One day Dad was pretty peeved at Michelle and I for assuming it was ok to let our friends come over and play with his boxing gear without putting any of it back in its proper place and without asking him first. When he entered the garage to workout on his bags, he couldn't find his boxing gloves in the spot where he kept them or anywhere in the gagage for that matter. He always blamed us for anything missing anyway, or for random lights being left on around the house or in the garage, while no one occupied that space. But this time he placed the blame correctly. He came into the house and asked Michelle and I where his gloves were and we told him they were in our room. We then got a lecture on putting things back in its proper place as well as a lesson on never assuming that it was okay to take his things without asking. He brought us back into the garage where he set up his easell and clipped on a piece of paper where he wrote the word "assume". He then proceeded to explain to us what happens when you assume. He separated the word by use of slashes and explained that when you "assume", you make an ass out of you and me, ASS/U/ME, everyone's favortie lesson. Well, alrighty then. Is our meeting over? "Can we go back outside and play now Dad?"

Michelle and I loved to step up on to the 2x4 on the back side of the gate on our side yard. We would do this at first because it was fun to swing back and forth on the gate, it was like a ride. Dad had warned us not to swing on the gate. Ugh! Ok, fine. We would not swing, we would just perch ourselves up on to it and chit chat. It was fun to stand on the gate because we were able to see over the gate and into the culdesac. He yelled at us to get down. He had told us time and time again not to swing on the gate. I thought, "Excuse me Dad, correction, we were not swinging, we were simply standing." Isn't that different? He didn't think so. He determined that there needed to be a bigger consequence since we did not listen the first time. He said he would have to spank us like other kids were spanked when they disobeyed. Spank us? I was in 6th grade. "Dad, no." He had made up his mind. Michelle and I had never been spanked before and we always handled things with family meetings.

Most parents spank their child out of anger or frustration but our dad had to plan the entire event out first. By the time he was prepared to spank us, the momentum had passed. He placed a kitchen chair in the middle of the family room and sat in it. He told us to line up and he would spank us one at a time. It was obvious that he was also uncomfortable with this task, but was determined to follow through.

He said, "Um, ok, now fold yourself over my lap and I will spank you."

"Dad, really? This is weird.", I said.

Dad said, "I see no other choice."

"Like, oh my god, dad, this is like totally weird."

I laid my uppper body across Dad's lap and he said, "Ok, ready?"

"Dad, just get this over with."

His hand came down and he smacked my bottom once with a sharp sting. He then said, "Ok, you are next Michelle." He did the same to Michelle. Awkward. We never stepped up on to that gate again.

We prefered our family meetings. Usually Dad would lose his temper and yell, send us to our room to "think about it" and then come in to talk about what happened, why we should not have done what we had done and how to make sure it would not happen again. Dad would then apologize to us for yelling and losing his temper. He always apologized, and we always ended our discussions with hugs.

One summer afternoon, Lia, Joyce, Michelle and I all rode our bikes down to the local *Sav-on Drug* store in the Mervyn's parking lot. The four of us stopped in the hair brush isle and noticed there were packaged brushes with a tiny "sample" brush attached. It did say, "sample". So we each grabbed a brush, lifted the corner of the plastic cover and took out the cute little sample brush so we could take it home and actually sample it, most definelty on one of our doll's hair. We each shoved the sample brush in our pockets and continued on our way around the store and to the junk food isle. We each picked up a snack to munch on, I picked up my favorite, Doritos Cool Ranch, and went through the register to pay for our snacks. When we walked out the store door, the store manager followed us and told us to come back inside the store and empty our pockets. What? Crap, the sample brushes. We were shocked and scared. We were caught. The store manager proceeded to give us a lecture about stealing, threatened to call the police, but instead called our parents to come pick us up. Joyce's dad drove her back to the store to apologize for stealing. And boy was Mom mad! She grounded Michelle and I for a week, but agreed not to tell Dad. We were not grounded from television, just from playing outdoors for a week. So as we sat in the front room and watched tv for an entire week during summer time, Dad, on his way out the door for work one day, was perplexed.

He said to Michelle and I, "Why are you girls in front of the TV so much? Why don't you go outside and enjoy the outdoors?"

We said in harmony, "Oh no, that's ok Dad, we're fine."

"Ok, suit yourselves. It is a beautiful day."

He left for work, and we looked at each other with a sigh, "Whew! That was a close call."

I was always picking on my little sister, isn't that what big sisters were for? We were only 20 months apart, maybe that had something to do with our constant bickering. *Bumble Bee Tuna* had a tv commercial out with a very catchy tune. Michelle had very buck teeth due to all of her finger sucking, and I always made fun of her by forcing my top jaw over my bottom to make very exaggerated buck teeth. Michelle walked outside one day while Lia and I were hanging around in the front yard and I started to tease her and sing the commercial to her with my exaggerated buck teeth face, "Bum bum bumble bee, Bumble Bee Tuna. I love the tuna they call Bumble Bee!". Lia and I would laugh hysterically. We thought is was so funny. Michelle did not. She would run into the house crying. Mom would tell me not to treat Michelle that way and I would just roll my eyes, "Yeah, like, ok Mom. For sure."

I was in the 6th grade and I was curious one day about my middle name, Susan. I asked Mom and Dad why they chose the name Susan as my middle name? I was just curious. As my inquiring mind wanted to know, where did my middle name come from? Was there a story or a special reason for my middle name? As I asked the question, the two looked up at each other and locked eyes. Mom spoke first, "We had a friend named Susan." I thought to myself, "Hm. That's funny, I never met any friend of theirs named Susan, nor have I ever heard either of them mention ever having a friend that they called Susan", other than their recent buisiness partner, Susan Tuttle.

I said, "Why have I never heard you mention your 'friend' Susan before? She must not be that close of a friend."

Silence.

I said, "I don't like the name 'Susan' for my middle name."

Dad: "Well, if you don't like it, go ahead and change it."

Me: "Really? I can change my middle name if I want to?"

Dad: "Sure. I didn't like my name and changed it. So, why not."

Well, there you have it. Dr. Spocks philosophy applied again, "you be you". I just got permission to change my middle name. Did I really need to change my middle name? No. But I was in the 6th grade, and Dad said it was ok, so I did; legally. Mom took me down to the Social Security office and I changed my middle name offically from "Susan" to "Suzanne." I know, huge change, right? I look back and I laugh at myself; all that effort for such a minor adjustment. But, Dad said I could, therefore I followed through.

Dad smoked cigarettes. Michelle and I did not like it. Mom didn't like it either. Back then, people smoked anywhere they damn well pleased, which was in the house, at restaraunts and even on airplanes! People were not concerned with smoking around children or the second hand smoke issue. Michelle and I told Mom how we despised his smoking, it was stinky and gross. Mom advised us to express ourselves to him and tell him our concerns. So we did, and in addition to telling him how we hated his smoking, we also posted signs saying, "NO SMOKING", around the areas where dad sat. We metioned how much we hated the cigarettes and exaggeratedely coughed each time he lit one up, we nagged him constantly. Boy did that piss him off, but we didn't care, we were persistant in expressing our dislike and Mom supported us, so it was okay. Apparently our persistency paid off because he finally quit smoking after more than 40 years, then proceeded to write and publish a booklet on, "How to Quit Smoking". He utilized these booklets to help his patients quit smoking too.

Like most siblings, Michelle and I were always fighting for the front seat in Mom's car. Neither of us wanted to be in the back seat. There were no seat belt laws at this time and Mom was so sick of us arguing all of the time that it seemed like the perfectly acceptable solution for the two of us to share the front seat. If I ended up on the side closest to the door that meant I was closer to Michelle's burnt arm, which was her right arm. I refused to touch her burnt arm or let her arm touch mine. I was obvious at first about this little rebellion and would pull away and say, "Ew, gross!", but if Mom heard me, she would remind me that it was hurtful to Michelle and her feelings. I didn't care about her feelings at the time, we were kids. So instead of protesting out loud, I nonchallantly moved my arm away and scooted as close to the side door as possible so we wouldn't touch. Being that we were nearly butt cheek to butt cheek in the front seat, this was a difficult task.

Whenever we took a family trip, we were the family who would sing songs in the car to pass the time. We would sing The Andrew Sisters, "*Three Little Fishes...Bim bam didum dadum whadum shoo, and they swam and they swam all over the damn*". I loved when when Mom or Dad would lead us in song, especially that song, it was my favorite! My parents were entertainers, what else would you expect? "*I've been working on the railroad, all the live long day. I've been working on the railroad just to pass the time away....fee fi fidly i o, fee fi fidly i o o o o*", another family favorite. I was surpised to learn later in life, that not everyone's family sang songs together "*just to pass the time away*".

When we went to Disneyland, we went in style. Our family would stay at the Disneyland Hotel for the entire weekend. These were the days that Disney was actually affordable, the days where they had the ticket books, in which you would use a certain ticket to get on a particular ride. We would do Disney all day and then by night we would have dinner and listen to live blues artists at the restaurant next to the hotel, Dad loved the blues. I often heard Dad playing the blues on his harmonica, harmonicas and the blues went hand and hand. We had many musical instruments in our household growing up. Dad had a couple sets of bongo drums, a ukylele, several guitars, Mom's piano, harmonica and a tamborine.

We were still performing with Edward's On Stage. When I was awarded solos, Mom would take the time to really work with me on them. I wanted to be as good as little Debbie Cohen! Mom and I would set aside times to rehearse, just her and I. The piano Mom had in the house belonged to her as a teenager in Boston. Once we moved to Verda Court, the piano was shipped by Grandma from Boston. Mom would play my solos on the piano and I would sing. She bestowed me with tips and suggestions to improve. Mom chose what I sang. *I Enjoy Being a Girl* was a show tune from the Rodgers and Hammerstein musical, *Flower Drum Song*, and Ella Fitzgerald's *De-lovely* to name a couple.

One day Dad called a family meeting to inform us that his half-brother Douglas from New York, could not handle his father any longer and was dropping him off for Dad to "take care of". (I look back and cannot understand what happened here and why Dad agreed to take this man in to our home.) This man, my Dad's father, who I had heard so many horrible stories about, was coming to live with us? Why didn't Dad say no? So, Dad's father was coming to live with us, huh? Interesting. We never met the man and all I knew was that he was a very bad man, a convicted pedophile, and now he was coming to live with us. I never called the man "grandfather", I don't feel that he deserved that title. I was still in the sixth grade at the time.

Uncle Doug came to Simi Valley from New York to drop off Dad's dad. The visit was very brief, there was no tourturous tickling this time around from Uncle Doug. The circumstances of this visit were far different, this was not a pleasure trip. It was a visit to get this man off of his back and out of his life. Doug dropped him off and left, literally, he didn't even stay for dinner. That was the last time I ever saw my Uncle Doug. (I learned while researching for this book, that Uncle Doug would pass away at the young age of 50 years old. I was unable to determine the cause of his death.)

## CHAPTER 11

# EASE ON DOWN THE ROAD

It was 1980, Dad's father was 85 years old, he was a small man with a big attitude and a had constant scowl on his face. A very grumpy old man. He was short, bald and round in the mid-section and wore thick glasses. He had no control of his bladder, or quite possibly he was just being an asshole, he would urinate all over the chairs and couches. Dad warned him to stop peeing on the furniture. He flat out ignored Dad. Dad again had a stern talk with him as he sat in one of our living room chairs, he looked Dad straight in the eyes and he intentionally urinated in the chair! So, let's go with "asshole" as the reason for his lack of bladder control; it was clear at this point that it was an intentional act of rebellion. With little recourse, our parents bought plastic and covers for our chairs and couches to protect them from this old man's urine. Yeah, we were THAT house now, the plastic house.

It was a typical day and all of the neighborhood kids were gathered at our house hanging out in the garage. We had a pool table in the garage and we were all playing and laughing and having a good time, when Dad's dad burst into the garage and yelled at us, "Shut the hell up!"

I think I was born a smart ass (must be an Irish/Italian thing) because I lipped off to him immediately and told him that, "No, we were not going to shut up!"

We all ignored him and continued to play.

He yelled again and said, "If you kids don't shut up, I am going to get my shot gun out of the closet!"

I said, "Pffff, yeah right! Go ahead and get your shot gun!"

Of course I knew he didn't have one. And I, of course, told Dad what had happened when he got home from the office. As I recall, the old man did not live with us much longer. That may have been the straw that broke the camel's back. Dad found him a "home" and shorthly after being placed in that home, Charles Hoyt Sr. would pass away.

I will never forget the day Dad told us of his passing. Dad said he was numb, said he had no "feelings" about his dad dying. He didn't know how or what to feel. He was struggling with the fact that he could not shed a single tear for this man. While most people lose a parent and mourn the loss, Dad would not mourn. He would not cry, he could not cry, then again, Dad's dad had not been much af a "dad" at all. Dad knew this was not typical behavior, and this was his struggle. But then he reminded himself, nor was his upbringing typical. He expained to us that he felt conflict about not feeling emotion for losing his father. There was no father/son relationship, there was no love, there were just horrible memories Dad carried of his father. He felt nothing when his father passed. Therefore, we felt nothing.

Life continued. Our house was the house that the door was always open and the cupbords were always full. Dad did not want to ever run out of food. He was often starving as a child and would make sure WE never starved. Dad's philosophy: We will have food, and we will have plenty of it. We had a "goodie drawer". All of our friends knew where our goodie drawer was, and were always told to help themselves. The goodie drawer was filled with Hostess treats like *Ding Dongs, Suzie Q's, Zingers, Twinkies, Hostess* pies and donuts. It was perfectly acceptable to eat "junk" in the 80's, we were a very active generation. We never stopped moving and we burned off every last calorie. I had never heard of, or knew anyone who was a vegetarian, a vegan, no one was lactose intollerant, or gluten free in my entire childhood. And in the 80's, California was the "fittest" state in the nation. Go figure. It was a "calories in, calorie's out" kind of world.

Mom was very talented with a knitting needle, as was our grandma, she both knit and crochet. Michelle and I would receive handmade afghans and handmade quilts for our beds at Christmas from her, items that got plenty of use. There is something very special about handmade items from loved ones. Mom had so much patience; she could focus for hours at a time and would knit project after project, sweater after sweater and purse after purse. I was always amazed by her focus, I had none. She was able to sit in one spot for long periods of time, I could not.

The four of us flew to Boston for the first time to visit with Grandma and all of our aunts and our uncle. Well, I went to Boston when I was a baby, but it doesn't count if I don't remember. We would also meet many of our cousins. I was still in the sixth grade, Michelle in the fourth. (It appears looking back that the 6th grade was a very eventful year!) We stayed at Grandma and Auntie Tootsie's house; they lived together. It was a dual occupancy home, an apartment type home with a home upstaris that Grandma and Auntie Tootsie occupied, and a home downstairs in which were for renters. Grandma had a basement. We didn't have any basements in California so I was fascinated by this, although it was used only for storage and I found it to be cold, dark, and creepy. I loved Grandma's backyard because she had a garden, I was particularly facinated by her wild tomato garden. There was a line running across the backyard for drying the laundry, like I had seen in the movies. Michelle and I slept in the sewing room which was a very narrow, attic type room on the back side of the house with a pitched ceiling along the roof line, and a tiny window where we could look out and see the tomato garden. We loved Boston! It was far different from California. We visted the historic Paul Revere house, which was so tiny. Every thing was tiny, the house, the height of the walls and the beds. It was hard to imagine people living like this. We also went to the Hancock Building along with many other touristy attractions. It was also fun to see the place where Mom grew up, and it was nice to be able to meet our distant family members.

Mom and Dad both got into making stained glass. Dad built a wooden work table in the garage and placed it behind the pool table in a position that would not interfere with our play space. They took on projects such as stained glass inserts for our kitchen cubbords, stanied glass wall hangings as well as other pretty projects here and there.

My best friend was Sandra Ramirez, whom I met in the 6th grade at Justin Elementary. We were both new to the school and both in the same class, Mrs. Smalley. Mrs. Smalley was known for wearing a lot of perfume and the boys called her Mrs. Smelly. Sandra and her family were originally from Columbia. They then moved to Florida and then when Sandra finished the 5th grade, they drove across the United States to Simi Valley, CA. Sandra was a good Christian girl, and although my family did not practice any kind of religion, we still became close friends. I already knew Stepanie Broad at the elemetary school, she was Jewish. I would introduce Sandra and Stephanie and the three of us would become glued at the hips.

My friend Sandra loved to come over and participate in our family crafts. We dabbled in the stained glass art during the holidays, she attemted to make a standing Christmas tree and I attempted to make a standing snowman. Cutting glass and using a saudering iron was tough business. I was unable to get mine to stand up very straight, it would be a leaning snowman.

My dad owned a Scooter. He's had a scooter since the time we lived in Los Angeles. Mom was not keen on motorcycles, they scared her and she did not trust Dad to own one. John Oddone down the street had a "real" motorcycle and Dad was very envious. Somehow Dad convinced Mom to let him get a bike, a big bike. Not sure how long he owned it, but one day when he was pushing the thousand pound bike up the driveway, it tipped off center and the bike began to lay down, but not without a fight. Dad held his ground as the big piece of heavy metal tried to lay on the ground and take him down with it. He managed to hold that thousand pound bike, never allowing it to touch the ground. I will never know how he was able to lift that bike and park it safely, but it would not be without consequence. Dad tore his bicep muscle, tore it in half. Literally, half his bicep was missing, sunk in forever. I had never seen anything like it.

Dad was always in a bit of pain. Not from the bicep tear, I never heard him complain about that. It was his neck. Dad had many different sorts of chiropractic devises for his neck issues. The chiropractor told him he believed his neck problems derived from when he was a kid, from being punched in the head so many times before his bones had developed. Dad owned what I used to call, the "upside down hanging machine". It was one of those contraptions that you would lay on and then tilt it upside down and hang there by your ankles, for traction. He also had a bag full of water hanging beind the garage door of which came with a chin strap. He would place his chin in the strap, sit in a chair, and let the weight of the bag perform traction on his neck. This always made me laugh, seeing him upside down or in traction.

For Christmas, Michelle and I would always get the same exact things; but different colors. Michelle got Raggedy Ann and I got Raggedy Andy. I do not understand why she was given Ann and I was given Andy. Could we not both have Raggedy Ann? We both received Monchichi dolls, both received the same pajamas, etc. When we got older, if we didn't get the same things, we got exactly the same amount of presents and the same amount of money would be spent on each of us. They never wanted us to feel any favoritism.

Dad had some over-purchasing issues, he loved buying in bulk. We had so much food in the house and we had a giant freezer in the garage, where Dad could store even more food. He loved purchasing from the meat trucks in bulk. We would never go hungry, that's for sure. A commercial on TV that advertised Arbey's roast beef sandwhices at $1 a piece for a short time only, prompted Dad to take a trip to the nearest Arbey's, which was the next town over. Mom, Michelle and I waited for our $1 roast beef sandwhiches to arrive. Dad always seemed to get side tracked. When he would dart out to the grocery store to pick up a few items, forever and a day later, Dad would show up with bags full of groceries. It did not seem possible for Dad to have the opportunity to become side tracked at Arbey's. We waited patiently. When Dad finally arrived, he stepped through the garage door, into the kitchen, with bags full of Arbey's. More bags than there were people, let's put it that way. Each bag was filled to the top with Arbey's sandwhiches. Dad had come home with 100 Arbey's sandwhiches, in a variety of flavors. I do so wish I could have been there to see the reaction of the Arbey's emloyees. They must have thought, "Is this guy kidding around?" We would all get a good laugh. We couldn't lie, we were all a bit excited about the thought of 96 more Arbey's sandwhiches at our disposal. These sandwhiches would be stored in the garage freezer, I have no idea how long it took us to eat all of those sandwhiches, but we did. Thank goodness the microwave had just been invented.

Mom completed her Masters program at CSUN while we were still in elementary school. She had recently completed her years of interning and was eagerly anticipating her degree in the mail. Mom received many of her interning hours at the local *Free Clinic* in Simi Valley as well as at *Interface* of Camarillo, an interim home for foster kids. I remember the day Mom received her notice in the mail that she had earned her Masters degree in Marriage and Family Therapy. She had been waiting for the mailman for days anticipating the notice. I will never forget her scream of delight when she opened the manilla envelope and pulled out a letter that said, "Congratulations on earning your Masters degree". Her feet may have even left the ground for a brief moment. Time to *"Ease on Down the Road"*, like the *Wiz*. Mom received countless hours of training at the *Free Clinic of Simi Valley* and was appreciative. In return, Mom donated her time back to the *Free Clinic* for the next 15 years or more, training the psychology interns, paying it forward many times over.

Now that Mom and Dad both had their desired degrees in psychology, it was time to open up their own practice. They began their journey by sharing an office with a third person, Susan Tuttle. At this time both Mom and Dad worked at Southern California Edison (SCE) as the staff psychologists. Dad was able to give Mom some of his patients at the facility. Dad's load would lighten as Mom stepped in, therefore they were both home at a decent time every day.

In order to be successful in their new endeavor, they would have to wean out of SCE. The office space they acquired was down the street from our house. They named their business, "Center For Growth". After many years sharing an office with Susan, Mom and Dad would branch out on their own, leaving Susan with the original office space to continue her practice, while they moved to the new building.

It was Michelle's and my job to clean their offices on the weekends, work for which we would be paid the flat rate of $5 each. We had a regular allowance but were given the opportunity to make more money and we were all for that. Our allowance wasn't just handed over to us, we had to earn it by cleaning the house. If we didn't do the work, we didn't get paid. They taught us at an early age that if you wanted money, you had to earn it.

The word "try" was not allowed to escape our lips, we either did or we did not. Mom and Dad would not accept "try". Mom and Dad offered my best friend Sandra an opportunity to work with us as well. We would not have to share the money, we each received our own $5. Sandra was grateful for the opportunity.

Dad was constantly seeking approval from others or a pat on the back for a job well done. If there was something Dad was proud of and we did not pat him on the back in a timely fashion, he would pat himself on the back.

"I think I did a really good job!" He says with a grin ear to ear, "What do you think?"

We would giggle and answer, "Yes, Dad. You did a great job."

While we were at the mall one day, Mom, Michelle and I found the perfect Christmas gift for Dad's office. It was a wood framed mirror with the words, "Damn, I'm Good!" etched on the center of the glass. He got a good laugh out of that one. He took it to his office and hung it in the waiting room.

Both my sister and I had braces, we both had buck teeth. Michelle's were far worse from her aforementioned finger sucking so she had more extensive orthodintic work done. We both had to wear head gear and neck gear to push our overbites back. Mom and Dad never let us slip. We would try to run outside for play time without our head gear on and Mom would stop us dead in our tracks and make us put them on before we went out to play.

"Ugh! So embarrassing Mom!", we would complain.

"There is nothing for you to be embarrassed about. You cannot go outside and play until you put it on."

We would do as we were told. The boys may have laughed for a moment, but that was it.

After we got our braces off, we had retainers. We would often walk down to Carl's Jr. on the weekend and have lunch with our friends. Michelle would always forget her retainer case, she would wrap her retainer in a napkin. We had both already lost a few retainers by this time. We finished eating and went about our day. By the time we got back home, Michelle realized that her retainer was missing and that she left it on the tray at Carl's Jr. and threw it into the trash. Mom and Dad were furious! They were not going to endure yet another expenditure for another lost retainer. Dad drove us back to the Carl's Jr. He approached the manager and explained what happened and asked if Michelle and I could go through their trash, Michelle remembered which one she threw it in. The manager let us know that all of the trash recepticals inside had been emptied throughout the day and had been taken to the dumpsters out back. Dad asked then if the manager would unclock the dumpster gate so Michelle and I could start picking through the trash. The manager's eyes almost popped out of his head, but he led us to the dumpster. Dad told us to get in and start going through every napkin we came across.

"Wait, what? Dad, really?" I said, "It's not even my retainer. Why do I have to do this?"

"Because you were there too.", he said sternly.

He helped us each climb into the large trash dumptser to begin our search for Michelle's retainer. Boy did this dumpster stink. Michelle and I proceeded to go through each trash bag and open up each napkin. Dad supervised from the outside of the dumpster. Wouldn't you know it, we found her retainer at the bottom of the dumpster in one of the few remaining bags. We then had to put all of the trash back into the dumpster. Did this stop either of us from being irresponsible with our ratainers? You would think so, but no. So the next time we lost a retainer, that was it. No more retainers.

Mom and Dad were very involved in our community, they were members of the Simi Valley Rotarty Club and did their part to pay it forward to the people of Simi Valley. They also wrote and published monthly newsletters for their patients to keep up on their mental health. Mom and Dad were very social beings and very active on many levels; business and pleasure. Dad would also somehow talk Mom in to participating in one of the local stage productions that he wanted to star in, he wanted Mom to experience it with him. She was not much of an actress, but would be a good sport and participate with him.

Our Uncle Jim had continued to visit us and stay for the weekends.

Dad and Uncle Jim would usually drink together, although typically we only saw him have one drink, he called it a "night cap". I never saw Dad drunk. He would wait until us kids went to sleep before he and Uncle Jim hit the bottle. Mom did not drink, "Don't drink, don't smoke, what do you do?", as Adam Ant said. Yup, that was my Mom, pretty straight laced. Uncle Jim would drink until he passed out, he would always show up with a large bottle of bourbon on Friday and it would be empty by Sunday.

I was in Junior High School at the time, and I walked into the family room where Mom, Dad and Uncle Jim were watching TV. They always gathered in the family room. As I entered the room, Uncle Jim exclaimed, "Oh my, looks like you are starting to bud", as he stared directly at my chest. I think you could have heard a pin drop. I brushed it off because I was embarrassed, and went about my business in the kitchen. I noticed my Dad glaring angrily at Uncle Jim. I woke up the next morning, which was a Saturday morning, and Uncle Jim was gone. Hm, I wonder why he left on a Saturday? He always stayed until Sunday. I asked my parents where Uncle Jim was and they simply said, "He won't be coming around for a while Tania". We never saw Uncle Jim again.

Our parents were always very fair, or at least I thought so anyway because I was the oldest. I was able to get my first 10-speed bike when I was 12 years old, Michelle had to wait until she was also 12 before she could have her 10-speed. We shared a room untill I was 13 years old. When I turned 13, Mom and Dad let me pick out a water bed and gave me my own room. We would omit the spare room in our house, apparently there was no longer a need for this room. I was going to have my own room and a cool new bed! I chose a waterbed with beige, courduroy cushoin around the outside border and head board and a bag of water in the center. I was so excited! I also postered my walls with pictures of cute male actors from *Tiger Beat* and *Teen Magazine*. Of course, Michelle would also now have her own room but she would have to wait until she was 13 to get her own water bed. It wasn't like that for every thing, just the big stuff. When I started shaving my legs,

Michelle started shaving hers as well, the boys on the block made fun of her hairly legs. Mom was always sympathetic.

Grandma came to visit. I always loved when she came to visit us because we would all make homemade ravioli as a family. I loved ravioli! It was a lot of work, but in the end there was great reward; the satisfaction of having made food from scratch and the delicious dinner that evening. " Mangia, Mangia!" which means "Eat, Eat!" in Italian.

Tania, Grandma, Michelle, 1981

Soon cousin Bobby would move out to Simi Valley. Bobby was Uncle Sam's son and would follow in his Dad's footsteps in a career in insurance. Bobby had cancer as a child and survived it, he lived with Grandma and Auntie Tootsie for more than a year so he could be closer to the hospital where he was recieveing treatment. As a young adult, Bobby wanted to start anew and what better place to be near his Auntie Phyllis in sunny California. Bobby would do very well for himself in the insurance industry.

He would join our family every Sunday for dinner. Mom was very excited to have her nephew living here in town. Uncle Sam would visit every year now too. When Uncle Sam came for a visit, he, Michelle and I would walk down to *Gemco* and he would let us pick out a new Barbie doll, we looked forward to this.

As you can probably imagine, since both Mom and Dad were in the field of psychology, we talked a lot. I mean, a lot. We had recuring family meetings. We talked about our feelings constantly. Dad would constantly say, "How do you feel about that Tania?", or "Tell me how that makes you feel." I did tell him how I felt and was conditioned my entire life to talk about my feelings. Many people were raised not to talk about their feelings and have a hard time understanding the need for me to share mine. Dad expressed himself at all times, which may include calling people out on their bullshit. People don't like to be called out on their bullshit.

Mom and Dad would come home from double dinner dates and Mom would say, "Well, we will not be having dinner with them again." Dad would then explain how he disagreed with the other couple's husband and all hell broke lose. Dad did not seem to be worried about it, he did not like that guy anyway. Mom would retain a relationship with her friends independently.

If Michelle and I were punished, we were sent to our room on "time out" to think about our actions. Afterwards, when Dad thought we had spent a sufficient enough time thinking about it, he would knock on our door, come in and sit on the edge of one of our beds. We would talk about what happened, why he got mad, why we should not have done what we did and then he would apologize to us for blowing his top. Dad had a temper, he was a reactor and would get mad and yell. But most of the time, his angry eyes said it all. He wouldn't have to say a word, you knew from the look in his eyes that you were busted. It was a scary look. We were always allowed to tell him how we felt about him yelling at us, after the fact of course, but he made sure we understood why he got mad in the first place and not to repeat that behavior again. We typically would not repeat our mistakes because we did not want a "talk" from Dad.

Dad cursed, my Mom did not. I picked up the cursing thing at a young age, Michelle did not, well not openly anyway, now she curses as much as me. We never heard Mom use curse words other than "damnit" and maybe an occasionaly "shit", but never the "F" word. Until one day; we had just gone school clothes shopping at *Miller's Outpost* in the "Pepto-Bismall" shopping center. As we were leaving the parking lot, a couple of teenage boys darted out on their bycicles in front of Mom's car. She slammed on her brakes, avoiding hitting one of them. As she stopped the car, she was so angry that she started shaking. Her hands came off the stearing wheel and next thing you know, Mom spats out, "Oh…fuck you!" as her middle finger came popping up towards the boys. Michelle and I couldn't help ourselves and we burst out in laughter. We could not believe our ears! Mom just said the "F" word! Not only that, she flipped the kid's off! As we were laughing, we noticed that it hurt Mom's feelings that we were laughing at her, so we stopped. We didn't want to hurt Mom's feelings. Of course the kid's never even looked over their shoulder's at her or gave her a second thought. We went home and shared the story with Dad.

I was so much like my dad, much to my mother's dismay at times. Dad was a great burper and of course so was I, we were proud of our burping skills. The two of us would have burping contests while at the dinner table. Mom was not thrilled, she would sigh and say, "Richard!". Dad and I would laugh and continue with our contest, unless Mom was super mad. We could tell when her lips became thin, tight and pursed together. Not a word spoken. At which point we would stop and continue with our meal.

Dinner time was family time. It was important to Dad that we share this time together. The dinner table was where Dad shared all of his crazy stories. I was fascinated, Mom, not so much. Mom was sometimes uncomfotable with the stories Dad chose to share with us. Michelle did not really pay attention as much as I did and tuned out a lot of his stories, possibly from shock. I enjoyed every story, always fascinated by how he was able to pull himself up, dust himself off and turn his life around. Dad was my hero.

One night at the dinner table Dad told us the story about his dad and being a convicted pedophile. "Whoa Dad! That's crazy!", I say. He then casually mentioned that his father also "liked little boys".

"What the heck? What do you mean?" As I asked this question, I noticed dad had looked over at Mom. I then hear her say quietly, yet firmly, "Richard!" Dad looked down at his plate and took a bite while thinking of a way to change the subject.

Dad said, after he finished chewing his bite of food, "Michelle reminds me a little of Julia."

I ask, "Which one was Julia?"

"My mother", he responds.

Michelle was a bit clumsy at the dinner table, often not watching where she was reaching and knocking things over and spilling in the process. This happened many a time, so often that on a particular night, Michelle reached over to grab a roll and her full glass of water toppled over and spilt on to the dinner table and all over the plate of meat. Dad had enough and reacted, he grabbed his glass of water and without any hesitation at all, poured it over Michelle's head! We all sat in complete shock and disbelief for a few seconds trying to absorb what just took place. Michelle finally cried while the water dripped from her head onto her shoulders and down into her lap. Dad was furious with Michelle and now Mom was furious with Dad. She never yelled, I never heard Mom yell and I never saw her lose her cool. She looked him squarely in the eyes and she firmly said, "Richard, that was NOT the appropriate way to express your anger." Dad agreed and apologized to Michelle. Dad asked what he could do to make it right. Mom felt that Dad should be punished equally, an eye for an eye. Therefore, as Mom supervised, Michelle picked up a full glass of water and slowly dumped it over the top of Dad's head. We all laughed, dried off Michelle and Dad's heads, and continued on with our meal.

Along with the end of the week and recurring family meetings there was also a "disappearing" box. During our family meetings if there were any items in the box, we would discuss it. Any and all items that were left out and not put away by our bedtime were put in the disappearing box until the end of the week at the meeting. If we left a toy or game out, it would disappear into the box. If we left a shoe out, bye bye shoe, into the box it would go. It appears as if they were tired of picking up after us. Come meeting time, we would discuss why the item ended up in the box and would then discuss how to avoid having the item end up back in the box in the future by simply picking up after ourselves.

I attended Hillside Junior High School. In the seventh grade, I had a crush on a basketball player, Joe Pugh, who was in the ninth grade. He was the tallest kid in school, light brown hair and blue eyes. I thought he was the cutest guy I had ever seen. But he was in Ninth grade and I was just a little scrub. ninth graders didn't look at seventh graders. Also in the seventh grade, Sandra, Stephanie and I would all try out for the drillteam and make it. We would be on the drillteam together through our eighth grade year.

In the eighth grade, there was a movie out called " The Outsiders". Sandra and I were obsessed with *The Outsiders*. Obsessed. It was during a passing period, I happened to be leaving my P.E. class. The girls locker room was near the front side of the school, so I would walk past the teachers' parking lot to get to the main buildings where my locker was. I saw something out of the corner of my eye and my head snapped to the left. I saw my best friend, Sandra, strolling across the street and off campus. I was shocked! Sandra was one of the most education driven, book smart individuals I had ever known, and here I was, witnessing her ditch school.

Naturally, I called to her, "Sandra, what are you doing?"

There were no yard duties around and no school personnel. She called back to me, "I'm going to go watch *The Outsiders* at Mann Theater."

I didn't have any books because I just came from P.E. I ran across the street and joined her. The two of us walked all the way across town to the Mann Theater, it took at least an hour. We were not worried about not being able to get into the movie theater, we happened to know someone who worked there, Tommy. He was a friend of the Czarnetskis in Los Angeles, who moved out to Simi to attned Moorpark College. Tommy let us in frequently for free. Sometimes we would pay if he wasn't there, but when he arrived, he would let us stay in the theater and see multiple movies.

In the ninth grade I tried out for cheerleading along with my two best friends, Sandra and Steph. I was confident that I would make the team because I was a dancer. All of my friends thought that I would make the team too however, that is not how it went down. Sandra and Steph both made the cheerleading team, I did not. I was devastated. I cried to my parents and they suggested I go talk to the cheerleading advisor and ask her why I didn't make it. So I did. I approached the cheerleading advisor and asked her why I didn't make the cheerleading team. She appeared not to be comfortable with me asking her this information as she refused to look me in the eyes. As she looked down, she was very short with her answer. She said sharply, "Someone else had a higher written test score."

I said, "Well, that doesn't seem fair to me. I had the lowest test score out of all the girls?"

She kept her eyes down on her desk, she refused to look me in the eyes and she refused to answer my question. I turned around and walked out of her classroom.

Since I didn't make the cheerleading team, I tried out for the girls volleyball team and made it. Rad! I was totally stoked! I would be a starter! Who knew I could play volleyball? I didn't! I loved playing volleyball and enjoyed being part of a sports team.

Steph, Sandra and I liked nearly all of the same things and we especially loved *Duran Duran*. The three of us were pretty tight. We called ourselves "The Three Musketeers". *Duran Duran* was going to be playing in concert at the Rose Bowl. Sandra was not allowed to go, but Steph and I went. We were only in ninth grade so we needed a ride, it was not cool back then to go to concerts with your parents, but Steph's Mom, Nini, was a trooper. She would give us a ride and pick us back up afterwards. Nini was always chauffering us all over town, she didn't seem to mind. She would drive Steph and I all the way to Pasadena to see our first concert. Nini would keep herself busy somewhere and then come back and get us when the concert was supposed to be over. There were no cell phones then, so she had to guestimate. Parents had a lot of trust for their kids back then. Steph and I were just 14 years old and were trusted to fend for ourselves at the Rosebowl and somehow we managed.

By the time I got to high school, I made the cheerleading team and would be on the team throughout high school, with my two best friends, Sandra and Stephanie.

Tania, Sandra, Stephanie, 1984

I would formally meet Joe Pugh, my crush from the seventh grade, who was captain of the basketball team at Royal High School and also on the wrestling team. Joe and I would date for a year. We would both also join the track team together. Joe would do the high jump, the pole vault and running long jump, while I did the 100 yard dash, the 220 yard relay and the running long jump.

One morning while I was curling my hair with my cordless *Clicker*, Mom sat behind me on the toilet seat like it was a chair and asked me if Joe and I were having sex. Oh my God, did my Mom just say that word out loud to me in a sentence? So embarrassing! I couldn't lie, we do not lie to each other, so I told her that, "Um, Yes." Mom then took me to our doctor and put me on birth control pills.

Michelle was madly in love with Chad who lived around the corner from us and who was cousins with the Oddones. Chad was an Italian kid with tanned skin and blond hair. Michelle and Chad would date for a year. Michelle's heart was broken when they split up, she was crushed, her first love. Michelle maintained a friendship with his mother Francis and his little sister Tara. It was part of her routine for the past year to stop in and chat with them after school, although now she would make sure Chad wasn't around so it wasn't awkward.

When I was 15 years old, Dad decided to enter me in a Miss Teen California beauty pageant. I was walking into to kitchen one day when he said, "Oh by the way, I entered you in the Miss California Teen Beauty Pageant. It's this weekend."

"Dad! What the heck? Why did you do that? You couldn't have told me sooner?"

"It slipped my mind.", he said without taking his eyes off his newspaper.

"Can't you cancel it?"

"No. It's too late."

Mom took me to get a one piece bathing suit (which I normally wouldn't have been caught dead in) and a fancy dress with a petticoat under the big hoop skirt for the pagent. I had no idea what I was doing or why I was there, but I was there. I clicked with another girl in the pageant and had a friend for the day, that was the fun part. I never did the pageant thing again. No thank you, but it is a good memory and an interesting experience. There was a talent portion as well, so I did get to perform a jazz solo.

Dad also enrolled me in a modeling program in Hollywood during summertime, Caroline Leonetti's. He asked my boyfriend, Joe to take me to and from modeling school in Hollywood. He did and was paid as if it was a job. I really enjoyed it, I learned how to do my makeup and how to be in front of the camera for print work. Each girl who was enrolled in the program, got a full photo shoot to use for our portfolio. In the end, they did not represent me because they said I was not tall enough. Oh well, didn't break my heart. I didn't want to be a model. I wanted to be an actress and a dancer.

Tania Hoyt, 1985

After a year, Joe and I broke up. We would attempt to work it out. When Joe showed up to pick me up for a date, my parents could see that he was distraught about our break-up. As one of my favorite childhood artists, Neil Sedaka, sang, "Breaking up is hard to do", and that it is. They would ask him if he wanted to talk. When I came out of my bedroom, I noticed they were all sitting at the "meeting area", the kitchen table. When Dad started with the arm rubbing, I would back away and not disturb them. Most people found it easy talking to Mom and Dad, they cared about your feelings and there is comfort in that.

I wanted to learn how to knit better. When I was a kid I knitted a blanket and pillow case for my *Snoopy* doll. Mom was so good at knitting sweaters and I wanted to knit one of my own. I chose smokey blue yarn and proceeded to knit myself a sweater with the guidance of my mother. After working on it for many weeks, I managed to get the entire front side of the sweater completed and then ran out of patience, lost my attention span, I was over it. Mom was gracious enough to finigh it along with many other rad sweaters she would make for me. She loved to knit!

When I was just a child, Dad had Mom take me to seek an acting agent. He neglected however, to prepare me for it, to teach me how to "read" and how to talk to agents. I had no idea what to expect at all. I read the script as if I was reading a book in school. Pretty funny in retrospect. In junior high school, I enrolled in drama with Mrs. Mohler. Mrs. Mohler was also my teacher at Royal High School, she chose to transfer over the same year I did. I took classes in the evening with a woman named Ruth Devron, who was a talent agent who held acting classes for kids in her living room in Simi Valley. My friend, Allan Tagg, from school would be in my classes. We would both be represented by Ruth as our commercial acting agent. She taught us how to read lines in all kinds of tones: angry, sad, happy, excited, etc. It was fun and I enjoyed it. Allan and I showed up at the same audition one day in Los Angeles. It was pretty rad because we would somehow be chosen to read with each other.

I was becoming more and more fascinated with dance. Michelle enjoyed dancing and continued to do so but she wasn't planning on making it her career. Mom always wholeheartedly supported me in the arts, but especially in dance because she knew this was my passion. Mom paid for me to have private dance instruction from a new teacher at Dance Unlimited, Jill. I really liked Jill and looked up to her. She was a tall, beautiful blonde with long legs. Jill was also working as an extra on television sitcoms, like "Cheers". She helped me take my dancing to the next level and offered to choreograph my first solo. Back then you had to be invited to do a dance solo. Not just anyone could pay a dance teacher and get a solo like today. I was so flattered. I was the only one in the studio to have a solo! My costume was fierce. It was a bright white, shiny spandex, longsleeve body suit. I wore black jazz briefs over the white spadex and a totally bitchen, silver, braided, forehead band which was mostly covered by my bangs. Oh, the 80's! Envision the movie *Zanadu*.

As I got older, this acting and dancing stuff got a little tougher. Everything was about size and weight. I was considered a "skinny" girl. I was always thin, in fact in school people would call me "Skinny Bones Jones". Why didn't the dance teachers and agents think I was skinny? I was 5'6 and a ½" and weighed 115 pounds. Mom would drive me to see my agent only to be told to lose twenty pounds and come back and see them then. Until then, they would not send me on any auditions. What? Twenty pounds? Are you talking to me? I didn't realize I had twenty pounds to lose.

✳ ✳ ✳

In high school, I had a black, VW Rabbit GTI. It was acting up, so Dad called a mechanic to come over and fix it. The mechanic was a small, brash, Irish man with a giant leprechan on the side of his work truck. I am positive my Dad chose him because of the Irish thing, Dad was, afterall, a proud Irishman. I walked outside to ask about my car. The guy was finishing up. I asked him what he did to fix the car. The man said, "Eh, I nigger rigged it."

"Oh", I said, "I will go tell my Dad that you are done."

I walked in the house to retrieve Dad. He was sitting at the counter stool as usual. I told him that the mechanic was done.

Dad asked, "Oh, ok. So what did he do to get the car to work?"

I said, "He nigger rigged it."

I repeated what the guy said. Dad lost it. His eyes narrowed, his face turned red and I swear, steam began to come out of his ears!

I was confused, what did I say? I did not stop to think about what I said or what it meant. I was a little naïve like that.

Amongst the many other things he yelled at me, he harshly forbade me to EVER say anything like that again. That word may never be allowed to escape my lips in his presence or at any other time. And, I did not. Ever. (I find it very uncomfortable to even write.) Prejudice was not a part of our family, in any way, shape or form.

✳ ✳ ✳

Dad was from the Speedo generation. He chose to wear Speedos to the beach and to the pool confidently. It didn't bother me as a kid, but I was quite embarrassed throughout my teenage years. We had a pool in our yard and would constantly have the neighborhood gang over to swim, and school friends too. And there Dad was, marching around in his Speedos.

When our friends would come over, Dad would actually answer the door in his Speedos. He saw nothing wrong with it. I was horrified and so were my friends. Way too much information. I would see the embarrassment cross over my friends' faces when they attempted not to look at Dad's little swim suit. Dad also wore platform thong sandals to make him taller. He also added lifts to his shoes. Dad did not like being or feeling short. He claimed to be 5'9", but I think that was with the one inch lift. Dad was very confident in himself in his speedos however, he never thought twice about it and would walk out to get the mail wearing his Speedos and his platform thongs. I wonder what the neighbors must have been thinking.

Friend: "Hi Mr. Hoyt!"

Dad: "It's Dr. Hoyt."

Friend: "Oh sorry! Dr. Hoyt."

Dad was proud of his accomplishment and wanted to be acknkowledged for it. That I could get over, but the Speedos, I was over my dad and his Speedos. I found it too embarrassing to bare any longer. I took Mom aside one day and asked, "Mom, can you PLEASE ask Dad not to wear Speedos to answer the door or in public at all? It's so embarrassing!"

Mom said, "Tania, he's been wearing Speedos for a long time and he's not going to stop now, so you will have to learn accept it."

"But Mom, does he have to anwer the door like that?"

Our family is under the philosophy of, you be you. So, Mom explained again, "This is who Dad is and what he is comfortable wearing. He isn't embarrassed, why should you be?"

"But Mom!"

"I'm sorry Tania, he has been wearing those his entire life, he will not stop wearing them now."

I threw out an eye roll then turned around and headed towards my room. She was not going to tell him to stop answering the door in his Speedos. Great. My Dad, the Speedo man. My friends and neighbors most likely got a big kick out of it. I however, did not.

Dad used to keep the needle for the manual air pump in a special spot. He used it to keep his speed bag pumped with air, we used it for inflating bicycle tires and handballs and such. I needed to put air in my 12-speed bike tires. I went to Dad's jewelry box to retrieve the needle for the pump, that is where he chose to stash it. As I opened the top of his jewelry box, I noticed something and I said to myself, "What the, what the heck is that? It looks like a joint. Why is there a joint in Dad's jewelry box?"

I took the joint and I walked out to the front room to inquire about this with Mom, Dad was not home. Mom simply said I should ask Dad what that was in his jewelry box.

I waited until he came home from the office and I asked him, with the joint in hand, "Dad, what is this?"

He said, "Hm. Looks like a joint. Where did you get that?"

I said, "I found it in your jewlery box."

Dad answered calmly, "No. In MY jewerly box?"

"Yes Dad."

"Show me where you found it."

Wow, he was really milking this one.

I proceeded to take him down the hall to his bedroom and to his jewelry box which sat on top of his dresser as we entered the room. I opened the top and pointed to the spot where I found this mystery joint.

Dad said, "Hm. Well, that must be a really old joint that I forgot about."

"Oh, ok Dad" I said, "What do you want me to do with it?"

Dad said, "Flush it down the toilet if you want."

So I did. I flushed it down the toilet. I thought to myself, I don't recall ever seeing that joint in there before and I had been in there many a time.

As a teenager, I started pulling away from my parents, as most teenagers do. Dad would do his best to keep us all one big happy family, as this was his life long mission, one big happy family. Family dinners were not only important, they were a normal part of our everyday lives, as you recall. Michelle started taking her dinner plate to her room to eat by herself. I guess she was over Dad's stories. I continued to sit at the table with my parents and listen to Dad however.

Dad felt us pulling away. He attempted to keep the love and communication going around. I would be running out the door for school and find Dad chasing out the door after me, "Wait, wait! Let me give you a hug!"

Ugh! Really Dad? And as I rolled my eyes and turned around to let him hug me I said, "Oh my god Dad, really? I'm late for school." I let him hug me because I knew it will hurt his feelings if I din't, but pulled away quickly and headed to my car. At least he wasn't wearing his Speedos.

Dad and Mom would participate in our High School Career Day. They would both be talking to my peers about their careers in the psychology profession. Talking about their path in getting there; college degrees and interning. Speaking about their experience working in a corporate environment as well as their private practice. I was always very proud to have my parents on campus inspiring my friends. I found that my peers repspected their profession and that made me proud, although I would never tell them that.

I was in my favorite teachers class, Coach West. He looked like Robert Redford, swoon! I just loved Robert Redford! Coach West was my weights class teacher, my health teacher and was also the football coach. One day in his health class, he was running a film. I was totally bored with the film, therefore began to doodle on my PeeChee folder instead of watching. As I was doodling, I heard my dad's voice. What the heck? Why is my dad here? I looked around the room and then assumed I was hearing things because clearly my dad was not inside of my classroom. As the film continued to roll, I glanced at the film. I noticed a number of adults and children sitting in a circle on the floor in the film. The film discussed the value of a babysitting co-op. Hm. That term sound familiar. I looked back down a continued my doodling until I heard my Dad's voice again. Where was my his voice coming from?

As looked up at the screen I blurted out, "Hey, that's my Dad! Hey, and my Mom! No way, that's me!" Michelle and I were both in the film, as very small children. Coach West was fascinated that my mom and dad happened to be in a film that he was showing in his classroom. A very interesting coincidence indeed. When I got home from school, I told Mom and Dad and they got a big kick out of it. They said they filmed that while they were in college for one of their psychology projects. They had no idea it was in the school system. Mom and Dad asked me to ask Coach West if he had any information on the film. Mr. West said he would be happy to give my parents any information he had. They attempted to retain a copy of it, however were unable to do so for some reason.

One evening, Dad came home from work and proceeded to check our home phone messages as per usual. This was during the times that we had an actual "answering machine" equipt with a cassette tape and all. One could leave as long of a message they wanted until the tape ran out. On this particular evening, Dad pushed play having no preconception of what he was about to hear. I happened to be in the living room stretching after dance class, practing my splits. I was in ear shot. There was a woman on the recording, she was drunk and she was angry. The woman on the recording said her name was Christine and that she was my father's daughter.

Christine then proceeded to curse the hell out of Dad dropping all kinds of "F" bombs! She called him a piece of shit, an asshole, a mother fucker, etc. She screamed, "How could you! How dare you!" She went on and on sreaming and crying for what seemed like forever, until the cassette tape ran out of room. The screaming, crying and cursing was over. The room was now filled with silence. I watched as Dad paced in front of the answering machine after it all ended. He was in the den as he paced back and forth, side to side, scratching his head, biting his fingernail and was in complete confusion.

"Dad, who was that? What was that all about?", I asked.

Dad was straining to figure out who Christine was. He did not know. He finally told me that he believed it could be the woman in Nebraska, the woman he cheated on Mary with when he went away to do the movie "Song of the Loons" had had a child. He had a relationship with this woman for a year and now assumed she must have become pregnant and did not tell him about it before he moved back to New York. Did she not tell him because she had no way of getting in touch with him? Or was it because she knew he was already married? Or was this even the correct assumption that was playing out in his head? He was unable to come up with any other logical conclusion. Or could Christine be a product of the woman in Boston during Summerstock Theater, that Dad had an affair with while married to Mary? I will never know the answer. We never heard another word from Christine again. This was not the time of redial, *69 or caller I.D.

My dance training was becoming more intense and I out grew my dance studio in town. If I wanted better ballet training, wanted to be able to be on pointe, I had to go outside of Simi Valley. If I wanted to be in a dance company, I had to go to the San Fernando Valley, (the valley for short). And that is what I did, I went to the valley to find a new dance studio. Mom did the research by looking through the phone book and calling around. She drove me down to Roscoe and Parthenia to view a class.

We pulled up to a studio in a little shopping center on the corner, "Dan Duhman's" Dance Center, as I sat on the floor to view the jazz class, there was a girl who caught my attention during the jazz warmup. She seemed nice as she looked over at me during the warm up and give me a welcoming smile. I would later come to know her as Faye, who would end up being my best dance friend.

I chose to attend this studio! The studio was owned by a very young male dancer, Dan Duhman, who was 21 years old at the time. Dan danced with both Joffrey Ballet and Boston Ballet. I was fascinated by him and upon viewing classes, I was also fascinated by the talent in his studio. I wanted to be a part of it.

## CHAPTER 12

# GOODBYE MADDIE

M y brother Philip served his time in jail as an adult, although he was only 17 years old, he would be released in a year's time. Jail, yet again, did not seem to have any "scared straight" effect on him. He would continue on his path.

His step-father's gambling was beyond control. Philip could not stand this fucker. He was always gambling their money away and his mother was still struggling, she was supporting all three of them. It was bullshit. Philip couldn't stand by and watch his mother struggle. He was 18 years old and pretty fed up. One night he laid into John about his lazy, gambling, worthless, good-for-nothing, drunk ass. The fight escalated pretty quickly and began to get out of hand. Mary was scared of the outcome and angry with John for fighting with a teenager, her son. She kicked John out of their apartment and out of their life. John moved back to Pennsylvania, where he was originally from. Philip and Mary never saw him again.

By the time Philip was 22 years old, he began dating a gal named Maddie, she was three years his senior when they met. Maddie was already on drugs, in fact, they were both addicts. Maddie was a cute little Irish gal with brown, curly hair and smiling eyes, she was a true daddy's girl. A few years prior to their meeting, Maddie's dad had gone down to the corner store one day for what was supposed to have been a quick stop. He had been gone for quite a while, too long actually, Maddie decided to go out after him. When she neared the corner where the store was, she came upon a big commotion; there was an ambulance out front. When she approached the crowd she saw her neighbor, who ran to her and informed her that it was her father, he'd had a massive heart attack inside the store and had died. Just like that, her father was gone. The pain was more than she could handle, Maddie turned to drugs; heroine would become her drug of choice.

After a year of partying together the couple decided to get clean together. It was December 1983, coming down off heroine was not without its consequences, they knew it would be hard, brutal even. There could be severe depression and anxiety to go along with the actual physical symptoms of withdrawal.

Philip and Maddie admitted themselves into a program for methamphetamine addicts. This program provided them with treatments that were medicinal and assisted in weaning them off of this terribly addicting and deadly drug. They had to be consistent about their program or it would not work. It was not an in-patient program. It was out-patient so they had to be responsible.

Maddie and Phil were not very responsible, they overslept one morning. They were in Brooklyn and had to make it to Manhattan for the program. They jumped in their car and drove to the program in a frantic rush. They had hope that they would make it in time. The car began to sputter. They pulled over to the curb as they ran out of gas.

They then hopped on the nearest subway. When they arrived to the program, they were turned away. They were too late.

They made it back to the subway feeling defeated and panicked. They were at the station on 34th Street and 8th Avenue underneath Madison Square Garden. Maddie and Phil were beginning to get sick. The only way to help them through this sickness was with the help of the program or to find some heroine. The latter would have to suffice as their first option was no longer available, not today anyway. Maddie was worried that they were not going to make it back in time before they got violently ill. Maddie and Philip paced around the subway station, anxiously awaiting the next train that would take them to their meth dealer.

Maddie was sinking, and fast! It was the middle of the afternoon and the subway was teeming with people rushing here and there. By now Maddie was distraught and was completely losing control of her emotions; the drugs always kept the emotions at bay, they kept her numb. Without them she had no choice but to "feel", feel the loss of her father and the emptiness she felt in her heart. Philip assured her that they would be on the next train and that much closer to getting the *fix* that would help them get over the hump which would take them to their sweet oblivion.

Maddie continued to spiral deeper and deeper, crying uncontrollably now, she could barely breathe and Philip was worried. There was a train approaching, but it wasn't the one they needed to be on, it was on the other set of tracks. He could see the headlight approaching and feel the vibrations emanating from the tracks themselves up through the subway floor. The train was approaching at high speed, before his mind could even register what he was seeing, Maddie ran, she ran with full force and determination towards the oncoming train. She leapt onto the tracks smack dab in front of the train, Maddie turned and waved goodbye to Philip as the train violently hit her.

Philip started yelling, "Where is she! Where is she?", as he looked under the train. He didn't see her.

There was an off duty police officer who witnessed the entire event, from the other side of the tracks. The officer shouted to Philip and pointed to where Maddie laid. Philip had to run through a tunnel under the floor in order to get to the other side of the platform. As he approached, he could see her limp body, awkwardly positioned. In a way he knew was not right. He could see that her head was split open. Philip attempted to get over to her, but the officer stopped him from going any further, he advised him against it. He would not allow Philip to endure the brutality that lay ahead. Maddie was gone. Maddie always talked about wanting to be with her father again, Philip hoped that she was.

Can you say, Post-Traumatic Stress Disorder? Philip would suffer with severe PTSD from this mind blowing event. I am not sure that anyone could witness something of this nature and not suffer greatly. That was it for Philip; it was his turn to lose it. Philip became distraught and enraged. He could not get the horrible images of Maddie's death off of his mind and out of his head. He took on the burden of blaming himself. He was angry. Why Maddie, why? He should have been able to save her. He should have made sure that they had showed up to their treatment on time.

Maddie and Philip, 1982

Philip went on a rampage and a crime-spree throughout the town, causing a ruckus wherever he went, as his father had before him. He did not know how to deal with his emotions. He dealt with it the only way he knew how, by robbing and stealing, which was not an unusual thing for Philip to do. The unusual part was that he did it at an outrageous level. Phil was pulling approximately ten robberies a day; armed robberies. "Fuck everything!" he thought. And since he did not know how to talk about what he was feeling, and did not know WHO to talk to about that, he distracted his thoughts by keeping himself busy, busy breaking the law.

Philip stole taxi cabs at gun-point and robbed liquor stores every day for about a month straight, until the authorities finally caught up with him. Philip, along with a buddy of his, James Mateo, was convicted of 20 armed robberies, who was his partner in crime at that time. Philip was sentenced to a term of six years in a maximum security prison in New York.

On January 20, 1984, the *New York Times* published an article stating that "Philip Hoyt and James Mateo were arrested and suspected of committing 20 robberies." Although we know there were many more than 20 robberies committed.

Philip was going to be in prison for a long damn time. He chose to make the best of it by enrolling in a prison college program. He aspired to pursue a career in psychology, like his father back in California. During the duration of his stay in prison, Philip earned his B.A. in Social and Behavioral Science at the prison college, known as Mercy College. Philip also occupied his long prison stay by taking on a job at the college, working as the Dean's assistant. Between college and work, the 6 years were more bearable.

Mary, his mother, visited every weekend and brought him care packages of cigarettes and homemade food. Yes, every weekend for six years unless there was something to prevent her otherwise from visiting. This was her son and she would continue to love him regardless.

While in prison, Philip had a lot of time on his hands to think. To think about the past, the present, and the future. As Philip sat listening to Led Zepplin in his prison cell, he thought about what happened back in California. He thought about what could have been, and what it is now was. Philip chose to place a collect call to his dad in California to let him know what had become of him. Philip inquired about Michelle and I.

# CHAPTER 13

# THE APPLE DOESN'T FALL FAR

**D**an Duhman's Dance Studio was in Reseda, California. Mom drove me to the Valley and back until I obtained my driver's liscence at age sixteen and could drive myself. Michelle would eventually join me at this studio. Mom would drive her seperately most of the time because our schedules differed. I joined the dance company, therefore my dance schedule became more intense. Dan put a lot of focus on ballet technique. As I mentioned previously, ballet at this level was not offered in my hometown. If I wanted to become a better dancer, I needed to take more ballet and If I wanted to be in a dance company, I needed to be in the Valley.

I was fascinated by Dan Duhman and the fact that he was a former professional member of both the Joffrey and the Boston Ballet companies. Dan was tough and he expected his dancers to work hard. Hard work would pay off, he would acknowledge it with a pat on the back or a verbal appraisal of delight. At times just a simple look of approval, if his eyes narrowed and a crooked smile appeared, he was proud. It was not easy getting Dan's approval, we had to work for it. He did not just hand out compliments.

We were expected to take ballet daily if we wanted to participate in his dance company. I was at the dance studio daily, taking ballet along with other classes like jazz and tap. I learned more ballet technique from Dan than I could have ever envisioned. Dan often had a live pianist accompanying us in class. Dan would quickly blurt out the combination, we were expected to pick it up from his one time verbal and visual instruction. At times, it was only a verbal explanation of the combination. We learned to think quick on our feet. At times he was gentle in the way he gave technical corrections and other times he was irritated, but he always took the time to explain, both physically and verbally to reiterate his expectations. Dan took the time to manipuate the dancers body in to the position he was looking for.

Mom set up weekly private lessons with Dan. I loved my time with Dan! This was when my technique began to grow immensely. Taking private lessons was a privilege and an opportunity; I seized it as well as valued it. Dan was molding me into the best dancer that I could possibly be.

One day during jazz class, we were going across the floor; we danced across the floor two at a time. I chose to go last which put me in position to perform with Robin, the best dancer in the studio. I did not plan it this way and would not have. I did not want to dance next to Robin. Dan would never look at me if I am danced next to her.

It was our turn to go. Dan shouted, "5,6,7,8" as we began our combination: chasse', turning pade' burre', grande jete'then side jete'. As I was in mid-air during my first jete', something prompted me to look at Dan. As I did I noticed that he was looking at me! His eyes shone brighter than I had ever seen! Upon completion of the combination he squealed with delight and ran towards me to reward me with the most amazing hug ever! As he pulled away he placed his hands on my shoulders, looked me in the eyes and said, "Tania! That was amazing! I am so proud of you!" My heart just about exploded! That was probably one of the best days of my life!

Dan began taking me to dance classes with him, where he, himself, took classes. He took me to the professional dance studio, Joe Tremaines, where he and I would take classes together. He introduced me to Joe's jazz classes, Douglas Caldwells lyrical classes, (before they labled it lyrical) and jazz with Marcea Lane, who was an aspiring leotard designer. I would purchase one of her leotards in class one day. The leotard was shimmering black, french cut, open back, long sleeve and high colar. It was beautiful! (I still have it to this day.) Marcea would later become a big name in the costume making industry.

The ballet world was crazy and anyone who was a ballet dancer was expected to be skinny. In fact the entire world was obsessed with being skinny back then; it was the 80's. Aeorbics was in full force, leotards & sweat bands were worn in the gym, not just in the dance studio. Leotards were everywhere. We had no problem pumping gas or strolling around the grocery store with our leotards and legwarmers after an aerobics class or a dance class. There was no such thing as "jazz pants" or yoga pants as of yet, and girls wore heels to tap class. Wearing heels to tap class was a sign of a promotion and an advanced tapper. Tap was in classical form. Gene Kelly and Fred Astaire were my tap idols, as well as Gregory Hines, (although Gregory was not a classical tap dancer, he had his own amazing style) and Baryshnikov was the most worldly ballet master around at this time.

I loved aerobics and spending time working out at the gym. Jane Fonda was my hero, my idol. I spent many hours with her VHS tapes in front of the TV, performing her aerobics routines. Dad got us a family membership to *Coast and Valley Gym* in the *Larwin Square Mall*. Dan heard me talking about working out and was angry with me for lifting weights. Dancers do not lift weights. He did not want me bulking up with muscle in my thighs, it was not condusive to a dancers body. I did not stop doing aerobics and working out, I just did not partake in weight training as per his request. I loved aerobics so much that by 16 years old, I would teach an aerobics class at Coast and Valley for $5 a class on Saturday mornings. Shortly thereafter, I would take on a few more classes at *Mary's Workout*, an all female gym.

After my acting agent told me to lose weight, I began to gain weight. Telling me to lose weight in such a way, a threatening manner, made me angry and somehow made me want to eat more. As the pounds began to creep up on me, Dan called me in to his office. Dan would also tell me to lose weight.

"Whatever it is you have to do to lose weight, do it.", he said. I don't care if you are anorexic, bulimic, I don't care if you do drugs, just do it."

What the heck is happening? I had no idea that I was fat. In the ballet world, eating disorders were common, and quite possibly expected. Dan did not just expect me to lose weight, he expected everyone in his company to lose weight, even those of us who were not "overweight". It was a common theme for the era.

There was a popular talent show on television called, *Star Search*. It was a show which discovered various talent's. Dan brought all of us company members to the *Star Search* audition. We had a very weight diverse group, and after our audition, Dan was told by the *Star Search* casting directors, that there were too many "fat girls" in the group, therefore we would not be accepted on to the show. I wonder if I was one of those "fat girls". Dan was humiliated and furious. He increased his nagging for us all to lose weight. Dan brought in a scale and placed it in the classroom. When the scale was brought in, we were to weigh in before shows and competitions. Most of us would be threatened that if we did not lose five pounds before the show, which happened to be the very next day, that we would be removed from the performance. Now, that never actually happened, but we all sincerely believed that Dan would act on his threats. None of us wanted to be kicked out of the show, we all loved to dance and we wanted to please him. Another dancer in the company took me aside one day when she heard me complaining that I could not lose weight. I had tried Dexatrim, the Slim Fast Diet, I tried not eating, I tried exercising more, nothing was working.

She said, "All you have to do is eat an entire box of *Ex-lax* the night before. You'll be up all night in the bathroom, but you will lose the weight. It works for me." So that too, I added to my weight loss regimine, but it was not as simple as she made it sound.

I attempted not to eat. I tried not to eat, I tried to be anorexic. Maybe that was my problem, I was "trying", not "doing", hearing my Dad's voice in my head. After attempting to starve myself, I would end up binge eating because not only was I hungry, I was angry with myself. Happy people do not try to starve themselves, nor do they eat everything in sight then purge. I was not happy and I thought if I were skinnier, that I would be happier. The anorexic thing was not working for me, so I worked at being half anorexic by putting myself on a strict 500 calorie-a-day-diet. That always ended in a binge session because again, I was hungry and I was anrgy that I was hungry. I started gaining more weight. I was desperate to lose weight, this evolved into my mission and apparently the most important thing in my life at this time.

I finally saw no other choice but to throw up after my binge sessions. I had to throw up, the guilt over eating so much and gaining more weight was too much to bear. My binge sessions were either late at night or when no one was home. I started to feel severe hopelessness and depression. I starting feeling that I was never going to be able to act or dance profession-ally, because I was just too fat. (And here is the thing, I was not "fat" by any means.)

I joined Weight Watchers and then Jenny Craig. The ladies would all look at me strangely when I walked in to the weight loss establishment, like "What the heck are YOU doing in here little girl?". I couldn't seem to stop myself from eating when I was angry. I was angry with myself for not being able to control my eating, angry with myself for bingeing and purging, an-gry that I was being told I needed to lose weight in the first place, angry that I was unable to lose the "extra" weight, and therefore angry that because of this, I was unable to go out on auditions. I ate so much that I could not possibly throw it all up, hence the reason for me continuing to gain weight. As I continued to gain weight, I continued to become more depressed. It was a vicious cycle.

It was 1986, I was now a Senior in high school. I heard cocaine made you skinny by supressing your appetite. "Skinny" was all I needed to hear. I needed to get my hands on some cocaine.

I began hanging out with a junior on the songleading squad, DeDee was her name. It happened naturally because the two of us were the "party girls" and the rebels of the squad anyway. Birds of a feather flock togeth-er. We would cruise the backyard parties on Friday and Saturday nights, drinknig and dancing, dancing and drinking. I started smoking cigarettes and every so often I bought a pack of Cloves. I must have been born with a very high tolerance because I could pound down the alcohol, hard alcohol, even as a teenager.

At age 16, I drank almost an entire gallon of tequilla by myself. DeDee, Barbie, and I cruised the parties that night. I drank so much, I began to throw up. I did not want to go home however, so I went with the girls to the rest of the parties that evening, although I was too sick to make it inside to the next party, so I told Barbie and DeDee to just leave me on the lawn while I puked my guts out, and to come back and get me on their way out. I figured I would feel better once I was done throwing up all the poison that I had ingested. I was unable to pull myself out of it. By the end of the evening we somehow made it back to our friends' house, whose parents were gone for the weekend. I was so drunk, I was unable to walk. I would be carried up the stairs to bed by my friend, Greg Jones, who was a gentleman. (I guess I wasn't too fat to be carried upstairs!) I woke up a few hours later, ready to continue the party. I walked downstairs to find Greg asleep on the couch. I searched the other rooms and found everyone was sleeping. I found my way back to bed and slept the remainder of the night away. I was sick for three days. I guess a gallon of tequilla and a 16 year old girl, do not get along. No more "to-kill-ya" for me! On to Barcardi!

DeDee and Tania, 1987

I wanted some blonde highlights in my hair. DeDee and I bought a tinting kit and went to her house. She put the plastic cap on my head and pulled some hairs through. When she was finished, I told her it was not enough and to pull more hair through. When we were finished and DeDee pulled the cap off of my head, I was a bleach blonde. Oopsie, too much hair pulled through apparently, my bad. The next day at school, we were walking to class with our friend Barbie and after we arrived at our lockers several minutes later, Barbie looked at DeDee and asked, "Where is Tania today?"

DeDee and I looked at each other and busted up laughing.

I looked Barbie in the eyes and said, "Barbie, I am right here!"

Barbie gasped and jumped back in shock and laughed as she said, "I didn't even recognize you!"

Mom was not fond of my new hair color, but Dad said, "Hey! I like it!"

In the 80's, the laws were not as strict and I was usually able to purchase cigarettes and alcohol although I was under age. It didn't matter anyway, because also in the 80's, there were ways to easily obtain a "California ID", you could purchase one even if you didn't have a drivers liscence. There was a booth at the Saugus Swap Meet, which was about an hour away, where I was able to purchase myself a fake identification card for $25, without showing any proof of my actual age. Imagine that. Totally bitchen! I am now 21 years old according to this "California I.D".

Since I had a fake ID, I figured when the police broke up the backyard party I was attending with my girls, DeDee, Elizabeth, and Barbie, that I would just walk out of the party with my 181 proof Bacardi. I didn't have a lid for the bottle, I lost it inside the party. I figured I could just drink it as I walked past them to my car and drive away, since I was "21" per my ID. The police officer stopped me and I showed him my fake ID, he fell for it. He said although I was of legal drinking age, I still had to dump out the alcohol because I couldn't drive with an open container. I dumped the Barcardi alright, dumped it down my throat. They looked at me and shook their heads in amazment but were satisfied because there was no longer an open container issue. I then got in my car with my girls and drove away as the officers watched. Oh my god, really? Yes, really. I laughed my ass off about the stunt I just pulled and got away with. This fake ID is Rad!

The next morning there was a knock at my door. I opened the door and shit, it was the officer from the night before!

After I opened the door, the officer said, "Hi Tania, remember me?"

Damnit, "Yes, I remember you."

He asked if he could come in and talk to me, so I let him in. My parents were in their bedroom "taking a nap" (or so I thought). I was hoping the officer would make this quick so my parents would not come out of their room and see an officer at their kitchen table, taking to their daughter about her shady behavior. The police officer sat down with me at my kitchen table, gave me a gentle lecture and a new ticket with three violations: open container, minor in possesion of alcohol, and false information to a police officer. Woops. He would be there for quite a while. He would also confinscate my fake ID. I was so thrilled that the entire time the officer was at our kitchen table, my parents were napping and never knew. I thought I got away with it and apparently I did since we would never speak of this event. Coincidence? I think not. In retrospect, there is no way they could not have known, but hey never said a word to me about it…ever.

That did not stop me from purchasing alcohol as a minor. The Palm Deli Liquor store had already been selling to me, he was no longer asking for my ID. My friend Elizabeth Garcia and I were on our way to yet another party. I purchased a bottle of Bacardi, some wine coolers and a case of beer. We got in my car and proceeded to exit the parking lot. Before I entered the main street, two police cars blocked my exit and two more police cars pulled in behind me. Uh oh! Snagged. They took me back into the liquor store and asked the man why he sold to me and if he saw my ID that night. He screamed repeatedly, "But she told me she was 21! She told me!" Palm Deli would lose their liquor liscence for six months.

Meanwhile back in school, there were pep rallies at the high school that the cheerleaders and songleaders typically performed at. My junior and senior year in high school, I was on the songleading squad, which was cheerleading and a dance team mixed as one. It was so totally bitchen, I loved it! I loved cheering, I loved dancing, and I loved performing; this was when I was happiest.

After a lunchtime pep rally, us songleaders were hungry. We were unable to eat lunch because we had to perform in the quad area of the school, while everyone else ate. Stephanie, Anissa, Katie, Bonnie and I saw no problem in walking off campus and across the street to Fosters Freeze to get some grilled cheese sandwhiches, french fries, and ice cream cones or malts. Sandra did not particiate as school was her priority, she went back to class hungry.

On our way to *Foster Freeze*, a police officer drove by. We watched as the officer flipped around to meet us in the parking lot for a little chit chat. We explained to him our dilema, we did not get to eat lunch and we were very hungry. He humored us, but told us all to hop in his police car so he could take us back to school to talk to the principal. We assured him that our principal, Mr. Hanke, would be ok with us getting something to eat off campus. The police officer thought otherwise. We all laughed and giggled and expained how we were really going to be hungry now! How were we supposed to perform adequetly in class being this hungry? The officer walked us in to Mr. Hanke's office and explained where he had found us during school hours, then left. Mr. Hanke laughed along with us, but explained that walking off campus without a pass, was probably not the best method for us to chose. We would be sent back to class hungry.

There was another silly rule they were implementing at my high school; if you were not actually, physically sitting in your seat when the bell rang, you were considered tardy and would have to do Saturday school. You could no longer just walk through the door when the bell was ringing and be safe. There were randomly placed school personnel by classroom doors to enforce this rule.

"What a lame rule!", I thought. I didn't like that rule.

I was on my was to English class with my friend Stephanie, and wouldn't you know it, the damn bell rang and as we were just walking through the door. Who was the person enforcing this rule by the doorway entrance? Who other than the vice principal of the school. She stopped Stephanie and I and told us to step aside for our detention slips.

"Um no." I said.

Stephanie was a good girl and did what she was told.

I did not. I turned away from the vice principal and walked over to my seat and sat down. The English teacher was shocked at my rebellion, I watched her eyes widen in disbelief. The teacher came over to my seat and asked me to please go talk to the vice prinical.

I said "No."

She urged me to talk to the principal. I again rebelled. The vice pricipal came over to me, by this time she was furious. I told her how ridiculous

155

this entire thing was and that I wasn't going to detention on Saturday. "I was not late, I was right on time!"

We argued in front of the entire class for several minutes. I was not afraid to throw out "F" bombs. She was now enraged. I am not entirely sure how she convinced me to leave the classroom with her, but I finally did. We ended up in her office. I cursed her out the entire time. (The "F" word is my favorite word, I find it to be very descriptive.) As I stubbornly protested and told her to fuck off in as many ways as I knew how, she suspended me.

I protested again, "Oh fuck you bitch! You can't suspend me! I will show up anyway, you fucking bitch! This is fucking bullshit!"

She finally called my house and Dad answered. Oh shit. She spoke to my dad and told him how out of control I was, he asked to talk to me. I got on the phone and told Dad that I thought that rule was bullshit and that being suspended was bullshit and I wasn't going to accept a suspension.

I said, "Dad, she is such a fucking bitch!" He told me he understands but to stop saying it out loud because I was making matters worse.

After I hung up with my dad, the vice principal told me to go home. "Yeah, ok, whatever!"

I went to my weights class, my favortive class, with Coach West. I wasn't going to miss my weights class. As I was standing outside the weight room with my friend Dean Keene, I see my Dad approaching from the parking lot. "Oh Shit!", I said to Dean, That's my dad!"

Dean laughed, "You are fucking busted!" Dean was the cutest boy in school. He was a surfer, with sun bleached hair and very tan skin.

Dad came down here to get me? I thought, I have my own car. What am I going to say to get out of this one? He approached with a smirk on his face. I was shocked for a minute because my brain expected an angry dad, and here he was smiling. Was it an evil smile? No, it did not appear that way.

I said defensively as he approached, "Dad, this is bullshit! She's a total bitch and the rule is ridiculous! I was walking through the door as the bell rang! I was on time!" He says, "I know Tania, you're right. Come on, let's go home". I wasn't going to challenge Dad's understanding gesture.

I went home that day, but decided to go back to school the next morning, ignoring my suspension. My first teacher would not let me in the classroom as she knew I was suspended. So I figured I would spend some time in the library doing school work. Well geez, the libraian wouldn't let me come in either, so I called her a bitch too and she yelled for me to leave or she would call the principal. She called the principal anyway, Mr. Hanke met me outside of the library and calmly urged me to go home. As I protested, I saw my friend Howard Green on a hall pass, headed for the drinking fountain, his long black trench coat caught my eye! Howard was the shy guy, a sweet soul with chubby, pink cheeks and a gentle smile. He always surrounded himself with girls, and us girls welcomed his friendship with open arms. Howard and I casually made eye contact, he lifted his arms, bent at the elbow, hands by his head in a "what are you doing?" kind of gesture. Howard laughed silently at my rebellion, shook his head and mouthed to me to "go home". I returned my attention to Mr. Hanke and continued to argue with him for a few more minutes about the fact that they were refusing me of my education. I finally gave up after his calming tones urged me to let it be. I went home for the remainder of the week. Boring.

I could never seem to make it to my first period class, which was cinema. I was either very late, or I skipped it entirely. I did not really care so much for the elective class, plus, it was much more important for me to stay home and work on taming my unruly hair. It would take me hours to blow dry it straight because my hair was wiry, curly and quite frizzy. There were not many hair products on the market yet other than *Aqua Net* hair spray. The straightening iron was not yet invented.

Both Anissa Lopez and I had younger sisters on the cheerleading squad. Michelle and Trisha were sophmore cheerleaders, while Anissa and I were both seniors, they would already know each other because of the friendship that Anissa and I had and would become the best of friends throughout high school. Michelle only participated in cheerleading her sophmore year. She was also a cheerleader in the ninth grade at Hillside Junior High School. She would participate on the track team in her sophmore year and continue throughout high school. Michelle was fast, she loved to run and she was good at it.

Michelle was the "good one" but she had a few tricks up her sleeve. Mom and Dad purchased Michelle a yellow, VW Bug. It was at the house prior to her obtaining her drivers license. When Mom and Dad were at the office, Michelle and Trisha took the bug out for joyrides often. Michelle made sure to observe the exact position of the car prior to the joyride and then precariously park it in the same position upon return.

One afternoon after Mom and Dad left the house to go to the office, Trisha asked to drive the car and Michelle, of course, agreed. As Trisha drove out of the neighborhood and onto the main street, she arrived at a red light and came to a stop at the corner of Erringer and Cochran. She was preparing to make a right turn. As they waited at the stop light, they noticed Trisha's parents were on the road waiting for the light on the other side of the street. They were preparing to make a left turn. Trisha's family lived up Erringer Road. As the butterflies in their stomachs fluttered away, they did the natural thing, they ducked. As they both lay their upper bodies sideways in the vehicle, hiding from Trisha's parents, they carfully peeked one eye over the dashboard as Trisha completed the turn. They then immediately pulled into the Carl's Jr. parking lot to hide and wait for her parents to pass. At this time they felt it was a good idea to return home, carfully returning the car to its original position.

Trisha was so comfortable driving Michelle's bug that she would ask Dad for permission to use the vehicle for her driving test. Dad had no problem with it. He was cool like that. Trisha would pass her test in Michelle's VW bug.

My grades dropped to a 1.2 average and I was suspended from the songleading team. However, when the cheerleading advisor was not around, I stood up and cheered anyway. Did you doubt that I wouldn't?

My songleading teammates noticed I was changing, noticed that I was headed down the wrong road. They attempted to rectify it and get me back on the right path by having a "value circle". A value circle was a group talk where we litterally sat in a circle and shared our valuable thoughts. I respond much more pleasantly when I do not feel like I am put on the spot, but they did not know this, nor did I at the time. I had developed quite the rebellious attitude. Steph, Sandra, Bonnie, Katie, and Anissa planned the value circle in hopes of brining us all back together. DeDee and I entered the circle. The girls explained that they noticed me pulling away and that I focused all of my attention on DeDee. They felt this was detrimental to our team as we were losing our bond. I immediately stood up, feeling attacked, I responded with anger and walked away, pulling DeDee with me. Why was I angry? My entire life I was taught to "talk it out". Why was I not willling to talk it out now?

✳ ✳ ✳

Mom and Dad saved enough money to be able to take a cruise to the Caribbean. They would be gone for more than a week and were leaving Michelle and I alone to fend for ourselves. We were both teenagers, they saw no problem with it. Michelle and I saw no problem with it either, in fact, we were pretty stoked! The house to ourselves for 10 days? Let's get this party started! And that is exactly what we did, we had a party.

Word got around pretty quickly. What started out a friendly get-together, turned in to a full-on back yard block party. Except, there were too many people that showed up, filling the house, the garage and spilling into the backyard. Some of my neighbors were there as well, walking distance parties were the best! Vince and Eddie were hanging out in the garage, along with many other party goers. Cars were parked up and down the street, around the corner, and eventually completely filled up the culdesac. Cars blocked any one parked at the curbs and any neighbors from getting in to or out of their homes.

I attempted to kick people out of the house but received resistence from some jerks that I didn't even know. People would not leave. One of the neighbors called the police and for once, I was thankful. All of the neighbors knew our parents were out of town.

When the police arrived, they had people begin backing their cars out of the culdesac in an organized fashion and everyone left the party. Dad's car happened to be parked in front of our house but pulled in facing the wrong direction against the curb. The police asked who's car it was. I told them it belonged to our father. He must not have left us his key. Prior to the police leaving, they left Dad a nice little parking ticket.

The next morning I woke up started walking towards the kitchen. On the way, I noticed a trail of some sort on the carpet. Oh great, what the hell was this? I walked closer to the marks on the carpet and noticed these marks were cat paw prints that were dipped in paint! Paint? I traced the paint soaked paw prints back to the garage. I entered the garage to find a can of paint that had been knocked over, spilling its contents out onto the garage floor. How the hell am I going to get out of this one?

As I was in the garage, I looked up and saw Dad's heavy bag. Wait, what was that on his bag? I stepped closer and noticed that someone had drawn a giant happy face on my dad's heavy bag, with permanent ink marker. Really? Could this get any worse? I asked around and was told later that my neighbors may have had something to do with this. I never did ask them.

In addition to that, my ten speed bike was missing. I was told that punk rocker, Gary Roca took it. Roca was suspended in Junior High for coming to school with a mohawk. Apparently a mohawk was a sign of rebellion. He was known for having no fear, of anything, and took a dare without a second thought. He and Mike Hoolihan, (aka, "Hooli") were also both known for being able to control their saliva as they, ever so gently, guided the long string of saliva towards the ground while they stood over it. A small piece of paper or bubble gum wrapper would be waiting on the ground below. As the longest line of spit I have ever seen still extended from their lips, it would hit the piece of paper on the ground and they would suck the line of spit quickly back into their mouths pulling the paper up with it. Such a talent! I wonder how they actually figured out that they had such a talent?

Anyway, I called up Roca and asked him if he took my bike. He said he did and that he promised he had planned to return it to me. He said he did not have a ride home so borrowed my bike. Gary lived in the neighborhood across Cochran and Justin. Maybe he really would have brought my bike back or maybe it was because I called him out, but he was true to his word. I can't see a bad ass, punk rocker wanting a girl's 10-speed bicycle. Gary rode my bike back over to my house that day and I gave him a ride back home. Roca was actually a very nice guy, despite his "bad boy" reputation.

When Mom and Dad were back home from their trip, we had to explain the entire story and how it got out of hand, and then we had to hand Dad his parking ticket. Our parents actually took it pretty well, even the painted cat paw trail across the carpet. We were too old to "ground" and since we were honest, they gave us a break, I guess.

Since I was going to all the backyard parties, I started hanging out with all of the partiers. I was weaning out of my "good" friends and into the "party" friends. DeDee and I were becoming glued at the hip. She was a rebellious party girl, as was I now. Two peas is a pod. I expressed to DeDee that I wanted to do cocaine. She said she could get some. She hooked us up with a $25 bindle that weekend. She brought it to my house, we went in my room, shut the door and railed up a couple of lines. It was the day before my senior prom. I would do cocaine in the bathroom while at the prom.

When I do something, I never do it half assed. I always give it my whole ass and my full attention, which is how I proceeded with cocaine. I was doing what I had to do to get skinny. I began doing lines of cocaine in the bathroom at the dance studio, no one knew. I heard about a pill, it was called a cross-top, it was speed too, I was told this pill could also help me get skinny, so I bought a bunch of those because they were cheap. Bring it. Let's get this skinny thing going.

My party friends and I drank, and we drank A LOT! We were able to put down a gallon of hard alcohol between two or three of my gal pals, I no longer drank it alone. DeDee was a pretty girl, we always told her she looked like Michelle Pfifer with light brown hair. Denise was a new friend we met at the parties. She had strawberry blonde hair, a freckled face and big boobs. Denise was proud of her big boobs. DeDee, Denise and I would drink before we went out to the parties, while we were getting ready. It was our ritual. We would take our half drunk gallon of liquor with us to the parties and finish it off. After the parties, we would stop at the liquor store for another bottle to take with us to the "after party". There was always a party AFTER the party. We were all on coke (cocaine) so we had plenty of energy left and didn't want the night to end. There were a lot of people doing coke, therefore a lot of after parties to choose from. A town full of young people doing the same thing, drinking excesively and doing coke until the sun came up. There really wasn't much to do as a teenager in Simi Valley, we found other ways to entertain ourselves.

This life-style went on for a year or so, my weight was like a yo-yo. I was so depressed and thought, "What the fuck? Why do I just keep getting fatter and fatter?" I hadn't had a boyfriend in a year or so, and my peers were like, "Oh poor Tania, she doesn't have a boyfriend. How sad." Not sure why it was so sad, apparently being independent wasn't cool. So, I began to feel bad about myself, something else to bring me down. Here I was fat AND single.

I confessed that I was bulimic one night while drunk to two of my friends, Elizabeth and Garrett. Elizabeth was super pretty, super skinny and Garrett was her boyfriend. The girl could not gain weight to save her life. I was not jealous of her, she was my friend. She never tried to "be" skinny, she just was. The next day, I forgot all about my confession, I was beginning to black out whenever I drank.

I was at the point where bingeing at home wasn't enough. I frequented fast food Drive-Thru's ordering full meals, in fact, I would go to three fast food places in a row. After the third one, I would make my way to the bathroom and attempt to purge it all. It was usually in the Del Taco bathroom. Del Taco was always my last stop because the restroom was on the outside of the restaraunt. No one would be able hear me throwing up. Eventually, I would learn to purge without a sound, I had a lot of experience as I was bingeing about eight times a day by now.

Garrett saw me one day, chowing down by myself in my car in the parking lot of Del Taco. Right after he saw me at the Burger King drive-through across the street. Elizabeth and Garret were so concerned that they went to my house to confide in my mom and dad. I came home and walked into the garage to find all four of them suddenly silent. They looked guilt stricken. Mom and Dad were at a loss. They did not understand what went wrong, where they went wrong. They were psychologists, how could their daughter be such a mess? How did they not see it and what were they going to do about this?

Mom and Dad noticed my depression. They also had the displeasure of hearing me throw up in the bathroom late at night after I came home from parties. I would binge by myself in the kitchen and then go throw up in the bathroom which happened to be near their bedroom. I would turn on the bathroom sink and let it run to disguise my gagging. It was not working ostensibly. My parents would hear me. Disturbing, right? Dad could not take it any longer, he was furious that I was hurting myself.

In the middle of a puking session, Dad started banging on the bathroom door demanding for me to open it! I told him "Ok. Hold on."

As I hurriedly flushed the toilet and wiped off my face and tried to act casual, I was hoping the toilet didn't back up again; it had been doing that a lot lately after my binge and purge sessions. I was getting anxious, the toilet wasn't flushing fast enough. Seemingly it wasn't fast enough for Dad because next thing I know, the door is being kicked in! Oh shit.

The look in his eyes was pure fury. I did not even have time to think as I watched his hand come down upon my face. I felt the sharp sting of his hand! What the fuck? Mom was frantic. She raised her voice slightly to attempt to stop him from coming at me and to get him out of my face. She tugged at his shoulders from behind. I honestly don't remember anything after that and how that night ended. Mental block.

Mom and Dad sent me to a rehability center for eating disorders. I would have to go daily to group meetings and to a nutritionist. The nutritionist was easy. She would tell me what she thought I should be eating, and I would in return tell her what I would be eating, which had nothing to do with any of her suggestions. She would timidly allow me to defy her suggestions. There was one night for a group meeting which involved family members. Mom and Dad would be invited to share their feeling and experiences, along with other family members, as my lifestyle choices affected the entire family. Dad had confessed with tears in his eyes, that he too struggled with bulimia while young and entering the entertainment industry. Wow. Who knew? The apple doesn't fall far from the tree. A couple of months after I began attending this rehab center, it was shut down by the state for not having proper licensing.

Mom and Dad sent me to a phycologist. I was to have weekly one-on-one sessions with this woman as well as participate in group therapy for other people with eating disorders. She did not appear to be a "been there, done that" type of person. She would be easy to fool. I was "high" on something during all of my sessions. She had no insight and no knowledge of it. I was able to pull this off with a lot of people. I was not your normal spaz on cocaine, I was actually calm and super friendly. I could talk your ear off. But I was supposed to talk in therapy, right? I was 17 by this time and was able to tell her exactly what she wanted to hear.

At a USA Cheerleading camp in high school, I was selected to audition to be a USA Cheerleader! This was quite an honor! One of the USA employees found me at the completion of cheer camp to deliver my offer letter personally. I could not be more flattered. The audition would not be until the following summer, which was right about now while I was a walking disaster. By the time my audition date arrived, I was unprepared. I had many months to put together a routine but chose drugs and alcohol over the opportunity that had been presented to me. I had been up all night partying. I had half-assed my choreography, slapped it together for the first portion of my routine and improvised the remainder. It was obvious. I blew it. I look back and wonder why I bothered to show up at the audition knowing that I was ill-prepared. Well, I had better head home and get ready to go to the party tonight.

My alcoholism, drug addictions, and bulimia were taking their tole on me; my body and my mind. I was doing lines of cocaine in the bathroom before pointe class at the dance studio. I would then join my dance company members for rehearsal. Dan was angry with me for some reason, maybe because I took too long in the bathroom and left everyone waiting. Or maybe my shitty attitude was shining through.

Dan began to call me out for little things in our dance rehearsals. He told me my head was not angled low enough. I said okay and put my head back down. He snapped at me again and said my head still was not low enough!

He snapped, "Look at Nicole's head! I want it as low as Nicole's head!"

I looked at Nicole, who was frozen in fear, and when I looked around, as were the rest of the girls. I looked back at him and challenged, "Everyone else's head isn't as low as Niclole's!"

"Just do as I say!"

I said, "Fine." Then I mumbled, "Dick", as I proceeded to drop my head in an exaggerated way to make him see how ridiculous this was. That pissed him off. His eyes almost popped out of his head at my definace.

Shocked that anyone would talk to him that way, (no one talked to Dan that way) he spat, "What did you say?"

No one challenged Dan, but I just had. I looked up and looked him straight in the eyes, "I said, DICK."

That was it. Dan lost it. He could not believe that I would actually repeat that word again and even louder than the first time. The girls remained frozen.

Dan yelled, "HOW DARE YOU! You get OUT of my studio this instant!", as his arm extended and he pointed towards the door.

I said, "Fine. FUCK OFF!"

Dan yelled, "Don't you step foot back in this studio ever again!"

I walked off, grabbed my dance bag and ran out the door. I ran across the street to use the liqour store pay phone and I called my Mom crying.

I cried, "Mom! I just told Dan to fuck off!" She let me cry and allowed for me to explain what happened and then told me to come home. She knew I could not talk my way out of that one. I hurt Dan's feelings and in front of everyone, disrespected my director and studio owner; the man I looked up to.

For the next year, I traveled around Los Angeles County dancing anywhere I could. I frequented Joe Tremaines professionaly dance studio, the place where Dan took me to jazz class with him, and I frequented Debbie Reynolds Dance Studio as well for tap and jazz as well as a studio in Agoura Hills for ballet and pointe classes. One of the instructors at Tremaine's studio was Barry Lather, who was a dancer in a few of Janet Jackson videos. Janet and her dancers would frequently rehearse at Tremaines dance studio. I was able to catch a glimpse of her one day during Joe's class and was thrilled to no end, I saw Janet Jackson; my idol! At one point in my life, I wanted to BE Janet Jackson. I choreographed and pieced together a dance, imitating the dances from her music video's for the most part, for my high school variety show. Sandra, Anissa, and I would perform, *What Have You Done For Me Lately*. The three of us would take second place in the variety show contest!

After a year of cooling off time, Dan called my mother. Mom would ask me to call Dan and we would apologize to each other. Dan wanted to start a professional dance company. He invited me to participate along with Faye, Ralph and Moses. The four of us were all over 18 years of age. I would return to Dans studio for another year, taking classes and rehearsing for shows. Ralph would receive an offer to dance professionally in Las Vegas and would accept. Our team would then dissolve. Shortly thereafter, Dan would chose to submerge himself back into the professional world of ballet. He moved to Boston and resumed his dancing career with both Joffrey and Boston Ballet's. Dan would pass away a few years later from AIDS.

# CHAPTER 14

# WILD CHILD

After a party one night we planned, as usual to continue the party elsewhere. It was past 2:00 am and the liquor stores were all closed but we needed more booze, as my dad called it. I was with my friends', the "Johnson" brothers. They were both blond, both loved motorcycles, both loved to party but were very different from each other otherwise. "Sonny", the younger brother, was the more rational brother while "Blake", the oldest, was the wild child, much like myself. Blake was tall, super skinny with fair skin and was a dare devil! Blake was into motorcycles, rode a GSXR, and was dating my best friend, DeDee. DeDee got a ride and waited for us at the after party, while Blake, Sonny and I drove to the Vons Grocery store. We knew that it was too late to purchase alcohol. I told them not to worry, I got this.

We were in my car, Sonny hopped out and into the driver's seat, I told them to wait there for me with the car running. I walked into the grocery store. I passed all of the checkers standing around and walked towards the liquor section, it was roped off; no problem. I stepped over the rope, grabbed a bottle of hard liquor of my choice, stepped back over the rope and proceeded to walk past the checkers. I wore a big smile on my face. They looked at me oddly as I walked by with the bottle in hand.

One of them called out to me, "Hey! Where do you think you are going with that?"

I turned around and laughed flipped them off. I then ran out of the store with my ill-gotten gains. Two of the checkers chased me out to the parking lot, but I was faster than they were and was able to hop in my getaway car. I yelled at Sonny, "Go! Go! Go! Let's get out of here!" He

put the pedal to the metal and got us the hell out of there! We all laughed.
Whew! That was close!

New Years Eve 1989
Top Left to Right: DeDee, Barbie, Faye, Tania
Bottom: Karen and Jen

By the time I turned 18 years old, I got a three bedroom apartment with
two of my friends. I was working at California Yogurt and worked my way
up to assistant manager within two months. I received a raise from the
minimum wage of $3.25 up to $5.00 an hour and could afford to move out
of my parents' house. Yes! After just a couple of weeks in the apartment,
one of the gals moved out. She had already had enough of the parties.
Jennifer Montinez was my other roommate who I had known since the
sixth grade. Jen was cute as a button and had the most energetic, bubbly
personality. When the first gal moved out, Jen and I could not afford the
rent on our own. The rent was $875 for the three bedrooms. Jen and I
would need another person to share the rent with. My best friend DeDee,

who was only 17 years old at the time, jumped right in. Although it wasn't her that rented the room, it was her 18-year-old boyfriend, Blake. Blake and DeDee moved into the master bedroom and Jen and I took the other two rooms.

I reconnected with my half-brother Phillip. He was back in prison. Phillip called Dad from prison. Before they hung up, Philip asked for my apartment address so he could write to me. We became pen pals and through our letters, developed a close relationship

I stepped on the scale one afternoon and jumped off as fast as I could when I saw the numbers, 149. I was now up to 149? In one year, my weight shot up from 115 to 149? I was devastated. I was a dancer, I was an aerobics instructor at two local fitness clubs, I was using cocaine, cross-tops, Dexertrim and Ex-Lax. I was throwing up whenever I over ate; why was I still gaining weight? I was so depressed about this that I decided to eat. My roommates weren't home, I ordered a large pizza with peperoni. I was able to shove the entire large pizza down my throat in one sitting. So now I am angry at myself for eating an entire pizza. I went to the bathroom to purge it all up. I was gaining weight because I was eating too much food, I could not get it all back up, no matter how hard I tried, and trust me, I tried.

After I got off of work at *California Frozen Yogurt* one particular day, I strolled next door to the *Sav-On Drug Store*. I bought a package of Unisom sleeping pills and went back to my apartment. No one was home. I wrote a suicide note to my roommate and best friend, DeDee. I then proceed to cry as I popped one pill at a time through the tinfoil backing and swolled each pill. Geez this was taking forever! There were 36 pills in the package. By the time I got to pill number 24, I was tired of it. I figured 24 sleeping pills was plenty anyway. I layed down on my bed and cried myself to sleep.

I wish I could reach out to all young people struggling with depression and tell them that it is a temporary emotion; hold on, as this too shall pass.

I woke up from my "nap" and I had to use the restroom, my bladder was full. I attempted to get up and go to the bathroom, however I could not stand up. My body was heavy and I collapsed to the ground. Oh my god, I thought, what have I done? Never mind! Never mind! Never mind! I don't want to die, I changed my mind! I crawled to the bathroom and began to attempt to throw up what I had swallowed! I was really good at throwing up so I figured I could induce vomiting and get the sleeping pills out of my body. I was wrong. I was unable to bring anything back up. How long was I asleep for? Shit! I persistenly tried to thow up, now in a panic, I was unsuccessful.

During these purging attempts, DeDee came home. She heard me in the bathroom. She screamed, "What the fuck are you doing in there?"

I cried for her to help me. I hadn't locked the door. DeDee came into the bathroom and as I sat on the floor at the toilet, I told her what I had done.

DeDee cursed at me, "Damnit, you fucking bitch! What the fuck were you thinking?" As she pulled me up off of the floor and supported me, she quickly helped me walk me to my car and then proceeded to drive us to the emergency room.

She cursed me the entire way. "Damn you, don't you ever do that shit again! You hear me? Don't you do that again, you fucking bitch!" These were terms of endearment. No, seriously, I was grateful for her.

We got to the hospital and I was given Epikak which would force the purging of all contents in my stomach. DeDee sat with me in the ER. The hospital called my mom, and my psychologist. The nurse in the hospital was very condescending and asked me why I did not take all 36 pills? He said I was just crying for help. Thanks for your understanding of my situation, jerk.

My psychologist called me next and was furious with me. "This is quite embarrassing! How could you embarrass me like this?"

Oh, this was about her?

She must be embarrassed that I fooled her into thinking I was fine when in fact, I was sufferring. When my mom came down to the hospital, I told her what the Psychologist said to me. Mom was mad, I could tell because she was pursing her lips. Mom called the woman and then reported the psychologist to the State Board. Apparently it is not ok to tell your patients that they are embarrassing you while in the midst of a real life crisis. Thanks Mom!

Life went back to normal. I went back to the heavy drinking and the lines of cocaine with DeDee and Blake, every day, all day long it seemed, until all of a sudden, it all fell apart. DeDee, Blake and I had been up all night partying. Blake and DeDee decided to go on a motorcycle ride with several others down Pacific Coast Highway (PCH). I did not go; I had a headache from staying up all night. I was supposed to teach an aerobics class at Coast and Valley Gym. I called in sick. They were angry that I called in last minute, argued with me about it, said come in and teach or else.

I asked, "How do you expect me to teach aerobics with a migraine? I am not coming in."

They fired me. So I said, "Eh, fuck you then." I laid down to catch up on some sleep.

Two of our friends, Frank and Dino, dark haired, Italian brothers, who rode with DeDee and Blake to the beach that morning, came back to the apartment, but without DeDee and Blake. They asked me where they were. I told them I that they had not yet. They said that was impossible because they left the beach an hour before them. Frank and Dino expected that Blake and DeDee would be here by now. We called everyone that was on the ride and anywhere they may have stopped, and no one had seen them. This was not typical, we began to worry. We called the hospital. They were there.

Blake was in ICU. DeDee was ok, she was banged up and an emotional wreck, but she was alright. When we arrived at the hospital, DeDee explained what happened. Blake fell asleep at the wheel of his motorcycle on Olsen Road, the road between Simi Valley and Thousand Oaks, and ran into the center divder. Blake was thrown off his bike and into the street , tumbling alongside his bike. Luckily, DeDee was thrown onto the center divider which was grassy. Blake broke his neck. He was not wearing a helmet. Interestingly enough, he was told that if he had been wearing a helmet, things would have been worse, pulling a helmet off of someone with a broken neck can be a deadly maneuver. He would have a HALO screwed into his skull for the next six months; it would not slow him down.

I was supposed to go into work at *California Yogurt* that evening, I was planning on covering for another manager. I called her to tell her that my roommates were in a life threatening motorcycle accident and I would be unable to cover for her. The gal had no sympathy and said I better come in because she had a date. A date? A date is more important than my friends' lives? I told her that I wasn't coming in and she fired me. Wow! That's two jobs in one day that I was fired from.

Considering I lost both of my jobs, I was unable to pay rent. Blake was also unable to work due to his Halo. Jen moved out and we were up shit creek without a paddle. We hung in there as long as we could, until we were kicked out of our apartment. Blake, DeDee and I stayed at the apartment until they locked us out and turned out the electricity. Somehow, we were able to open a window and get in anyway. The three of us spent one final night at the apartment doing lines of cocaine and playing card games by candle light. Although none of us worked, it was fairly easy between the three of us to split a $20.00 bindle of cocaine. Drugs were cheap. One could blaze all night on a $10.00 square of LSD.

After this last hoorah, I decided to stop doing cocaine. I moved back in with my parents for a few months. Unfortunately, I lost all of my high school memorabillla and some furniture because I didn't get all of my things out prior to being locked out. You would have thought since we were able to get back in to the apartment that maybe I could have grabbed these special items, but no, I wanted to party in my apartment one last time. That was my only focus.

I moved back home into my old room and Blake and DeDee moved into my parents' garage for a few weeks. Neither of them wanted to go home yet and Dad said it was ok that they stay. There was a sofa bed out there. Mom and Dad were cool like that. Maybe too cool, because we would stay up all night partying. Dad would try to catch me, but I would hear him coming before the garage door opened and was able to lay down and fake sleep. The door would swing open abruptly and he would ask Blake and DeDee where I was as they focused on their card game. They would tell my dad that I was sleeping and point down to me on the sofa bed.

He would be satisfied with their answer and then close the door.

This was ridiculous. What on earth am I doing? I finally was done with this shit. No more cocaine for me. I was over it.

I was clean for a few months, not sober, but clean from cocaine and anything "speedy". DeDee and Blake had moved on to bigger and better drugs and wanted me to join them. They wanted me to experience free basing cocaine with them. We used to call it "rock". No pressure there. I turned them down a few times, until one particular night. They took me to some guy's house, his name was Scott and his parents were gone. There was a loud, obnoxious guy there with cazy hair and crazy eyes, named Danny Garzellie.

As I walked through the front door with DeDee and Blake, there was Danny holding a glass base pipe up to Scott's lips shouting, "Come on Scotty! You can do it! Come on! Take a hit! Don't go to sleep! Come on Scotty!". Scott would take a hit. Scott was tall, slender and had long blonde hair. Allegedly Scott had been up for seven days straight. I took my first free-base hit that night and would do this most every day for a year.

I was good at cooking up rock, they called me the master chef. I worked at the mall at a retail clothing store called, *Saturday's*. One afternoon at work, I received a phone call from my friends Blake and Lee. A phone call at the front desk of the clothing store. Cell phones and texting did not exist as of yet. My manager handed the phone over to me. Blake began to ask me for instructions on how to cook up rock. I explained that I could not talk and to wait for me to get off of work. They did not want to wait. I attempted to instruct them using vague words hoping my manager would not pick up on it. My manager looked at me oddly and motioned to me to get back to work. I had to finish my conversation with Blake and Lee and they would have to figure it out on their own. The following day at work, my manager asked to speak with me privately. We sat outside the store on the planter. She was writing me up for selling drugs at work. I laughed and defended myself, "I was not selling drugs at work." Well, I wasn't. Thankfully once she understood, she tore up my write-up and apologized for misinterpreting my conversation.

Scott and his older brother, Mike, would get into a big argument. Scott was at my house one afternoon when Mike came over to talk with him. The two of them began yelling at each other. The tension was escalating. Scott was a known smart ass and Mike had heard enough. Mike raised his fist! I instinctively wanted to protect Scott, so I stepped in front of him as Mike's giant fist landed like a brick on my face. Mike was 6'4" and over 200 lbs. It was too late to stop himself in mid-swing, although he pulled back as much as he could, he was unable to completely stop the forward motion, he decked me. The mood instantly changed from anger to sympathy. Mike felt horrible. I was not angry with him, I took complete responsibilty. I had a black eye for several days.

In 1989, Grandma was in the hospital for a heart attack so Mom was planning a trip to Boston. I asked if we could also go to New York so I could visit Philip in prison. Mom had no interest in going to New York but agreed to let Michelle and I go on our own for a few days. We would then take the train and meet her up in Boston to see Grandma. Dad called his ex-wife, Philip's mother, and asked if Michelle and I could stay with her. Mary agreed and was very excited to have us. She planned to drive us up and visit Philip in the maximum security prison where he was serving time in.

My brother and I spoke on the phone one evening prior to our scheduled visit. We discussed the possibilty of me sneaking in some marijuanna to him, yes at a maximum security prison! I agreed and he gave me instructions. I did not have much money, I was a teenager, so he wouldn't get much weed. I stashed the weed in small water balloons, per his instructions. I did not know why "water balloons" at the time and I did not ask.

Mom would fly to Boston. Michelle and I were to ride to the Flyaway together. I had been up all night drinking Bacardi and free basing cocaine with Scott and Garzellie. We always partied at Garzellie's house because his Mom worked graveyard shifts. Michelle had to track me down at Garzellie's because I didn't show up at home the night before to sleep in my own bed. She would show up and rush me out the door, follow me home so I could finish packing my suitcase and stash the weed-filled water baloons.

She was so frustrated and did not understand why I wasn't prepared for this trip. We still had to get to the the Van Nuys Fly Away, a bus service to the airport.

Once we made it onto the Flyaway, there was a crazy amount of bumper to bumper traffic on the freeway, which is typical. Michelle was panicking and I was playing it cool telling her we were going to make it, although I was beginning to doubt it myself. When we finally arrived at the airport, we had to then wait in the long line to check our bags. We literally ran to the gate. They were closing the doors to the airplane as we ran through the entrance ramp. The stewardesses and the passangers looked a bit peeved as we walked in and found our seats, delaying the take off. I could only imagine that Michelle was furoius as well as embararsed, but we made it on the plane and were on our way to New York. I slept the entire 5 ½ hours on the flight, catching up on some much needed sleep.

Michelle and I stayed with Mary, Phillip's Mom, Dad's ex-wife. I do not think Michelle was very comfortable with this, but for some reason she went along with it. As we were getting ready to visit Philip in prison, I took the two small marijuanna-filled balloons and placed them between the outside of my waist band on my pants and placed my belt over it. I then thought, maybe that wasn't such a good place. I instead placed the balloons inside my pants between the waistband and the bare skin of my stomach. Ok, I was good to go.

We walked in and were to walk through a metal detector. Shit. I got a little nervous. Then I thought, "Oh, don't be silly, marijuanna is not metal." As I walked through, the metal detector sounded! My heart dropped into my stomach. The prison guard asked me to take off my belt and try again. Whew, good thing I moved those balloons. I did as I was told and walked back through. This time it did not sound off. Whoa, that was close!

In this maximum security prison, there was no separation between the inmates and the visitors. It was easy to give my brother the goods. When we approached each other for a hug, he reached out to me as I reached back. The transaction complete, we completed it with a hug. This was going smoothly. Philip sat down and chatted with us for a few minutes then excused himself and went to the restroom, and that was that. Mission accomplished. We stayed for a while and then before we left, Michelle, Philip and I, had our pictures taken in polaroid by prison guards. The next day Michelle and I would hop on a train and meet Mom in Boston so we could visit Grandma in the hospital while she recovered from heart surgery.

✳ ✳ ✳

Scott and I, along with numerous drug addicts, free based cocaine, staying up for nights at a time. I was a wreck, but I was happy because I was finally skinny! I got down to 108 pounds. I was told I was too skinny, even my party friends told me I was too skinny, that my bones were starting to stick out. I can only imagine how worried my parents must have been.

To get our drug money, I used to pull what we called, "Mervyn's scams" with another party pal of ours, Steve Erskine. Steve and I would steal clothes from the Mervyns Department store in town and then return them without our receipt, in exchage for cash. Stores honored your word then, in regards to returns. We pulled this scam often. We could not go week-after-week to the same store or we would be caught for sure and so made our rounds to other nearby cities. Typically Steve would steal the clothes, and I would return them for cash. One afternoon, Steve went into our lo-cal Mervyn's to steal some clothes, but Steve would not make it back to my car, Mervyn's caught on. As soon as Steve stepped out of their doors, the police stepped up to him. For some reason, the police did not come after me. But at this time, Mervyn's would implement a policy of no receipt, no cash return.

One day as Dad sat at the kitchen counter, he asked me casually, "Are you on drugs?"

Tania: "Yes."

Richard: "Well, I am worried about you."

Tania: "Don't worry Dad, it's just a phase."

Richard: "You think so, huh?"

Tania: "Yes, Dad. I'm like you right?"

Richard: "Yes. But do as I say, not as I do."

Tania: "Well, didn't YOU get over it?"

Richard: "Yes, but…"

Tania: "I will get over it too, Dad."

He said ok and that was that.

Well Dr. Spock, how about that for individuality? Dr. Spock's philosophy in which Mom and Dad had followed and so whole-heartedly believed in was quite possibly backfiring. I just got a *ticket to ride white line highway*. Quite possibly they were too flexible with me, too tolerant with my idividuality. Why didn't my dad just say, "No! I don't want you to do drugs! Drugs kill!" I may have listened, or would I have?

The day I saw someone who I partied with "do the fish" as we called it, which was a seizure induced by an over-dose of cocaine, was the last day I would do cocaine. No more for me. This was getting out of control. Was this really my life? Did I really go from cheerleader to free-baser? Time to pull my head out of my ass. I did not want this life anymore. I made a decision, no more coke.

I chose to still drink excessively, as we Irish do. The cheerleading team would always invite back the alumni for homecoming. DeDee and I would attend. We had already managed to down a liter of Bacardi. DeDee and I were plenty drunk when we arrived at the high school. When I got drunk, I got loud and quite possibly, a bit obnoxious. I was standing on a cheerleading podium doing a cheer with someone's megaphone. When I was done shouting the cheer, I dropped the megaphone on the ground. Professedly, the cheerleading advisor had had enough of me and my behavior because she came down from the stands to scold me for droppng the megaphone.

I thought this to be a ridiculous complaint but I said, "Yeah, ok, whatever."

As she turned around to head back up to the stands, I flipped her off, arm extended into the air. When she returned to her seat, she was told about what I had done. She sent the security to have me thrown out. The young men asked me politely leave to leave as they did their best not to laugh with me about the incident. They told DeDee that the advisor said she could stay. We all had a good laugh about that as well. We left and as we did, the security guards waved us off and told us to enjoy the rest of our night.

A few years later, when I was in beauty school, my neighbor, Kim, was now a Royal High School cheerleader. She asked me to do her hair for her for the alumni football game.

I said, "Oh, I didn't get a letter regarding the game.",

Kim said, "That's because you have been banned. You are on the banned list, from ever being invited back to a Royal Alumni Homecoming game." Well, alrighty then.

Scott rode his bike one day to pick up some cocaine; (he had not yet quit). He was spotted by a police oficer while on his way back. This police officer was quite familiar with Scott and his drug use. Upon seeing the officer, Scott casually dropped his bindle of cocaine on to the ground and in to the gutter. By the time the officer turned his car around and stopped Scott, the bindle was no where near. The officer searched Scott and found nothing. The officer was not a fool, he retraced the path of which Scott rode his bicycle and was able to locate the bindle. Scott was arrested for possesion of cocaine and was taken to Ventura County Jail. Scott called me collect and asked me to find a way to bail him out. I went to my Mom and asked her if she could help me out, she gave me $500 cash to bail Scott out of jail. I was amazed that she agreed.

I waited for a couple of hours for the jail to process Scott's paper work, my name was finally called, "Would the lady waiting for Mr. Sabbe please come forward."

I stood up and happily approached the window. The woman behind the glass pressed the speaker button again and asked me to proceed to the door to the right. As I did, an officer opened the door and shuffled me through. There were a few officers waiting on the other side.

I was then asked by an officer, "Are you Tania Hoyt?"

I responded, "Yes", still oblivious as to why they had to call me back here to let Scott out. I didn't realize this was the process.

Seemingly this was not "the process" of bailing one out of jail, it was the process of arresting someone unaware.

The officer said, "You are under arrest for a warrant for minor in possession of alcohol.

I forgot about that warrant. Well this sucks; Scott gets out of jail and I
go in. When they searched my purse, I had weed and a marijuanna pipe.
The police woman asked who the pipe and the marijuanna belonged to,
and I said, "Um, it belongs to me. Who else's would it be?"

She laughed and said people usually lie and try to claim it is not thiers,
when clearly, it is. After they took all of my belongings, they made me strip
down and put on their pretty orange jail uniform. There was a pay phone
that they allowed me to use prior to putting me in the holding cell. I called
my parents collect.

Tania: "Hi Dad."

Richard: "Hi. What's up?"

Tania: "I'm in jail."

Richard: "Yeah, so. What do you want me to do about that?"

Tania: "Nothing. I just wanted to let you know that I won't be home
tonight."

Richard: "Ok. Well, thanks for letting us know."

Tania: "Yeah. Ok. Bye."

We hung up. Damnit.

They then put me in a holding cell with a couple of other ladies. I had
to hang out there for a few hours while they processed my paper work and
sent me upstairs. I would be spending the night. By the time I got upstairs,
everyone was already sleeping, so the guards showed me to my cell and
showed me in. I climbed up on the top bunk as the bottom bed was already
occupied, as I heard the cell door slam shut with a memorable "clank" as
the door was locked.

I woke up to the sound of the cell doors openning, it was breakfast time.
I stood in line for my breakfast. After finding a seat, I began to eat my first
jailbird breakfast. As if we were in a movie, another inmate asked me if
I was going to eat my apple, I said no, and then handed the girl my apple
with barely a glance. After breakfast, I went back to my cell and sat up on
the top bunk thinking how much this sucked. Shortly thereafter, my name
was called. Yes! I was getting out of there! My parents had shown up to

bail me out. I can imagine that my Mom was a wreck all night and did not catch a wink of sleep worrying about me. Mom and Dad were at the jail by 6:00 am and had me out by 8:00 am.

I skipped two periods and decided maybe I should take a home pregnancy test; it turned positive. I made an appointment with my doctor and he confirmed it. I was 20 years old and pregnant. I had been clean from hard drugs for about a year. Scott had been clean for a half a year and would remain clean, but would have to serve 2 months in jail during my pregnancy for his prior possesion charge. I was afraid to tell my parents that I was pregnant! What would they think? How were they going to react? Would they be angry?

I chose to tell Mom and was pleasantly surprised, she took it pretty well. Mom would be the one to tell Dad, and he too was accepting. Whew!

I expressed to Dad, "I know I am young but…"

Dad sort of chuckled and said, "20 years old is not young."

Mom was trepidatious about telling Grandma. Grandma was also suprisingly accepting. Mom was relieved. I was thrilled that this was going to be a positive experience for my family. Mom began knitting right away!

I felt great during my pregnancy. I exercised two hours a day, everyday. Being pregnant actually helped curtail my bulimia, I would not do anything that would jeopordize my unborn child. My party friends disappeared during my pregnancy, except for Denise. Denise would come to my parents house and do "sober" things, like work out with me. Michelle's old room was set up as a workout room. There was a stationary bike, a weight bench with free weights and a portable tanning bed! One of Dad's random purchases. Tanning salons were very popular at this time. In fact, in my late teens, Dad signed us up for a family membership to the first tanning salon in Simi Valley, *Midnight Sun*. We all went together to get our tan on. Didn't everyone's family go to the tanning salon together?

I turned 21 and five months later, on February 23, 1991, my baby was born. We had a girl and named her, "Amanda" after our favorite *Boston* song, which was very popular in 1990.

Seven months after Amanda was born, my parents decided to renew their wedding vows on their 25<sup>th</sup> anniversay. They did not have a formal wedding 25 years ago, they had been married by a judge in a court of law. They would immensely enjoy planning their wedding. My parents had a friend with a beautiful backyard and a gorgeous view, their ceremony would be held there. Dads Best Man was his long-time friend, Tony Miller, who he had met while teaching acting labs at Film Industry Workshops Inc. (FIWI), on screen training for actors, in which Tony was the owner along with his wife, Pat. Sally Field took workshops at FIWI and Jerry Lewis would teach a few Physical Action Labs (PAL). Dad would have the pleasure of working with them both. I would take acting classes and PAL classes for many years with Tony and Pat at FIWI. Michelle and I were the Bridesmaids. Approximately 100 guests witnessed their event and joined in on their celebration.

Tania, Phyllis, Richard, Michelle, 1991

# CHAPTER 15

# THE LETTER

By now, my sister Michelle was living with her boyfriend in the San Fernando Valley, however she would come home and visit with mom often, her routine was to check the mailbox before coming inside. One particular day, Michelle came over to vist, went to the mailbox as usual and found a letter addressed to both herself and me. Hm, it was from someone in The Valley named "Sandi Smith". Michelle opened the letter and found a picture. Michelle stared at the picture for a minute, something was very familiar about the girl in it. Who is that girl? She is pictured with her family it seemed. Dad appeared behind her and was curious about what had captured her intense focus.

As he looked over her shoulder, and before Michelle could speak, Dad snatched the picture, and the letter from Michelle's hands and said, "This is none of your business." He walked back into the house leaving Michelle standing by the mailbox, flabbergasted. Wait, "None of my business?", she thought, "It was addressed to us."

Michelle went home shortly thereafter and called me. She explained what happened and asked me to find out what was going on and who was the girl in the picture. My first thought was, "Shit, Dad has another kid out there somewhere, I am not surprised."

That evening my parents were sitting in the front room watching TV. I walked into the room and stood next to the couch and said, "Hey Dad, can I talk to you for a minute?"

Dad said, "Yeah, sure" and looked up at me as he sat still on the couch.

I said, "No, Dad, alone. Can I talk to you alone, please?"

Dad looked at Mom and then back at me and said, "Sure."

Dad and I walked to the other room. I explained to him what Michelle shared with me and asked him what was going on? He drew in a deep breath and began to explain.

Dad said, "You and Michelle have an older sister."

I explained to him, "I had a feeling that this was what it was about. You have another kid?"

"Yes, Tania. You have another sister. Your mother and I had a child five years before you were born. We were not married and therefore gave the child up for adoption."

I said, "Wait so, does Mom know?"

Dad, "Yes. Mom knows, it is your mother's child."

I said, "Ok, so we have a sister. A half sister?"

Dad, "No. She is your full sister. She was born five years before you. Your mother and I were not married yet and weren't sure if we would marry."

Mom entered the room and I hushed Dad because I had not yet comprehended that Mom knew that Dad had another child out there, let alone that it was also HER child. I was very confused. My brain had a different scenario played out.

He could clearly see that I was very confused and not understanding that Mom had any part in this. Dad repeated, "Your mother and I were not married when your mother got pregnant in 1964. We gave the baby up for adoption. We were married in 1966 then had you in 1969."

I said in shock as it started to sink in, "Wait, what? Mom? My mom? My mom and you? You and Mom had a baby before me?"

Mom now joined the conversation. It was her turn to explain it to me, yet again.

Mom explained, "Your father and I were not married and it was not proper for me to have a baby without being married in that day and age."

"How did this happen?"

"Your dad pulled out, and I became pregnant anyway."

I thought, Whoa! Way too much information, Mom!

She explained the she could have gone to Tijuanna and have had an abortion, but that was not an option she wanted to live with.

They also explained that this was a secret they kept hidden from the family. Mom's family back east did not know. The pregnancy was secret information to all but Lolly. I was shocked. I had no qualms believing that Dad would be involved in this type of senario, but Mom? No. I was having a hard time imagining my mother having a role in this type of shennanigan.

So, I have an older sister, huh?

We discussed calling Michelle and filling her in. We each got on a phone in a different room, and I called my little sister to explain. Michelle was just as confused as I was and then dumbfounded when the reality hit her. Michelle was furious! Furious with Mom. This is not our mothers personality. How can this be possible?

Michelle screamed at Mom, "I hate you!", and then hung up.

The next day, after Michelle cooled off, she came over to Mom and Dad's house so we could look at the picture and read the letter together. The letter read as follows:

"Dear Michelle and Tanya-

Where do I begin? My name is 'Sandi' and I was born on May 4, 1964 at St. John's Hospital in Santa Monica, California. The couple who gave birth to me were Phyllis and Richard Hoyt. At the time I was born they were not married, but did end up marrying in 1966, but by that time they had already given me up for adoption. I was adopted by the 'Smith' family and grew up in Northridge, California, where I had a nice life and two younger sisters. From as far back as I can remember, I always knew I was adopted and had another family somewhere. When I was 22 years old, I decided to find my "Real" family. So I wrote to the California State Adoptions Department in Sacramento to see what information I could obtain. I was sent a list containing background information on Phyllis and Richard (medical, religious, family history etc…). But no names were allowed to be released. Phyllis and Richard also wrote me a letter in 1977 which was waiting in a file in Sacramento which I then requested. (I have enclosed a copy of it). Again, no names were released. Anyway, in order to get their names, my parents (the people who adopted me) had to sign a waiver form allowing this information to be releaased, but in turn, my parents knew who Phyllis and Richard were and gave me their names and phone number. So I called them explaining who I was and they called me the next day (this was 3 years ago). They were shocked to hear from me! Eventually we arranged a meeting out where I live. My husband and I sat with Phyllis and Richard for over 2 hours. Richard spoke about himself the <u>whole</u> time, not really interested in the daughter he chose to give up 23 years earlier. This was a dissappointment to me but what was I to expect. They told me of the two of you – my full blooded sisters who did not know I even existed! Another dissappointment and lie they have had to live with all of their lives! I wanted to meet you and establish some sort of a relationship with you, but was stopped by Phyllis and Richard.

It has now been 3 years since I have known of you and I don't feel like it's fair or right that you don't know me or are allowed to make a choice on whether or not you would like to know me. I know you are shocked and probably hurt that your parents never told you of me. But you can verify this by asking Phyllis – Richard will probably deny it. I have also included the information and the letter I received from Sacramento. Here is a photo of myslef – I'm sure you can see the re-semblance as I saw when Phyllis showed me the pictures of you.

Please feel free to call me or respond somehow. Don't be afraid! I would love to meet the two of you.

Sincerely-<br>
Your sister,<br>
'Sandi Susan Smith'"

Michelle and I cringed as we read her angry words. Gee, I could see Sandi was self absorbed as she did not even take the time to check the correct spelling of my name. Is she seriously throwing our parents under the bus in one breath and in another breath, anticipating our delight in meeting her?

"Don't be afraid"? I said, "What was it that she thinks we would be afraid of?"

Her middle name is Susan? Ha! Well isn't that a coinsidence, or was it? My middle name is (was) also Susan.

That was a hard read and her tone did not sit well with Michelle. At this point, Michelle had no desire to meet our "sister". I, on the other hand, was curious and wanted to meet her, regardless of her shitty attitude. Michelle and I proceeded to read the next piece of information included with Sandi's letter. Sandi included the letter our parents had written to her in 1977, which they submitted to the adoption agency:

September 1, 1977

"Dear Daughter,

It may seem strange to you hearing from your natural parents in this manner, but you have been much on our minds since you were born. We write because we want you to know about the circumstances of your birth and how that affected our decision to let you be adopted into another family. Most importantly we want you to know, and try to understand that we allowed your adoption because we loved you and not because we rejected you. That may be difficult for you to under-stand but we hope the following will clarify what we mean.

Let us both relate to you what life was like for us at that time.

For me, your father, my own childhood was traumatic in that I was battered and rejected by my own parents. I was afraid that I would inflict the same type of upbringing on you. When you were born, my life was in a turbulant state. I had just come out of two bad marriages and was not certain I wanted to marry again. My first marriage ended when your half-brother was born in 1960. By the time he was three weeks old, I had battered him the way I was afraid I might batter you. I was afraid for you as well as myslef and wanted you to have a better chance than I did.

That is all in the past. I underwent extensive therapy and then de-cided to return to school. Now I have a Ph. D. in Clinical Psychology, a "Shrink", if you will. I work with children and families to help them better understand themselves so they can bring more kindness and love to each other. I hope to be able to share that with you someday if you decide we are worth knowing. Your mother and I did finally marry in 1966 and you have two sisters ages eight and six, as well a a half-brother (yes, that son now lives with us) aged seventeen.

For me, your mother, I was afraid of the responsibility of caring for a child without marriage. The manner in which I was brought up did not allow for "mistakes". It was a rigid and moralistic upbrining and I was afraid that not only would I bring you up in the same way, but somehow make you suffer for my mistake as well. I was not sure at the time your father and I would be married. For this reason, I feared using you as a scapegoat for my frustration and disappointment. I wanted more for you. After we were married, both of us grew up a lot. We made sure we were ready to have children. You now have two sisters who we are sure are equally as lovely as you must be. It is different now for me as I have learned more about parenting. Like your father, I am becoming a psychologist and plan to work with him doing family therapy.

We want you to know of our deep affection for you. We also want you to know that you are welcome into our (your) family at any time. We are open to your getting to know us and visiting or sharing our lives sometime in the future. There is a warmth in our hearts for you that will never be extinguished and we hope that our decision those many years ago has not caused you more pain than you can bear. We don't ask for forgiveness, we take full responsibilty for our decision. We only hope you can understand.

We want to thank your adoptive parents for making a loving commitment to you. To you, the parents, our heart-felt thanks and deep appreciation for providing our daughter with the love and care that we could not. We know it has not been in vain.

With love and affection,
Richard Hoyt, your father
Phyllis Hoyt, your mother"

# CHAPTER 16

# THE MEETING

My parents wrote the letter to "baby Iritano", Sandi, in 1977 and sent it to the original adoption agancy. This was the same year in which Philip was sent to live with us. When and if Sandi ever wanted to search for her biological parents, the letter would be released to her, as long as she was 18 years of age. In the original letter to their daughter, Phyllis and Richard would include their full names and an address in which to contact them if she chose to search for them. When she begin her search for her biological parents, Sandi was 23 years of age and she was curious. After contacting the appropriate agencies, Sandi anticipated receiving the documents in the mail that would lead her to her biological parents. Sandi was not privy to their information as it was blacked out with a permanent ink marker. The woman who adopted Sandi was the woman from *The Horn* who hired a private investigator to arrange for the adoption, the "Shatzberg's". Sandi Shaztberg grew up in Northridge, CA which was only about a 20 minute drive from Simi Valley. Mom, Michelle and I frequently hung out and shopped at the Northridge Mall, as I am sure Sandi did, we may have walked past each other an not even known.

Michelle and I eventually decided to meet with Sandi. We arranged to meet her at the Sherman Oaks mall. She was easy to spot because she looked a lot like Michelle. Michelle and I drove together, with my baby girl Amanda, who was just a few months old. By this time, Sandi was now pregnant. I don't remember much about the meeting, it's all kind of hazy, as if it was happening to someone else. I do remember being in bewilderment. This was all surreal.

Michelle had a hard time with this meeting and an even harder time accepting that Sandi was our full blooded sister. Michelle would prefer not to know that our parents had a past. Michelle's reality was now altered and she did not like it. It was very strange for her, as it was for me too, but I was more curious than angry or hurt.

Sandi was raised by a Jewish family. After they adopted her, they were able to concieve two more children, both girls. Sandi would grow up being the eldest of three girls, which is ironic because the same scenario would have applied had our parents kept her. Would our lives have been different if they did keep her? Would Michelle and I even exist if so? So much to contemplate. Sandi would meet "Ric Smith" at the gym when she was 19 years old and marry him by the time she was 23.

Sandi and her husband Ric (short for Richard) came to our home for dinner on a few separate occasions. What are the odds that she would marry a man with the same first name as her biological father, a man she knew nothing about at the time. Ric was 20 years her senior and was a professoinal body builder and worked out at Muscle Beach in Venice Beach, CA. Ric was also a working actor on tv along with many other credits including print adds for Marlboro Red cigarette's. Ric had two sons from a previous marriage, but they were never involved in our gatherings.

It seemed as if Sandi was ready to jump right in and be a part of our family, she must have felt left out. I thought she said she had a nice upbrining. We were all adults now, we could not go back in time to form a bond as siblings do while growing up together. Too bad there were no "do-over's" because we could use one right about now.

Although Mom and Dad attempted to make this transistion as normal and natural as possible, this was far from the norm. Sandi was filled with anger therefore we would all walk on eggshells because everything upset her. We all did our best not to upset her whenever we were with her.

Sandi soon gave birth to her daughter, born five months after my daughter, she named her Samantha. After Samantha was born, we would not see Sandi for a few years and I have no idea why. She did send letters and pictures to Mom and Dad but Michelle and I were never included.

Allegedly Dad and Mom had been meeting with Sandi and Ric "secretly" for the past three years, prior to the letter. It turns out that 3 years of secret meetings was but a handful of times. Sandi would often complain to Ric that she did not want to meet with her birth father, Richard, but only with Phyllis. Sandi told us that when she met Richard, her biological father, she could not stand him. She said he was narcissistic. She said he did not care about her at all, just about taking about himself. In Dad's defense, I explained that when he became nervous, that's what he did as he was uncomfortable with silence. Did she want him to talk about how sad it was that they gave her up? Ric and Richard did however, get along great! The two had much in common and hit it off! Both Richard's were outgoing and both were actors. The two of them kept the conversation going by each talking about all of their many accomplishments in the entertainment industry, their common ground. Sandi was not happy about this. If she did not like her birth father, nor should her husband! While Sandi sat with her arms crossed and a scowl on her face, Ric and Richard attempted to make this awkward meeting a little easier with their jokes and energetic conversation.

The whole Sandi situation was confusing. She wanted to be a part of our family but was furious with her birthfather and placed the blame on him exclusively for not allowing that to happen so long ago, and during the past three years of meetings. She wanted to be a part of our family, but would prefer if Richard was not, she had a strong dislike of her birth father. Sandi knew as far back as she can remember that she was adopted, her parents shared this with her at a young age. I can understand that it was shocking to find out that her biological parents stayed together and raised a family without her, but to have such anger about it was bewildering to me. She must have imagined a far different scenario. Why was she so angry at Dad? Mom had a significant role in this too.

It amazed me how Mom and Dad were able to keep such a secret. Three years of clandestine meetings with their love child, all that time to absorb this and they still could not come up with a good plan to introduce us? Looking back on the previous three years, I was unstable and heavily into drugs, maybe they thought this would send me into a deeper spiral.

Did they not anticipate that their biological daughter may come looking for them? Did they not wirte her a letter and leave that door open? Why were they trying to close that door now? Did they believe that they could keep having their secret meetings with Sandi forever? My questions are endless.

# CHAPTER 17

# LITTLE JEANNIE

Philip Hoyt, 1990

**P**hilip completed his six year term in prison while earning a Bachelor's Degree in social and behavioral sciences. He was 30 years old upon his release and would go right back to shooting heroine and crack, although on Parole. Philip was out of prison for a mere month when he tested dirty enough times that he was sent back to prison. He was sentenced for another 2 ½ to 11 years. He would spend five out of the 11 years behind bars.

After Philip was released again, after almost 11 straight years inside, he continued to land in and out of jail numerous times for breaking parole for dirty urine tests. Having three violations in one year, Philip was picked up and sentenced to another year for each of those three violations. Philip found himself back in prison for another three years.

By the 1990's, Philip was out of prison for more than a moment and happened to meet a woman named Jean Marie at a local bar. Philip and Jean Marie were married after just a few months of dating. The two of them would drink a lot together. After all, they did meet in a bar.

Philip and Jean Marie (Jeannie) had been drinking one night and Philip had the itch to get high, do dope, shoot heroine. He had not done it in a while and was able to talk Jeannie into doing it with him. Little Jeannie had never done heroine before this night.

Philip got into the bath tub and drew himself a bath. He then shot himself and Jeannie up with dope and he passed out in the bath tub. Jeannie was very high and very worried that Philip would drown. She began trying to pull her husband out of the tub but he was dead weight. She tried to position herself a different way to gain more leverage, and attempted again to lift him out of the tub, but was unsuccessful as water splashed out of the tub and onto the floor beneath her feet.

Why did she not just drain the water out of the tub?

On Jeannie's final attempt to pull Philip out of the tub, she slipped on the water beneath her feet and went down face first towards the porcelain tub. Jeannie's only reaction was to tilt her head to the side on the way down. As she did, her temple hit the tub with such a force; she crashed to the floor in a lifeless heap.

Jeannie's son, "Derrik", who was five years old at the time, found both Philip and his mommy in the bathroom and could not wake either of them up. Jeannie taught Derrik how to use the phone in an emergency; Derrik placed a call to his uncle. Philip woke up to the sound of Jeannie's brother screaming in his ear. Derrik had put the telephone receiver up to Philip's ear as he lay passed out in the tub.

Philip assured his brother-in-law that everything was fine. Philip pulled himself out of the tub and walked over to Jeannie who lay still on the

ground. She had a tiny little black and blue mark on her temple. He figured she was high and passed out, so he gently scooped her up off of the
floor and laid her in bed. He then walked Derrik back to his bedroom to
put him back to sleep and back into his own bedroom to lie down and sleep
next to his wife.

When Philip awoke in the morning, he reached over to wake up Jeannie, she was cold and stiff. No! Please no!

In shock and disbelief, Philip performed CPR on his little Jeanie but
his efforts were worthless, she had been dead quite a while now. He placed
a call to 911. After interrogation, it was determined that Jeannie's death
was an accident. Derrik would be sent to live with his father full-time, and
would never forgive Philip, nor would Philip forgive himself.

Philip would place a call to his father, and then me.

## CHAPTER 18

# THE BEGINNING OF THE END

In 1991, Mom found a lump on her breast and went to the doctor. Two of her sisters, Lolly and Tootsie had already been through breast cancer. One had a lumpectomy and the other a masectomy. Although the doctor was privy to this information, he told Mom to monitor it and come back in six months.

Two weeks later she went back to the doctor. She explained to him that this was not just a lump, there was something strange about this lump, she had a very bad feeling. She said it felt strange and that is the only way she knew how to explain it. She knew her body better than anyone else. She demanded a mammogram.

The mammogram revealed her worst fear. She would then have a biopsy, which reavealed that the lump was a cancerous tumor. Mom had breast cancer. She was prescribed estrogen during meopause, which I believe had everything to do with her cancer. Mom was 55 years old, it was the end of 1991.

Mom was devastated, as we all were. Although, in retrospect, I do not know how well I really understood the devastation at the time. We did not discuss what stage her cancer was in. Was this discussed at all in 1991? I do not know, but I do know that both my Aunt's had breast cancer and survived, therefore I assumed that my mom, too, would survive.

Dad began drinking heavily. Did he know more than we knew? I had never in all of my 22 years, saw Dad drunk. I had seen him with "a drink", his "nightcap", but I never witnessed him drunk. Was this the beginning of the end?

My parents were renovating their house. John Oddone down the street would be the general contractor on the job. Mom and Dad would have John add a room addition to the front of the house, which also opened up the dining room, making more spacious. Michelle and I both happened to be living back home at the time and were sharing a room. We slept on air mattresses on the floor. We were sleeping one night and Dad came into our room, he was drunk and needed to talk. Michelle rolled over and went back to sleep. I allowed Dad a moment to pour out his feelings. Dad kneeled down beside my bed and he cried, he cried a hard cry. He loved Mom more than anything else, she was his everything. He could not snap his fingers and rid her of cancer, but boy does he wish he could. He would not be able to perform a song and dance to get his happy ending. He did not know how to handle these emotions, he felt helpless. My entire life, I saw my dad as a strong man, I know that my dad was a changed man, and I know that my dad was capable of crying, but I never saw my dad look so sad. I was worried.

Phyllis had a masectomy. She did not have chemo-therapy because the doctors said the cancer was not in her lymph nodes, therefore she did not need the treatment. No treatment? Ok, well they are the doctors and they know best, right?

Auntie Dottie came out from Boston to help my mom, her little sister, after her surgery. Auntie Dottie and Mom were very close. The two of them would spend hours on the phone together. Auntie Dottie took me aside and shared with me that Mom was ashamed of her body. She felt like half of a woman with her breast missing. Auntie Dottie did not want Mom feeling bad about herself. She did her best to reassure Mom that she was still a beautiful woman. Our Aunt encouraged Michelle and I to do the same.

Being a new mother was scary. I used to always watch the show, "Rescue 911" with William Shattner, and would cry when something tragic would happen to a baby as if it happened to my own baby. I am overly empathetic and "feel" way too much emotion for something that isn't actually happening to me. I was always worried about my baby, but what new parent wasn't? I never wanted SIDS (sudden infant death syndrome) to happen to my child, or for her to drown in a bucket of water, or for her to burn her arm as my little sister had. I kept my daughter away from anything that was hot. And no offense to my mother and father, but I would also choose to raise Amanda a little differently than they raised me. I was a "mean mom", a strict mom. I did however, raise her with the same philiosophy in which my dad had, "Do as I say, not as I do." Because I was strict, she would do as I said. She was a very good girl, sweet and soft-spoken like my mother.

One day I was changing her diaper, she stopped to look at me and appeared to freeze and I could have sworn that Amanda stopped breathing! I panicked and ran out of the room holding her with my arms extended straight out, crying out loud, as I ran straight to Mom and Dad. I cried, "Oh my God, she's not breathing!" Dad grabbed Amanda from my extended arms, and my Mom grabbed me, both knowing I had lost it. I sobbed in Mom's arms as Dad rubbed my back with one hand, while he held his grandaughter in his other arm. He calmly assured me that Amanda was ok, she was breathing. Everything was ok. I pulled myself together. Thanks Mom and Dad.

Dad had many hobby's, but his current obsession was Tae Kwon Do, Karate. Dad would take my boyfriend, Scott, Amanda's father, under his wing and introduce him to Bruce Kanegai and Jeff McKendricks who were Dad's friends at the dojang. Bruce was the Art teacher at Simi High School at the other end of town, the high school Scott attended his sophmore year. Bruce would go on to be a contestant on the reality tv show, *Survivor*, in the 90's. Dad would orchestrate and present to Scott a 3-month scholarship to practice Karate with him and his friends. Scott was appreciative of the opportunity Dad so graciously gave him.

Scott and I would soon get an apartment together, but it wouldn't last long. By the time I was 23, we would part ways, Amanda was 1 ½ years old. Scott would take with him the knowledge of what a loving, accepting, supportive family was all about, as his own family was none of those. Scott was grateful for both of my parents and their guidance throughout the past five years. If you asked him today how he felt about my dad, Scott would tell you that Richard changed his life forever, for the better. Dad had a profound impact on Scott's life in many ways, but was most definitely a positive role model and a fatherly figure to him, making Scott feel welcome in our home and a part of our family.

Bruce and Richard, 1992

I guess I am a lot like my brother, Philip, because I dove right back into the party scene. Why continue to be clean, sober and responsible when I could party? I could be a mom and party too, couldn't I?

DeDee, Terri, Denise and I were always out causing a ruckus some-where. My friends and I would drink constantly. We always found any excuse to party, or no excuse at all. We could drink all day and night, pass out and repeat, day after day. Sunday Funday was a great time as well, we would all gather in the early afternoon at the nearest school field, set up lawn chairs, grab a drink and watch Dean Keene and the rest of the boys drink and play flag football. The only night we could not find anywhere to go and drink was Monday, we always hated Monday's, until football season came around! When we went out at night, my parents watched Amanda, up until they put their foot down because I took complete advantage of them. They thought I should be at home with my child playing the role of

"Mom", and I figured Amanda would be sleeping when I went out anyway, what was the big deal? I, like Dad, would never be "drunk" in front of Amanda. I would find another person to babysit.

Soon enough, Michelle also left her boyfriend and needed a place to live. I wanted out and away from my current roommate, so we rented a house together on Pacific Avenue in Simi. It was a tiny three bedroom house but the owners had converted the garage into a 4th bedroom. We would all have our own rooms and one to spare. The house had a deck and a pool in the backyard. There was a fire station on the corner and a grocery store and strip mall across the street.

That same year, the 1994 Northridge, CA earthquake would shake up our town. As the earth violently shook, Michelle got a rude awakening, the picture on the wall above her bed fell off and hit her in the head. Amanda and I were down the hall, I grabbed her and cradled her on my waterbed while the ground beneath us rolled. Michelle ran with fear down the hall to my bedroom. She leapt onto the bed with Amanda and I. I cradled us all in a protective embrace. We held on to each other for what seemed an eternity. Once we felt it was safe enough and the after shocks were declining, we rose from our huddle. As we walked around the house checking out the damage and trying to shake off the fear, Amanda's Dad, Scott, showed up to check on us. There were no such thing as cell phones, if so, very few owned one, I didn't know anyone who did. "beepers" and pager's were what everyone was in to. The phone lines were all down. After Scott drove away, Michelle, Amanda and I jumped in my car and drove to Mom and Dad's to check on them.

Mom and Dad's house was hit pretty bad, they lived in the middle of Simi Valley, closer to the fault line than we were. Mom had many curio cabinets filled with her cat knick knacks, her precious Hummel collection and Lladro's, many of which broke. Their dining room glass cabinet also fell over and broke much of their china. The earthquake never seemed to end and the aftershocks would continue for days to come. It was a frigthening time for many people. So many lost so much, some had to walk away from their homes alltogether.

When the town returned to normalcy, my best friend Terri moved in with Michelle, Amanda, and me. Terri and I walked across the street to the grocery store one day to stalk up the cabinets and refrigerator. While we were gone, Michelle agreed to watch Amanda. As Terri and I were in line to pay for our groceries, we saw Michelle running into the store with her arms extended out, holding Amanda. It reminded me of the way I ran towards my mom and dad the day I thought Amanda stopped breathing. When she approached us, she was panic stricken, she said Amanda had swollowed a red berry from the bush in our yard. She said she first ran to the fire station on the corner but no one was around so she ran to find me next. I took Amanda from her arms and assured her, like Mom and Dad assured me, that everything was going to be okay, Amanda was fine.

Michelle and I decided to take an adult jazz class together in town. I would bring Amanda with me and she would sit at the doorway quietly and wait. I could take her anywhere and everywhere. Being back in the dance studio brought me right back to where I left off, which was not in a good place. I guess I wasn't ready to step back into the studio just yet. Six months into classes and I was feeling those same undesireable feelings of my eating disorder coming back on, and coming on strong. I had been in control of my eating disorder since I became pregnant. Here I was, feeling "fat" again. I talked to DeDee about my feelings. She confessed that she had been doing crank for a couple of months now, unbeknowst to me. And so it begins, again.

Michelle and I discontinued the dance classes after the six months, as they were uneventful and I was back on drugs. This drug, "crank" was similar to cocaine, we lined it up and we snorted it. It was quite a bit more powerful than cocaine and a little would go a long way. We could drink all night, the party never had to end. DeDee and I were in deep.

I was able to get DeDee a job where I worked in the Valley, at Nuvo Holdings. She was the receptionist and I was handling the accounts receivable. We drove to work together and railed up lines of crank on the way. We were listening to KROQ on the radio when we heard that Kurt Cobain had died, it was April 5, 1994. During lunch we would make a runs to the liquor store to purchase a small bottle of vodka and a pink lemonaide Snapple. We would sip on our vodka's at our desks for the rest of the afternoon while we worked. But not before we headed to the bathroom to do another line of crank.

I lost weight and was high all day, everyday, on crank. Since I was on drugs, I was stressed out, clenched my jaw when I slept and developed TMJ. I was also drinking a lot of Segrams Seven at the time, I had moved on from Baccardi. In fact, I drank until I passed out. Upon waking, a half full, warm, Segrams Seven would be waiting, which I would toss down my throat prior to rising from bed.

I began sinking back into a depression. I was too depressed to get out of bed any more. I began calling in sick to work, I called in sick for two months straight. My boss, Kiran Sidhu, who was one of the owner's of Nuvo Holdings, was beside himself. He had to have been the kindest, most forgiving human on the face of the planet. Kiran began to call me every day trying to get me to come in to work. Trying to undertand what was going on and trying to urge me to just come in and I would feel better.

Kiran would ask, "Tania, what is wrong? Why won't you come in to work?"

Me: "I don't feel well, Kiran."

Kiran: "What do you mean you don't feel well? Are you sick?"

Me: "I'm not sick. I just don't feel well."

Kiran: "Please come in to work. Maybe you will feel better when you come in to work."

Me: "I can't come in."

Kiran: "Please get up and come to work."

Me: "I can't get up."

Kiran: "What do you mean you can't get up? Are you hurt? Do you need a doctor?"

Me: "No, Kiran, I am not hurt."

He finally had to let me go. I almost had to urge him to do so. I never had the chance to expain it to him afterwards; that I was on drugs. Nuvo Holdings would move out of the state, I was unable to locate Kiran from that point on.

I had exhausted Michelle's and Terri's patience. They were done with me and my friends keeping them up all night. My party friends would come over after the bars and while Amanda slept. She was a heavy sleeper. She was three years old now and would sleep for 8-10 hours a night. We could not wake her if we tried. When Amanda was a baby and I was living at home, Mom advised me to leave the bedroom door open as Amanda napped conditioning her to be used to "noise" while she slept. We would have loud conversatoins by the open door and run a vacuum as she slept. We did not "tip toe" around the house. It sure did work! Amanda always slept sound.

On weekend afternoons, my friends when they came over would engage with Amanda in a friendly manner. When Howard Siracusa was at the house, Amanda felt comfotable enough to grab him by the hand and order him to stand in the corner of her room on "time out". He obeyed graciously. The two of them were pals. Howard was a small, jolly guy and Amanda enjoyed his willingness to participate and let her boss him around. Michelle and Howard would become great friends as well, although he may have had more than friendship on his mind. He had a crush on my little sister but they would remain in the friend zone. My friend James Harris was also playful with Amanda. Whenever he entered the house, James broke out and sang the *Barney* song, Amanda enjoyed the fact that he loved Barney too. All of my friends were good to my daughter.

Tania and Amanda, 1994

As my depression increased, Terri began to lose her patience with me. She often came home from work to find me sleeping on the couch. Every blind in the house shut so it would remain nice and dark. When I was depressed, I could sleep all day. Depression made me feel heavy, in mind and body. Upon entering the house, Terri would open up evey blind to get some light back into the house. She then attempted to coerce me into getting my ass up off the couch, "Get the fuck up! What is wrong with you?" I would tell her that I did not feel well and she would tell me that it was all in my head. I would reply, "Yes, yes it is all in my head, that's the problem." She made her best attempt to pull me out of the dark hole that I was sinking into. Once Terri left the living room, I proceeded to pull myself up off the couch as I walked around from window to window closing all the blinds that she just opened and then resuming my position on the couch.

Terri left and went to her parents house for dinner. When I woke up, I walked into the kithcen to find that Amanda had to help herself to some cereal, she must not have been able to wake me up and she was hungry. The refrigerator door was left open and the heavy gallon of milk spilled over onto its side and all over the kitchen floor. I walked back to her room and found her empty bowl of cereal that she had just finished next to her on the floow. I picked her up and held her in my arms and cried.

Michelle and Terri decided they were going to move out together, leaving Amanda and me at the house, in hopes I would be able to realize that I could not continue with this lifestyle and choose another. Tough love. My attitude, "Fuck you guys then! I can do this without you." And so I did, for another year.

Dad called me one day and said, "Tania, I figured out what is wrong with us!"

Tania: "What is WRONG with us? Something is wrong with us?"

Dad: "I recently read about a new study they are doing on ADHD. I think we are ADHD."

Tania: "What the hell is ADHD?"

Dad: "Attention Deffecit Hyper Disorder"

Tania: "We have a disorder?"

Dad proceeded to expalin to me the symptoms that go along with ADHD and it made perfect sense. Dad made us appointments with a psychiatrist who would do some tests and give us a diagnosis. Of course, I went to see this psychiatrist while I was on drugs. There was a questionaire that he read from. One of the questions pertained to drug use. He asked if I did cocaine, I said no and he said, "Of course not, I didn't think so." Well, it is true, I was not on cocaine, I was on crank. Anyway, he dianosed me with ADHD and prescribed me Cylert.

I went to my family doctor and told him I was depressed, he prescribed me an anti-depressant, Zoloft. I took that for a while and I did not like the way it made me feel. I didn't feel like "me". I was depressed, I liked "me", I just did not like the "depressed me". I was also drinking heavily, doing crank, popping a variety of pills, as well as the Cylert. All of these drugs interacting together had to be a horrible combination. I chose to discontine use of the anti-depressant as well as the Cylert. I would give the prescriptions another try once I discontinued the street drugs.

*Why can we not be sober? I just want to start this over,* as Tool played on the radio. Why can't I just be sober?

When on "the shit" as we would call it, another name for "crank", we would pick. A picker kept busy by picking at imaginay blemishes on the skin, therefore creating more blemishes which often causes horrible scarring. I denied to myself that this was the reason for the rash all over my body. I went to the doctor. He concluded that the rash I had must be due to an allergic reaction to my laundry detergent. I went with that.

My friend Dean Keene came over to my house to hang out one day. As he walked in my door, he looked at me then suddenly jumped back and gasped.

Dean asked, "Holy shit, do you have the chicken pocks?"

I said, "No, my doctor said I am allergic to my laundry detergent."

Dean, "Oh my god, you look like shit!"

I said, "Thanks Dean. I love you too."

Dean: "Ha! I'm just messing with you, Tania. But you really do look like shit."

And that I did. I was a wreck.

DeDee had gone to San Diego for the weekend. DeDee and I were so deep with the drugs that we started turning against each other. She wanted to do drugs forever, and I was not on the same page. We got in an argument, an ample argument. Our friendship broke up. DeDee would move to San Diego in the weeks to follow. Greg Jones and some other Simi locals already made San Diego their home, as would DeDee. We would not speak again for more than 15 years, she would continue on the same path of self destruction.

Dean was very upset about my "break up" with DeDee. He begged for me please call her and rectify this situation. I was stubborn and refused. Dean married shrortly thereafter. I would only see him on occasion and would soon not see him for many years to come as well.

Michelle was dating a guy who I knew from high school. He also grew up on the same street as my friend Terri. His name was Eddie Pitassi and he was just as wild and crazy as I was. Terri introduced the two of them. I was surprised Michelle agreed to date him because he and I had very similar extroverted personalities. She did not really like me much, so I wondered why on earth she liked him?

It was Easter Sunday, We had been at Mom and Dad's house for an Easter Egg hunt with Amanda, and they agreed to watch her while Michelle, Eddie and I went to Easter brunch. We drank champagne with Eddie's younger brother, Warren, and his girlfriend. We finished with brunch, but we were not finished drinking, Michelle, however, was. She was not much of a drinker, like Mom. She went home and we all went to MVP sports bar and grill to continue our drinking.

The bar was packed. One of the gals we were with mentioned that there was a chick at the bar giving her dirty looks and a hard time as she was buying her drink. I looked towards the bar as she pointed to the bully sitting on a stool. The bully saw us pointing at her. As she and I locked eyes, her hands flew up in the air as if to say, "Yeah, What's up?" I did the same exaggerated gestrure back at her. She motioned at me to come over to her, I obliged.

I marched over there with the intent to tell her to back off. The next thing I knew, a fist came flying at me out of nowhere and clocked me in the head. I was knocked out. I went down. Why on earth am I always being punched in the face by a guy? The next thing I remember is being walked outside with Eddie's support. I asked him what happened and he told me some big dude punched me in the head and knocked me out. Allegedly the entire bar broke out into a fight preceeding this knock out punch. I was furious. I charged back in to the bar. The dude was leaning back against the bar watching the bar fight go down. I casually walked up to him, grabbed him by his tie to pull his head closer to me and proceeded to punch him in the face three times. A stranger grabbed me from behind and pulled me away from him.

The police showed up and before you know it, they were cuffing me and putting me in the back of their police car. The guy who hit me was pressing charges against me, for hitting him. What the fuck? He hit me first! This did not seem fair. Why didn't anyone ask me for my side of the story before I was put in cuffs.

I was furious and drunk. I started cursing and screaming only for the police to ignore me. I finally laid down on my side in the back of the police car and began to kick the window. Yes, I went temporarily insane. I was a crazy lady! This really made the officer angry. He opened the door, yanked me out of the car, slammed my upper body over the hood of his car three times, I guess that was my pay back for hitting the guy in the bar in the face three times, and angrily whispered in my ear, "Shut the fuck up or you will make matters worse!" Shutting up was not my strong point.

"Yeah but…"

He rufused to listen to what I had to say as he threw me into the back of his police car. I continued my protest. Finally another officer came over. I begged for him to explain to me why I was going to jail, and the other guy was not. He let me share my side of the story with him. At that point he asked me if I wanted to press charges against the man who punched me, and I said yes. So we both went to jail that night. The police let me cool off and sober up in a holding cell and would release me later that evening. I would work a deal to do work release, picking weeds at local parks in

Ventura County, in lieu of jail time.

✴ ✴ ✴

I heard from my brother Phillip, he called me and shared the tragic story of his new wife, Jean Marie. Whoa. That's just crazy. Two women he loved have died tragically? He explained that he needed to get out of New York for a minute and get his mind off of his troubles. So we planned for him to come out for a visit to California to stay with me for a weekend.

Amanda was about to turn four years old. Philip would come out for her birthday. I was heavy into the drugs still and Philip was aware of this. I told him I would get him some crank, but that I was not going to do it with him. I could not live with myself if I did drugs with my brohter. I knew Dad would be furious if he ever found out and for making that kind of choice. I introduced Philip to my friend "Baker", they hung out all night. I was no longer responsible, my hands were clean.

It was the morning of my daughter's fourth birthday party. My front door was unlocked as I was up all night, no need to lock it since we hadn't gone to bed. I was sitting on the floor in my roommate's room down the hall, flapping my jaws, as I see movement next to me in the doorway. It was about 8:00 am and there were my parents, in my house.

I was still up with my roommates from the night before. We had all watched the sun come up. Philip was still partying with Baker aparently because he hadn't come back yet. Mom and Dad announced that they had come to help me set up for Amanda's birthday party. I rushed them out and said I didn't need their help. They knew I was on drugs and were worried that I wouldn't be able to pull it together in time for Amanda's party.

They hesitantly left and returned for the party, surprised to see that I pulled it all together. Sure I did, I just snorted up another line so I could make it through! I was a complete disaster for my daughters' fourth birth-day party. I am lucky she was too young to remember this time in her life. Amanda's dad, Scott, wwould be there along with his entire family. And there I was, still up from the night before, looking like a disaster. Philip would leave that evening and I would not hear from him again for many years.

For Thanksgiving, Sandi and her husband Ric, invited the Hoyts over to their place. Michelle was responsible for picking me up and taking me there. I was running late as usual. I had no concept of time while on drugs, nor did I care. Michelle was rightfully angry, she was a very punctual person and had no tolerance for those who were not. When I was on drugs, I would be in the bathroom for what seemed mere minutes, when in actuality hours would go by and I had no idea. Michelle would wait as patiently as she could but as the years passed, her patience ran thin.

We made it to Sandi's about an hour late. Sandi and her family had no knowledge of me being on drugs, but my family knew. After we finished with dinner, Sandi asked if anyone wanted coffee, I answered yes.

Dad looked at me harshly (if looks could kill) and said, "Don't you think you're high enough?"

I returned the gaze and said, "No, apparently  not."

I am sure he would have liked to punch me in the face. I walked over and helped myself to a cup of coffee.

When we returned home, I continued the party at *Splash* where all my friends gathered. Terri was there waiting for me, Dean, Keith and Kelly Shannon and Erich Burkhardt, who we frequently ran into at the clubs and backyard parties, would all be there as well. Fun times awaited. *Splash* was a bar and dance club up the street from my house where my friends and I were locals. As I walked in the club, *Rump Shaker* was playing, *All I wanna do is zooma zoom zoom zoom and a boom boom*, as I strutted my stuff over to the dancer floor to join Terri, *"Shake it baby, shake it now, shake it don't break it!"* Michelle graciously watched Amanda. Fortunately, Amanda had a wonderful Aunt that was there for her when I wasn't.

After Kiran finally fired me from Nuvo Holdings, I collected unemployment for six months. It was July 4th and I decided to have a party at the house I was renting. Amanda would again stay with her Auntie Chell.

Several friends gathered in my back yard, drinking alcohol and while we stood by the fire pit. Terri and I used to call each other "T and T", both of our names began with the letter "T". We were also very similar in our personalities, we were known as "mean girls" because neither of us had a problem calling someone out or telling someone off if they crossed our paths. Brian (Terri's older brother) put a spin on our "T and T" while doing his best JJ Walker impersonation, "TnT, (clap) Dy-No-Mite!"

All of my wild and crazy guy friends were there, after we were all good and drunk, the boys decided to have a fireworks shootout with Roman Candles. What could go wrong?

Brian, Roca, Morgan Anderson, and Kelly Shannon, all positioned themselves in precarious hiding places. Roca was across the street and positioned behind the street sign, using it for cover. Kelly was hiding behind my fence in the backyard. Brian and Morgan were positioned in the back alley. They were in the midst of a Roman Candle shoot-out. Roca took aim and shot towards Kelly, he would miss as Kelly ducked. Kelly would pop back up and deliver the next shot from his Roman Candle right back at Gary. Morgan and Brian were behind each corner of the fence now, one in the back alley and one on the side street and were also taking shots at each other, causing quite the raucus in the neighborhood.

The police were called, I am sure by a frightened neighbor. The police saw Brian get a shot off, altough they did not see Morgan, the one he was shooting at . Two police officers jumped out of their vehicles as the four boys ran in various directions, the two officers proceeded to chase them. As the police were chasing my friends around my house, Brian made it to my front door and ran through as he slammed it shut and ran to the closet, stripped off his flannel and threw it in. Brian did not want the officer to recognize him. He then ran and hid in the back room.

The officer who was behind him, got to the door and beat a hole in it with his stick. The door was not locked, just shut. The officer was running on adreneline, he did not try to turn the door knob. He was furious that he could not catch these punks. When I heard my door being beat in, I opened the door and asked him, "What in the fuck are you doing?" Why did you beat a hole in my door? That's fucked up! Are you going to fix that?"

Just then, the police officers saw Morgan and ran past me to detain him. Morgan was one of the nicest guys and he did not protest. Morgan was wearing a flannel and the officers were looking for the guy in the flannel. The officers cuffed Morgan as they were sure he was the one they saw shooting the Roman Candle, as he was wearing a flannel, as was the shooter. Brian, from his hiding spot, heard his friend being arrested. The guilt could not be refrained, Brian came out from hiding and approached the police officers who had Morgan in cuffs, explaining that he was the culprit. The officers did not believe him, therefore Brian retreived the flannel from the closet that he had stashed. The officers then detained Brian and released Morgan. They drew up Brian's ticket, he would be released on his own recognance.

I apparently made the officer feel bad about beating a hole in my door, he called his superior asking him to come to the location because I wanted to talk to him about the door beating thing. Yes, I was drunk and I was cursing up a storm, because that's how I rolled. I was being more of a smart ass than a drunken fool, but before the chief arrived, the officers told me that I should watch my mouth when he arrived, because he was intollerant to cursing.

"Fuck that. I am not going to watch my mouth for anyone. He can get over it. He is not a child."

I mentioned this to the chief when he arrived and he just laughed and said I could curse all I want. So I did. The officers ended up apolgizing for losing their cool and beating a hole in my door. The rest of the boys came out from hiding and joined our little chit chat with the officers. We would all gather in my front yard talking and laughing with the officers for the next half hour. Nothing came of my door, I had to fix it myself.

One evening, Michelle, Terri, Tamie, and I mosied on down to Pelican's Retreat in Calabasas, to watch our friends band play, *April's Motel Room*. Hooli was in the band along with a couple of other high school buddies, Tom Kelly and Jon Baffa. Most of the establishment would be filled with Simi Valley people; there to support the band. We went through the back entrance and ran into Keith Shannon and Dean Keene who were smoking their cigareetes by the back door.

The Shannons were a large Irish family in town and were well known for their wild and crazy nature; typical of the Irish. All of the brothers' name's began with the letter "K". I knew four of the Shannons, there were a few more. Keith was the oldest of the four I knew, he was often told he looked like Billy Idol because of his fair Irish skin and his very blonde, spiked hair. Kelly was a year younger than I was with long brown hair. I frequently hung around the two of these Shannon brothers. Their younger brother Kirby would rent a room from me for a few months and their other younger brother Kory would work for a future boyfriend of mine. I would make my boyfriend lunch and at the same time, I made Kory a lunch as well. He was struggling and hungry. I can't stand to see someone hungry. Kory was very thankful, he expressed it to me on a regular basis.

Erich Burkhardt was standing at the bar having a drink. My high school buddy, Mike Middleton, who was also dating a former roommate of mine, was standing near the dance floor. You couldn't miss Mike, he was a tall drink of water! He stood about 6'5", heads above everyone else in the establishment. Rudy Frenes and his girlfriend Irene were in the house, Rudy was a good friend and a helping hand for the guys in the band.

As my favorite April's Motel Room song, *God,was being* played, Michelle, Terri, Tamie and I stood in front of the stage to sing along and dance. Tamie was one of the prettiest girls in town, she was petite, blond, blue eyed and curvy. As we danced, a gang of girls behind us began to intentionally and forcefully, bump into Tamie. After the first bump, sweet Tamie turned and apologized to them. Another girl in the group repeated the action of the previous girl, tossing Tamie back quite a bit. Michelle, Terri and I noticed Tamie get bounced. I turned around and gave them a warning glare and a "What the fuck?" As soon as I turned my back again, Tamie was pushed. No one bullies our friend! As a girl fight began to break out, my little sister surprised me. You must understand that if you looked at Michelle, you would see a very strong girl, able to kick some ass, but if you knew Michelle, you knew that she would not hurt a fly. So when a fist was flying in mid-air towards Tamie's head, Michelle's natural reaction was to catch the girls fist in her own hand, grab her by the elbow then twist the girls arm behind her back. Michelle scared the crap out of the girl. As this was transpiring, Terri and I were head to head with the other two bullies, spatting out profanities and threats. The girls backed down and then left the premises. Clearly, they did not know who they were fucking with.

After Michelle and Terri moved out, I had other drug addicts move in. Angela was one of my friend's who moved in. She had fair skin and long blonde hair. Angela loved to collect lunch boxes and Pez dispensers. She was getting her crank from some chick who lived in the condo complex across the street.

I noticed different activity around my house. Tangibly the police were watching this lady as well as Angela, since she frequented the lady's place often. Everyone accused me of being paranoid from the drugs but I knew something was up. Drugs and alcohol affect an ADHD person differently than that of a "normal" person; alcohol gave me energy and crank chilled me out. So while everyone else on drugs at my house was spun out on crank, I was kicking back on my patio getting some sun, relaxing. While I sat there, I observed. A yellow VW bug, on a daily basis, parked across the street at the laundry mat. There was a scruffy looking man in that VW. The man was not inside the laundry mat doing his laundry, he was just sitting in his car facing my house. Everyday for more than a week. Who has that much laundry?

I began standing up on my back patio to stare at the man in the VW bug. I decided to wave at the man while he sat in his car. He pulled out of his parking spot and drove away. Until the next day, then I would repeat the same and wave, letting him know I knew what he was up to.

Upon a jaunt to my mailbox to retrieve my mail, I took notice of a car that was unfamiliar to the neighborhood, parked a couple of houses away, facing my direction. There was a man with dark hair, sitting in the car. I retreived my mail and went back inside. The next day, same car, same man, so I decided to wave at this man as well. Were they seriously playing me for a fool? As he noticed me waving at him, he suddenly ducked out of my vision. Was this a game of peek-a-boo? Dude, I saw you and acknowledged you and you duck? I got a kick out of this guy. I stood there facing his car waiting for him to come back up, with my mail in one hand and my other hand on my hip. He peeked up over his dash board, noticed me staring and ducked back down. This is hysterical, although I was not laughing. When he noticed I was not moving my position, he popped up, started his car, turned it around as quickly as he could and pulled away.

I informed my roommate Angela, that we were being watched. She laughed and scoffed it off to paranoia. I said, "Ok, laugh all you want now, but mark my words, this house is under survailance and you better watch your back."

It was halloween day and I was planning on having a party at my house that night. Terri came over and the two of us, along with Amanda, went out to the grocery store to get alcohol and munchies. When we pulled up in the driveway, my house was in the middle of a drug raid. I wasn't worried about it, I had not done any drugs since the night before and they clearly were not there for me at that point. I had been in a previous drug raid at Garzellie's house when I was a teenager, so I knew what it looked like and this is what it looked like. I noticed under cover cars parked down the street and around the corner as I pulled into my driveway. I walked up to the door which was wide open, Terri and Amanda in toe. I walked through the door, there were a few police officers both to my right and left.

I asked, "Hi! What is going on here?"

The officer answered that the house was being searched for drugs, and they had found meth in Angela's possesion.

I looked to my right and saw Angela with her hands behind her back in cuffs, sitting at the kitchen table. Her head hung low and she was crying. She carfully looked up at me.

As I looked at her I said, "Angela, you refused to listen".

The officer in charge came out of the room with a few of my bongs, I smoked a lot of marijuanna. As he came closer, I recognized him.

I said, "Hey, Bob! I know you! You used to live across the street from me. You were dating little Jenny's Mom!"

Bob replied, "Yes, I remember you Tania. How are your Mom and Dad?"

After the small talk, he asked me if the bongs belonged to me, and I responded that, "Yes, yes they belong to me."

The officer said, "Well, we will leave these here for you so you don't have to go buy new ones."

Ha! "Much appreciated", I said and thanked them.

The officers finished their business and put Angela in the back of the car. Angela was going to jail.

When she was released, Angela shared with me that the officer Bob mentioned to her, on the car ride to the jail, that he and my family used to be neighbors. She said he also mentioned that my dad was "pro-marijuanna", it did not surprise him that I too toked. Wait. My dad is "pro-marijuanna?" Why didn't I know that? He must know more about that joint that I found in Dad's jewelry box that day, than I do.

# CHAPTER 19

# HOP, SKIP, AND A JUMP

It had been a year since my mother's mastectomy. The cancer was back. This time growing in the other breast, and in her lungs. Lungs? But Mom never smoked a day in her life? I did not understand. Mom reminded me that her father passed away from lung cancer. She was admitted in to the hospital, this time for chemotherapy.

My drug use still had a grip on me. I refused to be around my family during this phase of my life, shame I guess, or the fear that they would somehow convince me to stop, and I was not ready to stop. Apparently, even under the current circumstances. I was not in a good place. I visited my mother only once while she was hospitalized. I had been on drugs all night prior to my visit. I created a drug induced picture collage of the family, of which included pictures of Sandi and her family, to present to my mother as a gift. After I handed her the picture collage, the nurses came in. I was getting ready to leave. Mom said it was ok to stay while they performed their procedure.

The doctor entered the room and walked over to my mother as she sat on the hospital bed with her back turned. The nurse handed the doctor the longest needle I had ever seen. Have I mentioned that I loathe needles? The doctor proceeded to insert the long needle deep into my mother's back, between her ribs, and into her lung. He then began the extraction of the fluid that was in Mom's lungs, she had Pneumonia. As I watched the fluid drain into a bag, I was horrified and nauseated. That would be the first and the last time I visited her. I am not sure if I chose not to go back and visit the hospital because I was horrified by what I witnessed that day and scared for my mom, or if it was because I was sinking deeper into the darkness of drugs, alcohol and depression.

Between the Northridge earthquake frightening Mom, all of us really, and the news of the cancer returning, our parents chose to move. They found a community in Tuscon, Arizona called, Saddlebrook that they would fall in love with. They purchased a new home and were awaiting construction. Saddlebrook was a 40 and over community. They were going to be purchasing their first brand new home, built from the ground up. Mom and Dad were very excited about this opportunity to start anew. There was a cancer specialist in Tuscon that Mom would be able to see. Michelle and I were not thrilled about their choice to move, but neither of us were ready to pack up and join them either. Arizona was just a hop, skip, and a jump away.

Mom and Dad sold their house prior to the completion of their new home in Tuscon. Cousin Bobby, Mom's nephew, lived in a large house in Simi Valley. Bob, as you remember, was successful in the Insurance industry. He had enough room in his home to accommodate them and happily invited Mom and Dad to stay with him until their house in Arizona was ready. Cousin Bob and his wife Karen opened up their home to my parents for many months. Bob was all too familiar with cancer as he had bone marrow cancer when he was 12 years old. He survived it but walked with a limp. Earlier I mentioned that when Bob had his cancer as a child, he stayed with Grandma and Auntie Tootsie because their home was closest to the hospital where he had his treatments. He would extend the same compassion and convenience for his Aunt Phyllis. My family was filled with wonderful people, always paying it forward when and where they could.

Mom began to lose her hair. Poor thing, she did not want to be bald, she was ashamed of the way she looked. She was not comfortable wearing hats nor where they in fashion. Mom and I found a wig store in Hollywood. Mom chose a short brunette wig and felt a little better about the way she looked in public, but still did not quite feel like herself. I took her to my hair dresser friend who cut the wig and styled it for her. It was heart wrenching watching Mom go through this.

Eventually, Mom and Dad's house was completed and ready for them to move in. Before I could grasp what was really happening here, they were gone.

When I reached the age of 25, I decided it was time to pull my head out of my ass. I made the choice that I was no longer going to do drugs. I also made the choice to never throw up again. I was going to kick bulimia and crank to the curb. I looked fine. I had to reassure myself constantly, "I look fine." Self love is important in the healing process.

I was ready to chocse a new path. This is not the road I wanted to be on any longer. This is not the life I dreamt of having when I was a child. What the hell was I doing to myself? What kind of mother was I? This is not the environment for a child. I was not a good role model. I was miserable. I had finally had enough. I was done.

I needed to get away from my party house and my party frineds if I was going to get clean. Notice my choice of words, "clean" not "clean and sober". Even my idea of clean was pretty liberal. I still chose to drink, smoke marijuanna, and smoke cigarettes, but the *white lines*, would *blow away*. All of my friends were drinkers, drinking was an acceptable "drug". I could out-drink the best of them and still walk a straight line and keep my speech in check.

I was once challenged by my friend Denise's brother, Rick Farmer, to a drink-off. We had been at a party and he was comparing his beer to my bottle of Bacardi. I told him me and my bottle of Bacardi could out drink him and his beer any day. We chose a night for the drink-off. Rick and six of our male friends showed up with their beer. I was ready with my bottle. We sat around and drank our asses off, every shot of liquor I took, they finished a beer. We continued this pattern until one-by-one, the guys began to drop off. One guy was throwing up in the backyard, a couple of guys had tapped out and a couple of others actually passed out. It was down to Rick and me.

We drank a few more rounds until he finally looked at me and said, "Tania, I'm done. I cannot take another drink. You win."

I threw my head back as I laughed and said, "Yes! Cheers!" I put the bottle to my lips, tilted my head back and gulped down the remainder of the bottle, there were a few shots still left, not enough to save, I thought. I hated to waste alcohol.

✳ ✳ ✳

My little sister Michelle did not understand the marijuana thing. She asked me why I smoked it. I told her it helped me focus and helped me with my ADHD. She complained to Dad about it one day. She shared with him my reason for smoking marijuanna. Dad's response, "Yeah, I can understand that. That makes sense." I am sure that is not the response Michelle was seeking.

In order to get "clean" I had to separate myself from my drug friends completely. Terri and Michelle were living in a condo together at this time, a condo that Terri's parents owned. Amanda and I stayed on their couches for two months until I could come up with a plan. During this time I was evicted from the house I was renting for non-payment, my car was repossessed (and it had only a two payments remaining) and both Amanda and I would get the chicken pocks! Oh if Dean Keene could see me now!

Now that I was off of the hard drugs, I was able to allow myself to have a closer relationship with my parents. I know I put them through unnecessary anguish for many years, but I was finally out of my "phase" that I explained to Dad I would eventually outgrow. Mom and Dad always told me growing up, that I can do whatever it is I put my mind to. I now put my mind to being a better person. A drug addict was not who my mom and dad raised me to be.

I wrote Mom and Dad a letter apologizing for my poor behavior, my poor attitude, lack of good judgement and poor choices in my life. I took the blame off of their heads and blamed myself for my poor choices, not my upbringing. I told them how proud I was of the two of them, although I did not show it or say it often enough. I told them both how much I loved them. Mom called me and thanked me for the letter. She told me how much my letter meant to her and Dad and they appreciated it.

During one of our phone conversations, Mom told me that it was very inexpensive to live in Arizona. She had researched the cost of apartments. She said that rent was only $400 a month for an apartment and asked if

Amanda and I would consider moving there. I was still too attached to my friends and my life here in Simi, I told her no. I chose my friends over my family. I wonder how differently Amanda's and my life would have been if I had said yes.

Since my car had been repossessed, I would be dependent on rides from Terri or Michelle. I would have to ride my bike, with Amanda strapped in the child bike seat on the back, down a steep hill every morning to get to Michelle and Terri's condo. I now lived in an undesireble area in town, in a crusty guest house known as The Knowles, up in the hills. Every morning I would commute by bicycle to Terri and Michelle's, one of them would give me a ride to the train station and the other would drop Amanda off at daycare. They were truly amazing and I could not have done it without them. After being dropped off, I would take the train to Burbank and catch a bus to my workplace. It was a lot of commuting, but I had no choice, I had a child to support and no one else to depend on. I did not pursue child support, I was determined to do it on my own. It was my choice to have a child and it was therefore my obligation to keep it all going for the two of us.

I met a guy named Greg just two months after I cleaned up. Greg was tall with blond hair and was very friendly with me. He had a 2-year-old son, Tanner. Amanda was already six years old at this time. I had not been clean very long and was still comfortable around a ceratin crowd of people, party people. This crowd, which was a new croud, happened to be on crank too. It takes a while for your head to get back on straight after it has been in a constant battle with drugs, but I had already made the choice never to use drugs again, so I was not particularly concerned about hanging out with those that did crank and falling off the wagon. *Just say no.* They all knew I didn't use, there was no peer pressure.

Greg and I hooked up right away. Amanda and I moved in with him after knowing him for only a few weeks. Although Greg was an addict, I fell in love with him for some reason or another. Greg and I would remain together for five years, he was on drugs the majority of the time. I would put my foot down after two years, he would quit for a while and then pick it backup, unbeknowst to me.

✳ ✳ ✳

After Mom completed chemotherapy, her immune system was very weak. Mom began to feel again, that something was very wrong, she was very ill. After her doctor conducted many tests, it was determined that she had contracted Parvo.

What the fuck is Parvo? Are you asking the same question?

What exactly is Parvo? Parvo is a rare dog disease. How exactly did Mom contract a rare dog disease? Airborne. After the chemo, her immune system was not strong enough to fight it off. A rare dog disease, and my mom contracted it. Now what? See a damn Veterinarian?

Mom spent the next two years trying to keep the Parvo at bay until the doctors could figure out a way to rid my Mom of this disease. Mom was in the hospital five days a week, eight hours a day, having blood transfusions. The Parvo attacked and killed all of her white and red blood cells, leaving her with neither. No defenses. The transfutions were what was keeping her alive.

When they moved to Arizona, Dad sent Amanda a few VHS tapes of which included a children's music video that he was a part of titled, *You be You*. Also on the tape was another music video he had recently been a part of, a remake of the Depeche Mode song, *Never Let me Down Again*. It was covered by a German band named *The Farmer Boys*. Dad played the villain. Dad also sent her a copy of *Support Your Local Sherriff*, starring James Garner. Dad had a bit part in this movie and I wanted Amanda to see it. Amanda watched as James Garner shot and killed her poppa on the TV. She was horrified and began to cry.

I asked her why she was crying and she exclaimed, "Poppa is dead!"

I explained that Poppa was not dead, that it was just a movie. She was not convinced. I picked up the phone and called her poppa and explained to him that Amanda was very upset because she thought her poppa was dead after being shot by James Garner. I handed the phone to Amanda as Dad soothed her aching heart and assured her that he was alive.

Dad handed the phone to Mom for her and me to talk. After some chit chat, Mom said, "I'm afraid Amanda won't remember me."

I responded, "What? What do you mean? Why wouldn't she remember you? You are only in Arizona. We will see you again."

Mom replied with, "She is so young, she will not remember." She said this with such a sadness and melancholy, it was both heartbreaking and frightening.

"Of course she will remember you, Mom. You two have a very special bond. We will come for a visit soon."

"Yes, I know."

I was intrigued by her previous statement. I asked her, "Mom, are you dying?"

"No." She assured me, she said, "I am not getting better but I am not getting worse." She sounded hopeful, therefore I would be hopeful too.

Our Mom began studying Thai Chi. She loved it so much that she began to teach it in their home in Arizona. She had a small group of women who came to the house to participate. Most people who met Mom, loved her. She was a kind and gentle soul. What I failed to realize growing up, was that she was also a very strong and determined woman.

Mom was determined to continue to be active, to continue with her social life, even through this was a trying time. She made many friends in the community and was part of a hiking group. The hike was focused in Sabino Canyon. Mom thoroughly enjoyed it.

Sabino Canyon is a three mile hike uphill. One can choose to take an informative narrated tram ride up and down the mountain instead, and had the option to hop on it during any portion of the canyon at the designated tram stops. Sabino is also known for their plentiful presence of hummingbirds and butterflies. Mom really enjoyed the hikes, however she tripped and fell one day during one of the hikes and tore up her entire shin. Because of the Parvo, the wound would not heal, the lack of red and white blood cells didn't allow for her body to mend as it should. Her doctor advised rest, but when Mom persisted after a several weeks of rest, he acquiesced and allowed her to hike as long as the wound was completely bandaged and covered, protected from any outside elements. There was something very therapeutic about hiking with her friends. Mom needed to get back to nature amongst the beautiful hummingbirds and waterfalls.

Dad was making his own friends while doing what he loved best acting and singing. He was back on the stage. Dad gathered up other entertainers from the community and confounded Variety shows at the community Club House. He was doing what he loved and invited others with the same love and passion for music and theater to join him. The shows were quite the hit! Dad was happiest when on the stage. The stage was his world and the world was his stage.

Dad had earned his second degree black belt by this time and continued to train even when he moved to Arizona. Dad was now instructing his own Karate classes in the community fitness center a few days a week. His long time friend and karate practitioner Bruce, would come for a visit and teach a class for Dad and his students. Dad still held privatepsychology practices out of his home office for a few patients here and there, as did Mom, but otherwise, they were trying to enjoy life as best as they could, semi-retired, if you will.

Michelle, Amanda and I always traveled together to visit with Mom and Dad. During one of our visits, Mom was complaining about some facial hair she had developed while on steroid medication. I brought my scissors with me to give her a haircut anyway. I gently trimmed the baby hairs off of her face. Tears came to her eyes, she was grateful. She was afraid to shave it off as she heard it would come back thicker, she did not want a beard.

I observed the way Dad took gentle care of Mom. He was now her rock. She needed him and his love more than ever.

Mom and I were on the floor in the spare bedroom playing with Amanda. I looked up at her and whispered, "Mom, he takes such good care of you. Dad really loves you."

As she looked me in the eyes, she said with such pride, "I know. I am really lucky."

✳ ✳ ✳

Dad chose to dive back into the business of entertainment by retaining an acting agent in Arizona. He began auditioning. Dad landed a national commercial for State Farm, but was even more excited when he was hired for a starring role in a William Shatner film, a science fiction movie, *Groom Lake*. He was looking forward to working with William Shatner. Dad was a bit disconcerted about having to do most of his scenes however, in his underwear. Yes, in his underwear, and while blowing purple smoke out of his mouth. I was happy for him and proud of him, even in his underwear! I was conditioned to seeing Dad in public in his family famous Speedos, so seeing him on television in his underwear was evident.

My maternal grandma had Alzheimer's for a few years, we were out in California and she was way out in Boston so we did not experience what it was like to be around a loved one with this horrible disease. She lived to be 91 but passed away from Alzheimer's in March of 1997. Mom was not permitted to travel, per the doctors' orders, she was not healthy enough. Devastated and unable to attend her own mothers funeral, because of her cancer and its complications. I can only imagine how she must have felt.

Dad would travel out to California for a week long intensive for Karate training in Ojai, CA with his karate pals Bruce and Jeff. Michelle, Amanda and I drove out to visit him on the last day of his training, it was only a 45 minute drive from home. It just so happened to be Father's Day. We watched as Dad tested, had lunch, and enjoyed each other's company as long as we could, until it was time for him to pack up and go back home to Mom in Arizona.

While he walked us to our car, Dad stopped us and put on his serious face. This immediately concerned me. What was that face? Something was awry. Dad then took a deep breath and explained to us that during Mom's last hospital visit, he spoke with her doctor privately.

Dad asked the doctor while Mom was out of the room, "How much longer does she have to live? A year? A week? What?"

He then explained that the doctor just shook his head, "Yes."

"Yes? Yes what? A year or a week?" I asked.

Dad was optimistic and said, "Mom has a year left to live."

Dad explained that the blood transfusions were not working as they hoped. The doctor planned to discontinue the transfusions and schedule a bone marrow transplant.

My heart sank. I could not fathom this at all. I thought to myself, "but I asked her if she was dying and she said no."

✳ ✳ ✳

Two weeks passed. Michelle and I hadn't been speaking much because we were in an argument over our boyfriends. She did call me and ask me to cut her hair. Although I dropped out of beauty school to get a full time job when Scott and I parted ways, I continued to cut and color friends' and family members' hair. Amanda would not step foot in a beauty salon until she was a teenager and she would regret it, most people don't know how to cut curly hair. Her hair, like mine, did not become curly until puberty.

Amanda and I now rented Bill and Jane's (Terri's parents) condominium. As we were approaching our front door, Michelle pulled up. We waitied for her to join us on the doorstep, we heard the phone ringing. I inserted the key into the doorknob but did not get the door open in time to answer the phone. As we walked into the condo, the answering machine picked up.

It was Dad's voice, he exclaimed, "Come NOW! Your Mom isn't going to make it!"

I dropped to my knees and screamed out, "No! Please no! NO!" I picked up the phone and called Dad, sobbing. We made arrangements immediately to fly to Arizona.

# CHAPTER 20

# THE OTHER SIDE OF THE TRACKS

When we arrived in Arizona, Mom was in the hospital, in a coma. Dad explained that she broke into a high fever of 111 °. He was unable to get her fever to come down so he called her doctor. Per the doctors' orders, he was to place her in ice water, mostly ice. He jumped in his car and ran up the street to the corner store and purchased several bags of ice. When he got back, he filled the tub with the ice and placed her in it. His effort were futile. Unable to get her fever lower that 107 °, he raced her to the hospital.

Dad endured this frightening day alone. Dad loved Mom, she was the love of his life. I do not believe he was ready to walk this life alone, to do life without her. They had been married 31 years now and they did everything together; they did the grocery shopping together every Friday, they both participated in cleaning the house, the laundry and the cooking, a true partnership, since they both had also always worked. They were equals, each independent, yet dependent on each other.

Although I knew Mom was now literally dying, I did not want to accept it. Every fiber of my being wanted to deny it. I wanted this to be just a bad dream. I wanted the doctors to figure it out and save my mother's life! Why can't they figure this out? They are doctors! We rely on them to save us! Save my mom! But this was not the way it was going to happen. My mother was dying.

All but one of Mom's sisters and her brother flew out to be by her side. Their baby sister, the princess, as they so lovingly called her, was about to cross over to the *Other Side of the Tracks*. They just lost their ma, and now had to endure losing the youngest sister only four months later. Sadly, Auntie Dottie was unable to make it, Uncle Pat was ill, she was devastated and guilt stricken. Although Mom and Lolly had been distant since that abhorrent day that Mom unexpectedly asked Lolly to move out in 1964, she was right by her side today. Along with other family members, Lolly was there to say goodbye to her little sister.

By the time we all arrived the hospital was keeping her "comfortable" on morphine. We all gathered in her hospital room and talked to her and conversed with each other all day and into the late evening. The room was filled with many loud Italians. Even though she was in a coma, we were all convinced that she could hear us and that our presence in the room was felt by her. I held my mother's hand for hours at a time, reluctant to let go, and spoke to her gently telling her how much I loved her. I stroked her hair and put lip balm on her lips, they were dry from the oxygen and lack of oral fluid intake. I brought to the hospital and placed by her bedside, a music box of hers. This music box was a tiny round piano with a black cat and a white cat perched on top. The song which played from this music box was *Memories*, from Mom's favorite musical production, *Cats*.

While were all talking, reminiscing and laughing and I turned to look at Mom. As I did so, I watched as a tear drop escaped the corner of her eye and rolled down her cheek. I burst out in to tears as I shouted, "Oh my god, she's crying!"

She could hear us. I knew she could! She could hear us but she could not respond.

I mentioned this to the doctor, and he said, "No, she can't hear you."

I disagreed, "Oh, yes, she can!"

The second day as we all gathered in her hospital room, Mom sat up abruptly! She bolted upright and began flailing her arms in front of her frantically as she shook her head from side to side! None of us knew what to say, we all froze in shock as we waited for it to end. Luckily a nurse happened to be in the room.

I asked her, "What is happening to my mom?"

The nurse said very sympathetically, "Oh sweetheart, she is fighting death."

I bowed my head and sobbed. Mom did not want to die. I was not ready for her to die. I was only 27 years old. So much lost time to make up for. So much more to come in the future. She would never see me walk down the isle. She would not be able to watch my daughter grow up, Amanda would not have a loving grandmother to guide her and spoil her. I had no more female role model, no more motherly guidance. I would no longer be given the opportunity to grow old with my mother. I had so much more I wanted to learn from her. I needed her, why did it take me so long to see that? So many unanswered questions. Twenty seven years with my mother, that's all I get? Michelle had just turned 26 years old. I was feeling robbed of the opportunity to have a mother.

As I sobbed, I whispered, "Please do not go yet Mom. Please." I was not ready to let her go.

On the third morning, Michelle and I planned to be at the hospital at 9am. I was running late as usual and Michelle was furious as usual. It was July 3rd, 1997, we arrived at the hospital at 9:20am. As we approached Mom's hospital door, we noticed it was closed. It had not been closed any of the other days we'd been here. Michelle and I exchanged a glance and continued on. As we impend the door, we noticed there was a note taped to it. I assume Dad wanted some privacy.

The note read, "Private. Reserved to immediate family only."

Oh, okay, well we are immediate family. As I began to push the door open, Dad swiftly slid out of the room, closing the door behind him.

What was happening? Something was different about his face. "Dad, what's wrong?"

He said, "She's gone."

I was unable to control my legs. They seemed to melt from under me. Before I knew it I was once again down on my knees, my head bowed down so low until it rested on the ground, my body wracked. I sobbed violently.

As I sobbed, I screamed, "No! No!! NO!!! Mom, no!" I was traumatized.

I do not remember who helped me up, but I was now standing. I had to pull myself together to say goodbye to my deceased mother. Her body lay peacefully still, although I was not at peace with this at all. It was frightening, yet serene at the same time. Her body was completely still but her presence remained, I felt it, I felt her. *Only the Good Die Young*; you were right Billy Joel, you were right. I don't think she wanted to leave us, just as much as we did not want her to leave us. What were we going to do without Mom? I walked over to her, kissed her forehead and whispered, "Goodbye Mom. I love you." I could not stop my tears from flowing, they dropped on to her arm as I pulled away.

After Michelle was finished with her equally painful goodbye, Dad asked us to give him another moment alone with Mom. He needed one more moment alone with the love of his life. I was reluctant to leave that room, I knew once I left that it would be the last time I would ever see my mother again. As we looked at our mother for the last time, we honored Dad's request and left the room.

We made our way downstairs and outside. We were both in desperate need of a cigarette. After a couple of minutes, Dad approached. He looked towards me and said, "Give me a cigarette." (He did not want one of Michelle's cigarettes because she smoked menthol.)

Michelle and I both thought he was kidding around. He hadn't smoked for almost 18 years.

I scoffed it off and said , "Yeah right, Dad."

His eyes locked in on mine as he firmly spoke, "Give me a fucking cigarette!"

"Whoa! Ok Dad." I quickly pulled a cigarette out of my pack. I handed it to him and, shit, I lit the damn thing for him too. The three of us sat on the concrete bench outside of the hospital in silence, each taking long deep drags of our cigarettes. Dad would continue to smoke for the following year, until he chose to finally gave it up again.

When we arrived back at Dad's house, he secluded himself in his bedroom and wrote the following letter to our mother:

July 3, 1997

"Phyllis
You were colors I had yet to see.
Warmth I had not felt.

Laughter I had never heard.

You gave me sunbeams and took away the shadows.

You were my life…and my love.

You were softness I had yet to experience.

Sweetness I had yet to taste.

Rainbows I had yet to see.

You brought me the calm. The quiet, the tranquil and took away the turmoil.

You are my existence…and my love…still!

Richard"

Dad gave our mother a beautiful memorial service at their home in Tuscon, AZ. As we gathered with all of Mom's friends, I heard Mom's voice. Dad was playing Mom's song titled, *Other Side of the Tracks*, which ironically, is where she was now. I broke down sobbing again as I listed to my Mom's voice, the voice of an angel. It was bittersweet.

✳ ✳ ✳

At a later date, Michelle, Amanda and I would return to Arizona to spread our mother's ashes. Mom asked to be cremated. She did not want to take up space on the earth, but to be reunited with it.

Mom wanted her ashes to be spread in the mountains at Sabino Canyon, her favorite hiking spot. Dad, Michelle, Amanda and I hiked the three miles to the top of the trail and then a little bit beyond, off of the trail. Amanda was still only six years old at the time. It was summer, it was hot, and she was pooped, but she made it to the top alongside us adults. We searched for the perfect spot, a very private spot, where we could spread her ashes and later return for visits.

We found a spot that was off of the trail, and higher in the mountains, we all agreed that this was the spot. We found a large rock in the area and lifted it, placing it off to the side for the time being. Dad spread Mom's ashes, reuniting her with the earth, as tears poured down our cheeks. Dad laid a picture of himself and Mom together, placing it in her ashes. We all sobbed copiously.

Later at Dad's house, it was his house now, mom's home was no longer in the physical world, I was outside having yet another a good cry, I could not seem to stop my tears from flowing. A hummingbird buzzed right up to my face, within inches nonetheless, and held my attention. I was mesmerized. It was my mother, I felt her presence once again. I smiled from ear to ear. She sent me a hummingbird to soothe my soul. From that day forward, each time a hummingbird crosses my path, I have thought of my mother. A hummingbird brings forth a sense of peace and warmth to my heart.

We were not in contact with Sandi during any part of this trying time. Sandi was still very angry and stayed away although she was informed of our mother's illness and her death. She was still angry that she was denied the right to be a part of our family. She wanted to be a part of our family and renounce her own past. Although she had a good life, she wanted the life she was disavowed, no matter the reason's. Sandi continued to place the majority of her anger on our dad, blaming him exclusively for the reason she was given up for adoption. None of us have the power to turn back time, however she chose to hang on to her anger, claiming he was over powering and that we were all scared of him, especially Mom. Therefore, our relationship with Sandi faded before it ever really began. How do you have a relationship with a person who continues to bash the ones you love? Why would you want to have a relationship with someone like that?

Dad came to California to give Mom a "celebration of life" in our home town. His friend Dennis Merrit Jones had a facility which he would open up for Dad to hold Mom's service. The "house" was packed as Dad stood up on the stage at the podium and spoke about Mom. I don't think there was a dry eye in the house. It was a beatiful celebration for our beloved mother. Sandi and her husband Ric would attend.

Auntie Tootsie would also organize a service for Mom, in Boston. She approached the Church about a service and they did not agree to it because Mom was no longer a member of that Church nor had she been for decades. Auntie Tootise is a tough little lady, she refused to accept that anwser and persisted, the Church would allow it. Mom would be honored and respected in her hometown.

Dad, came out to California again for Christmas, we would gather at Michelle and Eddie's house that year. Dad brought with him a letter he received from Sandi. We assumed it was in sympathy regarding our mother's passing. Dad stood behind us and read over our shoulder. We would all read the letter from Sandi, together. When we reached the end, Michelle and I locked gazes, silently saying to each other, "Oh brother, here we go again." We then turned and looked at Dad.

Michelle said, "Interesting."

I said, "I don't even know what to say Dad. Was that a sympathy letter or a letter about how Sandi was so wronged?"

Dad did not say a word. We had no more words to exchange about this. Sandi chose to continue to bash Dad and still insisted on playing the victim. Sandi insinuated that Dad was a bully, that we all fear his wrath. Michelle and I felt her words were at the very least, unsympathetic and self-centered, which was ironic because she was continually claiming Dad was the same. The relationship with Sandi naturally seemed to fade on both ends.

Dad had a really hard time with my Mom's death. Michelle and I tried to get him to move back to California to live with one of us, but he refused. Stubborn, prideful man, I thought. He explained that he and Mom built that house together and he was going to die in that house. He wasn't leaving Arizona because Arizona is where Mom would forever be. We stopped asking him and respected his choice.

It was very difficult knowing my father was suffering. Mom was the love of his life and he was missing her terribly. Mom was his everything, his reason for living, and she was gone. His funds were terribly low due to Mom's inability to obtain insurance after she was diagnosed with cancer the second time. Her previous insurance company cancelled her policy, not even cousin Bob bould help her out, nor did Mom and Dad have a life insurance policy. Mom could not even qualify for Medicare. The bills were piling high and most of their retirement funds had been spent on the hospital bills. By the time Mom passed, Dad was left with fifty thousand dollars in his bank account, and a million dollars in medical debt. The doctors would be gracious enough to write most of it off. However, fifty thousand dollars was not going to last Dad the rest of his lifetime.

When Dad and I speak on the telephone, he would usually end up crying. My father was a very emotional being, he was not afraid to share his feelings nor was he afraid to cry. I had seen Dad cry before, but this was a different cry. I was worried. He began talking of suicide, said he didn't want to live without Mom.

"No Dad. No. Please do not do that. I love you. I still need you, Dad."

It was a frightening time and he was living in another state so it was even more nerve racking. He was so low on funds that he was having a hard time keeping food in the cupboards, and we know he likes to have plenty of food on stock at all times. I began mailing him checks for $100 each month for the next six months to come. I could not have sent more, as I was still a struggling single mother. I could not fathom the idea of dad experiencing hunger ever again in his lifetime. I did not want him to go down the dark roads he had once traveled.

Dad was feeling an emptiness, he was lonely and alone. The widowed ladies in Dad's community knew that Mom had passed and were knocking down his door. He was up for grabs! He received many messages from interested ladies as well as a few knocks on his door and handmade treats, in hopes of winning over his heart through food. No one wants to spend their life alone. There is comfort in companionship. Although he was very flattered by the attention, he always loved a lot of attention, he was not ready to have any involvement with another woman. He was in mourning. Dad would remain mourning for two years.

Two weeks after Mom had passed away, was my 10 year high school reunion. I had planned to go but then planned to back out once my Mom had passed away. For some reason, Mom popped into my head. I knew my mother would want me to go. I knew she would want me to reconnect with the friends I had before I so carelessly tossed away my innocence. I felt that she would want me to re-establish myself with the good times in my life and the good people who were in it. Mom would want me to reconnect with my long lost friends, Sandra and Stephanie.

I attended my reunion only to find that neither of them would be there. I did run into my old friend and neighbor, Rudy Frenes. Rudy informed me that Sonya was in and out of the hospital and that she was on a list waiting to receive a kidney transplant. Rudy wanted to give Sonya his kidney, but sadly, he was not a match.

I also was able to connect with my cheerleader friends, Anissa, Katie and Bonnie, as well as my dear friend, Christine (Chris) Barrett. My dear friend Howard Green was there but I did not recognize him! Chris grabbed me by the arm and lead me to him, we embraced in a long hug. He grew into such a handsome man; his cute, chubby cheeks were no longer! I was heartbroken about Steph and Sandra not being there, but I enjoyed myself regardless and was happy I chose to attend. All of my friends appeared to be doing very well.

Shortly thereafter I decided to get back to dancing. I had not stepped foot in a dance studio since my early twenties, I was not yet ready in my head yet to be back in the dance studio. This time the dance studio was calling my name and I was ready to jump back in. I had stepped away from dance, oh so long ago, and was longing to dance again. I had lost the opportunity to be a dancer, I missed my chance, drugs and alcohol consumed me instead. Let's face it, my experiences with dance were the reasons for my drug use, I had to step away as I knew the environment was not healthy for me. But I felt my mother gently urging me to go back. It was time, I was ready. Life was too short. I should be doing what I love to do.

I searched all over town, and other nearby towns, for adult dance classes and had no luck. I spoke to the owner of a dance studio in Simi and she informed me that she would gladly attempt to round up attendee's and call me when an adult class was available.

A couple of months passed and the studio owner called me. I would again, drag my little sister, Michelle to this adult jazz class. I signed Amanda up for dance classes as well. When Michelle and I showed up for the first adult dance class, it was just the two of us and one other woman, the teacher was a teenager. We attended a few classes but we weren't feeling it. Although she was a nice girl, I was 27, not 47 like the other class participant, I wanted more of a challenge. There was a teenage jazz class preceeding the adult jazz class which was taught by a grown man and I was very familiar with his style of jazz dance. I thought, "Why can't I just take that class?" I called and asked the owner the same question. The owner advised me to ask the teacher if it was allowed. Allowed? If I did not have a problem with it, why would he? Michelle gracefully bowed out at this time, as she was not interested in dancing with the youngsters. She was only accompanying me for support anyway. I approached the Instructor prior to class. His name, Dennon Rawles. I asked if it was okay if an adult took his class, meaning me. Dennon sort of chuckled, and said, "Of course you can take my class." So I did not feel like a complete jerk, I explained that it was suggested that I ask.

After my first class with Dennon, I was hooked! He was as jazz as jazz could be! I was thrilled! It felt comfortable to me, like I stepped in where I left off years ago. I later learned that Dennon and his wife Sayhber were the choreographers for the movie, *Staying Alive*, starring John Travolta. He was exactly what I was looking for in a dance class. I would take classes with Dennon for the next four years. Mom had guided me to this man, I knew this was where I needed to be.

Dennon asked a question one evening, "Practice makes…what?"

I responded cheerfully, "Perfect!"

He said, "No. Nothing is perfect. Practice makes Permanent." Great point, I thought! This would be a philosophy that I would adopt.

The teenagers had a hard time with a 27-year-old adult in their class. Funny because, in my head, I was still young! I did not think of myself as an "adult", and quite possibly, I wasn't an "adult" yet. I lost some of my maturity to drugs and alcohol. I was not received very well at all. But I was not worried about them, I was there for me, they could get over it. I was great at balancing and could hold a passe' in releve' for a very long time. This seemed to make the teenagers angry, so much so that when one of them fell out of her balance, she then charged towards me and pushed me out of mine. This would be a metophore of my future career in dance; someone was always attempting to push me down.

The students did not support me, they wanted me out, but I was not going to leave. Unfortunately for them, when word got around to other dancing adults that there was an adult in Dennon's class, the class grew. Dennon's teen jazz would double in size, half teenagers and half adults. Amanda always accompanied me to class, she was such a good girl, I could bring her anywhere. I would take two classes a week, Tuesday's and Thursday's. I felt that the best thing for Amanda was to be with me, not with a baby sitter, those days were over. Dennon was amazed at her quiet nature and her ability to sit still for such a long period of time. Amanda would do her homework on the benches at the studio, which faced the classroom.

Dennon would saunter over to the stereo, turn down the music and expeditiously ask her, "Amanda, what's 2 x 4?"

Amanda would look up and answer eagerly, "8!"

"Yes. Good job."

While the class was participating in "across the floor" technique, Dennon would again wonder over to the stereo and challenge, "Amanda, what's 8 x 4?"

Challenge accepted, "32!"

"Yes! Well done!"

And so on. Dennon was very playful with my daughter and did not mind that I brought her with me to every class. She was very well behaved.

After a few months, one of Amanda's dance teachers received an opportunity to pursue a new career and she would have to move out of town. The owner of the dance studio called me and asked me to take over the class, it was a tumbling class. The owner and I had spoke on the phone one afternoon for hours, she was aware of my experience. I agreed to take over and was excited about the opportunity to teach.

By the end of the following year, I had acquired another class. Another dance teacher was leaving the studio. I was now also going to teach kids jazz and was thrilled. For the next four years, I would create many of my own classes, including adult jazz, lyrical,tap and ballet. I wanted to give other adults the same good time as I was having with dance, but that I had such a hard time finding, adult classes were non-existant until now! There was not yet a place in town for the teenage recreational dancer and no one wanted to teach the recreational classes, so I created classes for these kids giving the beginning dancer a chance. By the end of the four years, I was teaching 12 dance classes: tap, jazz, lyrical, ballet and tumbling. My would take my dancers to recreational dance competitions, kids and adults alike. I would make forever friends at this establishment. In addition to instructing 12 dances classes a week, I was still a full-time employee in the office and at this time worked as an On-Site Purchasing Administrator for a home-builder, drawing up construction contracts and such. I loved it!

A year after my mom passed away, it was a hot afternoon in July as I laid my head down on my pillow to cry. I was on my back in my room on my bed, my hands covering my eyes as I sobbed. I ached for my mother. I missed her terribly. I did not feel I ever had the chance to properly repair our relationship, I lost time with her while I was on drugs. So on this day, one year after her death, I cried harder than the other days. It is said that the first year after a loved one's passing is the most challenging, the first of all holiday's, birthday's, and every other "first" experiece without them is crushing, what they said was true.

A day had not gone by that didn't have a thought and tear for my mom. As I lay there calming myself down, catching my breath, I folded my hands across my chest and lay quietly with my eyes closed. As clear as if she was standing right next to me, I heard my mother whisper my name. It was as if she was kneeling down next to my bed and speaking into my ear.

I gasped for my breath as I bolted upright in my bed, eyes wide, mouth hanging open and in complete shock! I looked quickly to my right, to were I heard her voice, there was no one there. I looked to the left, then I searched the entire room. I jumped up from my bed searching around the room. I came back to reality, Mom was not actually there. I then burst back into tears. I screamed out her name, "Mom!", then dropped down to my knees and burst into tears again. Mom was here, she was here and she spoke to me, I heard her say my name and I felt her presence. She was there to soothe my aching soul. Thank you Mom.

From that moment on, I believed in angels. I believed my mother was still here in some form.  Mom was still here for me.

I have never again however, had the pleasure of hearing her whisper in my ear again, but I am convinced she has learned to communicate with me in many other ways.  She was able to get my attention that day and she will be able to get my attention again.

I hear you Mom.  I am listening.

# CHAPTER 21

# HEAVEN WAS MISSING AN ANGEL

After two years Dad finally allowed himself to date. I wanted him to date, I did not want him alone and lonely, he needed company, he was a very social being. It was pretty funny listening to Dad tell stories about all the ladies who were trying to court him.

He chose a woman who was Mom's opposite. The woman lived down the street from Dad, her name was "Bertha Shleeb" and she was a widow and a multi-millionaire. She stood 5'11" to Dad's 5'8". Not only did "Big Bertha Shleeb" tower above Dad, she outweighed him by at least 50 pounds. Her hair was cut like a bowl had been placed over her head, she wore glasses and no makeup.

When I met her, it was obvious that she was whipped over Dad. She said that all of the ladies in the community wanted him, but she got him. They went on silly adventures together, like clown school and Cowboy school. Did you know these existed? I had no idea and am positive this was all Dad's idea and Big Bertha was just going along with it. A good sport. The two of them would also travel to China for six months to teach Chinese children the English language. I was content that he was busy traveling the world. Keeping busy doing silly things that only our Dad would enjoy, and someone to do it with. I couldn't stand the thought of Dad being sad and lonely and too far away from Michelle and I. He had distractions now and I was satisfied.

Michelle, Amanda and I would vist Dad a couple times a year. During one of our visits, Michelle and I watched as our Dad held hands with Bertha. It was a bit awkward seeing Dad hold anyone's hand other than

Mom's, but we brushed it off.

During another visit to Arizona, my boyfriend Greg and his son Tanner would accompany Amanda and me. We were all sitting in the family room after dinner. Dad was sitting in his chair reading a book. Bertha walked past us as we sat on the couch facing Dad's chair. She sauntered up to Dad and leaned into him. One hand was on the arm of the chair and the other hand reached down to grab Dad's penis.

Did I just see this woman reach down and grab my Dad's package? Yes, in fact, we all witnessed her grabbing Dad's package, not just Greg and I, but Amanda and Tanner as well.

Are you kidding me lady?

Dad hurriedly pushed her hand off of him as he and I exchanged a look, a long, deep look. I was disgusted and he knew it. He quietly scolded her and she sort of laughed it off and walked off.

Was she trying to let me know she has my Dad by the balls?

I was sick. Is there not an unspoken rule that there is to be no package handling in front of his daughter and grand-daughter? I guess she didn't get the memo.

He was embarrassed, as he should be. Later he informed me that he had a "talk" with her about it and that she wouldn't do that again. It was too late, I would never respect her. I could not un-see what I saw.

Later that year, Dad came down to California to speak at his friends' facility, Dennis Merritt Jones, on anger management. This was the same facility in which my mothers "celebration of life" took place. Walking through those doors brought back memories of my mother, as I am sure it did for Dad. Greg and I went to the event to support my dad. Although he retains his Ph.D, Dad has a way of speaking to you, not at you. He does not try to impress anyone with fancy words, he knows he will lose most peoples interest. He knew that in order to hold someone's interest, he must to be on the same plane, must to get people to relate. Dad spoke about effective ways to break yourself from becoming angry before you have regrets.

"If someone says, 'Fuck you!', the consesus is to say, 'Fuck you too!'", he says as he looks over at Greg and I and winks. Dad continues, "What you should do is turn to them and smile, because as soon as you retaliate your anger will go up a level. Retaliate again and the anger goes up another notch. Retaliate further and you may be kicking someones ass, or worse, they may be kicking yours." Dad spoke calmly and pronunciated each and every word that escaped his lips. When Greg and I left the premises, he mentioned that the words my dad had spoken had a profound effect on him. Dad had the abilty to sanction life changing impressions on people. Greg would forever remember my dads words and work on applying his methods to his everyday life going forward.

I quit smoking when I was 30 but would still have an ocassional cigarette when I was drinking, untill I was 33 years old. Michelle also quit smoking around the same time.

One night I tucked Amanda into bed then snuck out to the backyard to have a cigarette. I kept a "spare pack" for those "just in case" times and this was just in case. While I was taking a drag off of my cigarette, I noticed movement. I looked up at Amanda's window and the curtain was being pulled back and her face was peering out at me through the window. She burst into tears and shut the curtain. Shit. Why did I stand where she could see me? I put out my cigarette and went to her room to talk to her.

As she laid on her bed crying, I sat next to her rubbing her back, as Dad always did, and apologized. She said through her tears, "Why are you still smoking? You are going to die! Smoking kills and I don't want you to die!" That was it, she got me, I hugged her close as I promised her I would never smoke again, I was true to my word.

I had resumed guitar lessons with my cousin Sam Iritano. He and Lucille now lived in Newbury Park, CA. Amanda and I would visit with Sam and

Lucille every Saturday for more than a year. While Amanda and Lucille visited, Sam and I would head to the back of the house for a guitar lesson. Mom had covered and recorded a couple of *Beatles* tunes, once upon a time. I wanted to learn, *In My Life* and I wanted to be able to play it for dad. The next time he would come out for a visit, I would play it for him.

"Dad, sit down. I have a surprise for you."

"Oh yeah? What is it?"

I grabbed my guitar and sat on the edge of my bed as dad sat on the floor, leaning his back up against the wall.

"Cousin Sam taught me one of The Beatles songs Mom used to sing."

I began to pick the notes and strum the chords. About halfway through the song, I looked over at dad. His elbow was propped up on his bent knee, his head laid in his hand, and tears streamed down his cheeks. The music was stirring up memories.

I stopped playing and cried with him.

Dad had some time on his hands, so in addition to his continued karate practice, his volunteer work at the police station counselling battered and abused children in which he began when he and Mom moved to Arizon, his painting hobby, his directing and performing in the local community theater variety shows and he would also delve back into his writing practice.

Dad wrote and had published, a psychological thriller titled *Thrust Home*. Dad had conducted countless hours of research in order to complete his book, which included police ride alongs. I was very proud of him. He had worked long and hard to accomplish this goal. He could check that one off his bucket list.

When he submitted his book for publication, he was not able to publish under the name, Richard Hoyt, as there was already a published author with the same name. He did not have a middle name, but in order to publish his book he had to have some kind of variation in his name. Dad thought about using the middle initial "C" only, but that was also in use. Dad chose his old name, "Charles". It was published as such, *Thrust Home by Richard Charles Hoyt.*

Michelle was dating Brennan, a guy she met while working in the mortgage industry. The two were engaged to be married. Michelle was planning on having Dad sit next to an open seat in the front row. That open seat would have a rose on it, in representation of our mother. I thought this was a lovely gesture. Michelle chose to invite Sandi and her family to her wedding.

In March of 2001, I would learn that my childhood friend, Sonya Frenes, was in the hospital and it did not look good. Sonya's kidney was failing and there was no donor. I visited my friend in the hospital. As I entered the waiting room, her entire family was there and then some. The room was still and filled with silence, there was gloom in the air. All heads were hung heavy and low. I was able to go in and see Sonya, but only briefly. I left the hospital and I was filled with sorrow. I understood the feeling that hung heavy in that waiting room all too well. Sonya passed away in March of 2001. I attended her services and cried like a baby. Rest in peace my dear childhood friend.

After Greg and I broke up, I dated a guy who was 16 years my senior, John. We drank a lot, he was really into red wine, consuming 2 bottles a night. I drank chardonnay, or martini's. I also smoked a lot of weed, John did not. He drank daily, I smoked weed daily. We were about to visit his family members in Canada. I packed some weed in my checked bag to take with me on the trip. I never travel without it. I used it for focus and to keep the anxiety at bay. I was not interested in taking prescription medications, which never really made me feel "right".

I had never been to Canada. I carried a sneak-a-toke pipe that I carried around in my purse on any average day, but removed it for the flight and put it in my suitcase with my goods. We arrived in Canada and as we were walking to get our luggage, a large, black dog came up by my side. I looked to see who was attached to this dog.

Oh, It was attached to a police officer. I said, "Aw, can I pet your dog?" With a very solemn face he said, "No. Follow me please."

Shit. John and I followed him. He brought us over to two female police officers who searched my purse founding nothing. I explained to them that

I had a pipe in my purse prior to boarding the airplane back in California, but removed it. They then asked if they were going to find anything in my luggage and I said yes. John was sent to accompany the the male officer with the dog to find our luggage.

"Shit. This really sucks." I whispered to myself. I am not going to hurt anyone with my weed, shit I may hurt someone without it! I was not planning on sharing it with anyone. There was only enough for me. So while the guys were away searching our luggage, the ladies and I chatted it up. They wanted to know why I smoked marijuana.

I explained to them, "I do not want to take pills any longer and the marijuana helps me focus, helps take away my negative energy and helps with anxiety and depression."

The police officers understood my reasons for its use but it was still illegal. One of the women said, "I have actually heard that before and I understand."

She then explained that I was to follow the police woman to another room, so they could strip search me. She said, "I don't anticipate that you have any on your person, but policy says we must search you."

Yeah so, that wasn't humiliating at all.

They let me go with a warning on my international traveling record, and of course they would be keeping the weed. I was cool, therefore the officers were cool. I laughed and said, "You are going to make me spend five days without my marijuana?"

The two officers laughed in return and said, "Enjoy your time in Canada."

When it was all said and done, John and his cousins were waiting for me for several hours. Great way to introduce myself to his family, eh?

✳ ✳ ✳

My friend Terri's future sister-in-law was about to marry Terri's younger brother, Mike. Terri and I took her out for a bachelorette celebration. The three of us had dinner and drinks at the Martini Bar in Westlake. Those lemon drop martinis were going down way too easy; I had four of them with dinner. We then headed over to the bar for more drinks. I managed to down eight more lemon drop martinis, two khamakazi shots and a watermelon shooter.

Terri and I were all on the dance floor getting our groove on when I blacked out. Blacking out was a normal occurence when I drank.

Terri informed me later, that one moment I was on the dance floor and the next I was gone. Terri did not have nearly as many drinks as I had so she was in a lot better shape than I was. When she noticed I was gone, Terri left the dance floor and went looking for me. The place was small so it was not difficult to find me. I was outside on the patio with my head between my legs and under the table. One gal was gently rubbing my back trying to soothe me. A guy was holding back my hair and another gal was talking to me soothingly as I puked my guts out under the patio table, in front of everyone. But did I care at that point? No. No shame in my game!

Terri called John to pick us up. The next day, I felt very off, bad hangover indeed. John and I went to the grocery store. The car ride was difficult, I was feeling nauseous. He parked and got out but I could not move. I felt if I moved, I would hurl. So I sat there for a few minutes taking deep breaths. I finally felt a little better so I stepped out of the car. I took about three steps and felt the world spinning around me.

I said, "I can't do this John."

He did not understand what I meant.

I said, "I cannot go into the store. I feel sick. Please take me home."

He got back in the car as I carefully made my way back into the passenger seat. We began the drive home and suddenly my hands, my fingers, they started to involuntarily curl inward. I was scared.

I said, "John, my hands!"

He said, "What do you mean, your hands?"

"My hands! Look at my hands!" I was panicking. "My fingers are curling inward!"

My fingers curled harshly inward, then the hands, then the wrists. I felt it traveling up my arms. My arms were now also curling inward towards my chest, as if they were shriveling. We pulled into the garage at home. Next thing I knew, my feet and legs are starting to curl up as well! I felt much like the Wicked Witch of the East whose legs curled up after the house landed on her in *Wizard of Oz*!

Holy crap, what is happening? It clicked and I knew I needed water. I was dehydrated. Severely dehydrated. I shouted out for John to give me some water. I always had a water bottle around, I never left home without it. He handed me the water bottle. I looked at him. I could not grab it nor could I possibly open it. My arms were curled into my chest and I lost function of my hands.

I shouted, "Please open it John! I can't use my hands!"

He quickly opened the lid, then he shoved the bottle towards me again.

I then shouted, (I am Italian, I shout a lot) "John, please help me and place the bottle to my lips!"

I had a few gulps then pulled my head away as I was feeling sick. I needed to sip the water slowly. I sat for a few seconds and then asked him to pour some more water into my mouth. I jerked my head away as I violently threw up all over the garage floor, projectile style. As I recovered, I asked for more water.

I gently sipped on the water as my arms and legs began to un-curl. I then asked him to carry me inside the house and lay me on the bed; I could not walk on my own. He scooped me out of the car and laid me on the bed. I took a few more sips of water. It was Saturday morning, I would not leave that bed for three days, I did not go to the doctor. Good thing Amanda was at her Dad and Angela's house (her step-mom) for the weekend. Monday evening I got up to teach my classes.

I would not drink for eight months straight, in fact, I never got drunk again. I will have an occasional drink, a few times a year at the most, but drunk, I will never be. It is interesting that once there was a time when I could not imagine NOT drinking, now I am in a place in my life where I cannot imagine drinking.

Michelle and Brennan's wedding day was fast approaching. The two of them threw a big, fancy engagement party. Dad and his girlfriend Bertha came out from Arizona. Sandi, Ric and their daughter, my niece, Samantha, attended as well.

I was shocked to see that Dad looked so old and worn out. He had on a neck brace and a bandage over his nose from skin cancer he just had removed. He looked frail and thin since last I saw him. I was uneasy about his appearance. I shared with him that I was concerned, he assured me he was fine.

Uncle Sam and cousin Bob attended with his wife, Karen, and their young children, Kevin and Katie. This would be the first time Sandi would be meeting other family members. I always looked up to my cousin Bob and was excited for him to meet Sandi.

As we introduced Sandi and Bob, Bob said, "I have heard so much about you."

Sandi relpied dryly, "I'm *sure* only bad things."

Bob shifted his feet and answered, "No. Only good things, of course."

Sandi rolled her eyes and replied smugly, "Well, you never know with these two", as she proceeded to take her two thumbs and point them at Michelle and me.

What the hell did she just say? Why on earth is she saying these things? Why would she think we are saying bad things about her? Is she paranoid because she was the one actually saying bad things about us? That was my first theory. This was her way of greeting our family? By bashing us? How could she believe that her negativity was ok in this environment? We were at Michelle's engagement party for pete's sake. This was incredibly hard for me because I have a reactive personality, however I bit my tongue and went on with my day. But trust me, the anger was still there festering.

Michelle and I had been nothing but accomodating to this girl. We both attempted to make Sandi feel like part of the family when she made it clear that it was what she longed for. She was still very bitter however about being given up for adoption. Will she ever be able to get past this and move on with her life? There is nothing to be done about this now. How did this become Michelle's and my culpability? Why was she so angry with us? We had nothing to do with the choices Mom and Dad made oh so long ago. She could not get over the fact that our mother and father stayed together and raised a family without her. Funny thing is, she was in therapy and had been for many years. Why wasn't she given the proper guidance to deal with this and move on? Isn't therapy supposed to help you move forward?

I am not in her shoes, but I do have several friends who were raised by adoptive parents. Some wanted to find out about where they came from out of curiosity and others had no intention of seeking out their past, content with the lives they were given. None of them expected a do-over. I am however, standinng in my shoes. How does Sandi think we fltl about finding out about her? She never asked, maybe she never cared. We were affected too, our perception of reality had been severely altered. Damnit, why is it always about her?

The following day we sent Sandi an email letting her know that we felt her comment and her attitude towards Michelle and I, in the presence of our cousin Bob, was an awkward and uncomfortable moment. I asked Sandi what her intention was. What did she hope to accomplish with the comment, "Well you never know with these two."?

Sandi's reply, "Oh please. I was having fun and being silly." We failed to see the humur.

A couple of months later, I received an email from Sandi demanding me to, "Tell your boyfriend to stop sending my husband pornography all day long!"

What the hell is she talking about? First of all, I had no knowledge of this. Second of all, I did not care about getting involved in what my boyfriend and his friends emailed each other. If her husband had a problem with it, he should have taken it up directly with the sender of the email. It was like Sandi was looking to pick a fight. You got it sister. I just love me a good fight.

My first reaction, "Are you fucking kidding me?" There goes my reactive personality.

And then, "Why on earth does your husband sit at his computer ALL DAY LONG?" And it escalated from there, inclusive with plenty of "F"-bombs. Sandi and I seemed to be competing for who could send the nastiest email. Who knew that being a bitch ran in the genes. At least we had that in common. We not not speak again for another spell.

Sandi's other sisters were having a hard time with this situation as well. Sandi was only able to embrace one set of sisters at a time. When Sandi was in communication with Michelle and me, she would put her other sisters on standby and push them away. When Sandi was angry with Michelle and me, she would run back to them. It was a vicious cycle. Why could she not embrace us all and be happy that she has not only two sisters, but now four?

✳ ✳ ✳

I was working for a construction company, a home-builder, as a Contract Adminstrator for the On-site Purchasing Department. I worked with a woman by the name of Karen, she was a motherly figure. I respected this woman and her knowledge about life as well as the construction industry. The two of us worked side-by-side for several years. Our supervisor at the time was going through a lot of personal problems and left Karen and I to pick up her slack. Contracts could not go out without her signature and approval; there were construction schedules to keep. If we did not get the contracts to our contractors, the jobs would be delayed.

Karen and I were responsible for writing the contracts. Our boss, "Sue Beanstock", would leave our pending contracts piling up on her desk while she closed her door and cried to her friends about her boyfriend issues. Our contractors were unable to get through on the phone lines to Miss Beanstalk so they would call Karen and me to ask about the status of their contracts. I was becoming frustrated and time was of the essence. So while Karen and I rushed to meet deadlines, Miss Beanstalk ignored then. We would have to pull out the imperative contracts and shove them under her nose and stand hoovering over her desk waiting for her to sign off. While Karen and I worked our tails off, Miss Beanstalk handles all of her personal business.

Boss lady came over to our desks and was hemming and hawing about how busy she was and that there was so much work to be done still. "Ladies, we have a lot of work to do!"

I looked her in the eyes and said very dryly, "We?"

Miss Beanstalk said warily, "Yes, we."

I replied, "No. Not WE. US." As I pointed to Karen and myself.

Her eyes narrowed. Boss lady was furious, "Come in to my office, now!"

I said, "Please do not talk to me that way!"

Miss Beanstalk stood 6' tall and wore high heels, she said as she towered over me, "Come in to my office now, right now!"

"I am not following you in to your office like a little puppy dog. Please do not talk down to me!"

Karen gently urged me, "Tania, just go with her."

"No. I will not."

Boss lady stormed off and slammed her office door. She called HR. Ten minutes later she comes out of her office and again ordered me to follow her. Karen urged me again to go, so I did.

Boss lady was writing me up. I did not take that very well. I looked at her and said, "Are you kidding me 'Sue'? You are writing me up? This is bullshit." I got up and walked out. I refused to sign her little paper. She then wrote me up a second time for using the word, "bullshit."

The supervisor of all of the fieldsSuperintendents, Steve, heard all of the commotion. He and I were close, he approached me and said, "Tania, you are going to be fired. Do you want to come work for me in the field?" He understood my dilemma with Sue as he too struggled with her lack of concern for deadlines. I responded with a, "Hell yes!"

I escaped the office and being fired and hightailed it to field as a Finish Superintendent at a housing project in Simi Valley. I went from high heels and short skirts to work boots and a hard hat. I could be me in the field, foul mouth and all, the guys had no problem with it. Nice. Why didn't I get out of the office sooner?

I was working in the homebuilding industry doing physical work, as well as working in the dance studios. Michelle thought this was pretty funny and called me "Flashdance", like the movie in which the lead character was welder by day and a dancer by night. I had been experiencing chronic neck pain for several years now, I also tore my hamstring while instructing my jazz class warmup, and was having some shoulder pain. I was sent by my doctor to a physical theray office for some relief. I always brought Amanda with me to appointments, in fact, I brought Amanda with me everywhere. One of the physical therapisits, we will call him "Fabio", knew I taught adult dance classes. He asked if his wife could take classes from me and I said, "Of course!" Fabio called the dance studio I worked for and purchased a gift card for Christmas to give to his wife.

I had on my jeans, a gown and I left my bra on under the gown. Fabio was wearing a turtleneck under his white coat and his blond hair was combed and styled to perfection, not a hair out of place. Fabio was working on my neck and shoulder while Amanda asked him questions from her magazine crossword puzzle. As they were interacting, Fabio's hands went from my neck to my shoulder, then to my chest. I thought, *Hm. I had never had anyone massage my chest before.*

As Amanda and Fabio continued to joke and laugh, Fabio's hands made their way down to my breasts. What on earth is happening? Was he massaging my breasts? I was so confused. I had no idea how to handle this. My daughter was sitting right next to me laughing and joking with the physical therapist as I lay still, completely traumatized.

I was always that girl who rolled her eyes at women when I hear them say that a man took advantage of them. I would say confidently, "That would never happen to me! I would punch him in the face and kick him in the nuts!"

Well, that wasn't going to happen because his face was behind me and his nuts were under the table beneath my head. After the breast massage, when my head was still trying to comprehend what was transpiring, he took his thumb and his forefinger on each hand and proceeded to rub my nipples between his fingers. Oh great, this therpay session was inclusive with breast massage AND a nipple twister. I freaked out. But instead of jumping up and punching him in the throat, I lay there frozen. I was unable to move. I was paralyzed by fear.

When Fabio finished getting his jollies with my flat chest, he left the room so I could put back on my shirt. As I was exiting the room, he stopped me and said, "Can I talk to you a minute?"

I said, "Yes, you can have a minute." He felt my tension.

I walked back in the room with him and left Amanda standing in the hallway. The entire office had already left for the evening and had asked Fabio to lock up. The three of us were the only ones in the office.

Fabio said, "I am so, so sorry! I got carried away."

"Yes. Yes you did.", I said.

He said a bit frantically, "That won't happen again, I promise!"

"No. No it will not happen again." It would not happen because I would not be back. I walked out of the office.

I had an adult ballet class to teach immediately afterwards. I was in a state of shock. Amanda had no idea what transpired and I did not let her see how awful I felt. I put on my happy face for her. When I arrived at the dance studio, my students, Kelly Wylie, who was a former professional dancer in Reno, NV, Alisa Guthrie who was a school teacher and mother of 2, Nancy Martin, who worked at the bank and was a mother of three (two of which would also take my kid and teens classes, Jackie and Julie), and Amy Irwin who was a tall, thin, 19-year-old, were there waiting for me. I set Amanda up on the bench to do her homework as I walked to the back office and asked the ladies to join me. When we were all in the office, I shut the door and burst into tears. Kelly, Alisa, Nancy and Amy were all there for me that night and I am forever grateful. We never got around to doing ballet. The four of them consoled me for an hour and a half instead. It was suggested that I go to the police.

After a good night's sleep, I drove to my jobsite in Calabasas. I had since been promted to Assistant Superintendent. When I arrived, I expalined to my Superintendent what happened and why I would be leaving for a portion of the day.

When I explained what Fabio did to me, the Super says, "I wish a female nurse would do that to me!"

One of the Assistant Super's, and my peer, say's, "It's because you are too friendly. That's why it happened. You are too nice."

Wow, no sympathy from this bunch!

Finally, a true gentleman and another Assistant Super, Bryant, says, "I am so sorry Tania."

Bryant taught me how to change out a toilet. I would utilize those skills later down the road. Bryant also gave me a nick-name, "T-Bone". All my co-workers would begin to call me that. Bryant then proceeded to walk up to me and ask if I needed a hug, I did. Bryant gave me a nurturing hug. I was so thankful he understood my pain and conflict. Bryant was older than the rest of us, possibly old enough to be my father figure. He was a mature man with empathy and understanding. Forthgoing, I would stick closer to Bryant's side on the jobsite.

I drove back to my hometown and to the police station. I was able to get Fabio on the phone while the police recorded his apology. Unfortunately, Fabio did not break out and confess the details, just that he was sorry for what he did. Because he didn't say, "I'm sorry I gave you a breast massage and a nipple twister while you were laying there so trusting on the table", it was basically his word against mine. Altougth they were sypathetic to my situation, the police were unable to help me.

I was not satisfied with this and was not about to stop there. I refused to let this man get away with touching me so inappropriately while I laid so helplessly in front of my child. I retained a lawyer. Fabio moved his wife and children out of the state, however my lawyer caught up with him regardless. It was determined by his lawyers that I would be a good witness, therefore they quickly suggested we settle out of court. I would not however, have a massage for more than 10 years.

After two years on the construction site, I began to have a hard time. My tolerance for "joking" around was low following this incident. My encounter with Fabio had me doubting everyone. I had an electrician friend in the field, "Nick". Nick was married. I met Nick's wife and child. His family along with my daughter and I, would go to Magic Mountain together and get together on weekends occasionally. Just a week after the incident with the physical therapist, Nick chose to tell me that he wanted to "Pick me up, put me on the counter, spread my legs, and lick me till I screamed." Nice Nick.

I called my boss, Steve. I told him about this inappropriate behavior and that I was no longer going to tollerate this type of talk. I explained to him that I was having a hard time now after the "massage incident" and shared with him what Nick thought was an appropriate choise of words. He moved me to a different construction site. While working on this new job, the first week a construction worker asked me to lunch. When I said, "No thank you." He called me a slut and a bitch. Really guy? A bitch, ok, but a slut? Screw you! I found my Super and advised him of the situation that took place. He found the guy, told him off and then kicked him off the job site. What on earth is happening? Is there a sign on my forehead that say's, "Please abuse me?"

I would seek out Mom and Dad's former partner, Susan Tuttle, for some psychological guidance then went back to work in the office. I worked another year for the home-builder, now as an Off-site Purchasing Administrator. I would soon receive an offer from some former co-workers who started their own business, they offered me a job working from home reading contracts. I left the construction industry. I was done with working in an office. I still had solid income from the dance studios as I was teaching at two different studio's which totaled 16 classes a week.

I would soon leave my boyfriend John and pick up 20 more hours of dance classes to teach each week. Yes, that would now make a total of 36 classes a week, I refused to go back into an office. My energy and sitting all day in an office where there were "rules", did not go hand in hand. I would use my excess energy to teach full-time. I taught mostly beginning and intermediate level dance classes and was not privy to having a dance assistant to help me demonstrate, the demonstrations were up to me. My friend Terri warned me that this was not a life-style I could keep up with forever. I disagreed, I said I could do it forever. I would eat those words down the road.

Amanda's dad, Scott, married a gal named Angela, who was my saving grace. She had a flexible schedule and was able to pick Amanda up from school when I was working and take her to the dance studio or orthodontist appointments. I was very fortunate that I had help with Amanda, her dance schedule was rigorous; she was dancing 14 hours a week. We were able to get her into an "independent work study" program in place of her high school P.E. class. She was on the competitve dance team at Pam Rossi's Dance Ten, where I was also a dance teacher for 10 years. Miss Julia Felker, the woman who choreographed our numbers at Edward's On Stage back in the 1970's, would also teach for this dance studio. We would start up a friendship which continues to this day. Julia has energy much like myself but she is a petite, little thing. I admire Julia for all of the experience she has in the dance industry and while I admire her, at the same time, I am saddened to think of the kind of life I may have had if I hadn't been caught up in drugs and alcohol. I lost out on a lot of experiences and lost a lot of time; time of which I cannot get back.

Amanda and I moved around frequently for many years and for many reasons: everytime I left a boyfriend, everytime the rent was about to be raised or everytime I had a loss of income due to the dance studios closing through holidays and a good portion of the summertime. There is no such thing as paid time off when you are a dance instructor; if I didn't work, I didn't get paid, so I always worked. I could not afford a day off, ever. I was very fortunate that my best friend Terri would date and eventually marry Craig Miller, who helped Amanda and me move at least twelve times. On a few occasions, Amanda and I would struggle and move ourselves because we could not bear to ask Craig to help us move, yet another time.

Once we rented a U-Haul and moved all of our furniture into it from a second story apartment by ourselves then into a storage unit, it was hard labor. When we arrived at the storage unit and were ready to unload the heaviest item, my mother's antique dresser, the dresser she saved up and bought when she rented her first apartment in Los Angeles, Amanda and I each picked up an end. We took a step as the dresser began to tilt heavily to one side and was about to go crashing down. I reacted quickly by turning around with the intent to catch it with one hand. I was able to catch it alright, with my big toe. The leg of the dresser dropped squarely on my big toe and broke it, the toe, that is, not the dresser. I cursed up a storm because that is what I do when I am angry. Amanda waited patiently for my meltdown to end and we continued on, exhausted. I would teach tap class in my flip flops for a couple of months; until I was able to get my foot back into a tap shoe without pain. I could not take time off to recover, if I did not work, I did not get paid and I was not going to allow that snowball effect to happen. I lived paycheck to paycheck, there was no money left over for a "rainy day". I was running my body ragged but just kept pushing forward. If I didn't think about it, I was fine. I did what I had to do, never concerned that there may be consequences, physical consequences. I'm like that *Little Red Corvette… baby you've got to slow down, cause if you don't you're gonna run your body right to the ground."* I hear you Prince but I am not yet willing to accept it.

✷ ✷ ✷

Since I did not see them at our 10 year reunion, I decided to do a search for my long lost besties, Sandra and Steph, on classmates.com. I found their information and sent each of them an email. Steph replied. I was thrilled. The two of us planned to meet at a coffee shop in The Valley to catch up. She had been living in Isreal for nine years prior, the reason why she was not at our first reunion. I had not seen Stephanie for seveteen years.

Sandra never replied and not having a lot of patience, I drove to her parent's house in hopes that they still lived there. When I pulled up, I saw Sandra's Dad's working van in the driveway. I walked up to the door and rang the doorbell. There was a heavy metal screen over the door and as I heard the door creek open, I was unable to see the person behind the screen.

A voice behind the screen said, "Can I help you?"

I said, "Yes, Mrs. Ramirez?"

I heard the voice shockingly say, "Mrs?"

The screen pops open, it is my dear friend Sandra! She exclaims, "Tania!", and came outside to hug me on the front porch. She explained that she just happened to be there visiting with her parents on this day. I was so excited to see her again! We have not lost contact since that day. We picked up where we left off 17 years ago.

✷ ✷ ✷

By now, Dad and Bertha had been dating for six years and through those six years, Dad would drink a lot, unbeknowst to me. When Dad drank, he would get emotional. Dad missed Mom terribly. He would reminisce about Mom when he was drinking. He would sit out on the back patio with his drink in hand, strare up at the stars and sing love songs to Mom in the heavens as he sobbed. Bertha would retire to the bedroom as Richard cried into the night.

During the month of March, 2005, I felt a strong presence of my mother. I walked into my family room, "click" the light turned on. A few minutes later, the television turned on. Mom was trying to get my attention, I just knew it! She would show me stronger signals in the days to come.

Music is my world. Music has the power to soothe my soul, speaking to me when I am sad, when I am angry, and when I am happy, I relate to music. Music also has the power to pull me down, if I allow it, or lift me up, when I am willing. My mother was aware of the affect music had on me. She also knows that when music is playing, I am listening. Music grabs my attention, music brings me focus. She wanted me to stop and listen, there were messages she was sending me through song, music would be her method of communication with me.

When I was teaching at the dance studio, I walked over to the stereo system to turn off my iPod. I then turned around and began to walk back to the students. On the walk back to the students, the music began begin to play again. The iPod was back on and no one turned it on. It also worked the other way around: I would turn it on, and it would shut off on its own. I would smile and say to my students, "That's my mom!"

My students played along with me. As this continued on a daily basis for the next two weeks, they would say, "Ah! It's your mom! She's coming to say hello!" For two weeks, several times a day, this pattern continued. I was so amazed by this activity and the strong presence I felt of my mothers.

Dad called me during one of these incredible days. I told him what was happening, my music randomly turning off and on, as well as lights turning off and on. I explained that I thought it was Mom communicating with me.

The first time I told him of this phenomenon, he said, "Hm, interesting."

The next conversation I had with Dad about Mom's visitation, he said harshly, "Oh Tania, get over it!" I thought, "No. No, I won't get over it." I wasn't upset with him for being so rough on me because I knew he was saying this to me because he, himself, could not get over it. The loss of a loved one is not something to just "get over." The longer my mom was gone, the more I missed her. I longed for her guidance and was soothed by the thought of her spirituality.

I persisted in telling him my theory, and by the third conversation, he finally said, "You may have a point."

Dad then proceeded to tell me that he was scheduled to have heart surgery to have a valve replaced.

I gasped. He scolded me, "Tania, you can't go around thinking everyone that goes into the hospital, is going to die! Every situation will not result in death."

He assured me he would be in and out in three days.

I said that I would schedule Amanda's and my flight so we could be there with him. Dad said, "No! I will be fine. It's a simple procedure. The only thing they are worried about is my age and calcium deposits, but I am not worried about it. I am in great shape. I will call you in three days." I respected his wishes and I did not go.

Michelle did not care about Dad not wanting us to make a big deal of his surgery, she and Brennan flew to Arizona

The day of his surgery, Michelle called me. She said Dad did not wake up from surgery within the recovery period expected. She approached to the doctors and they explained to her, due to his age, he may take longer to come to. Michelle and Brennan waited several hours longer, Dad still had not yet awoken. The doctors were now concerned.

Michelle called me again, "Please come now! Dad never woke up from surgery." Amanda and I dropped everything and flew to Arizona.

The doctors had taken Dad for an MRI. One of the doctors asked the family to follow him into a room where there was an x-ray machine. AS he clipped up the results of dad's MRI, he explained that calcium deposits shot straight up to his brain during surgery, which caused more than a thousand strokes. He was brain dead. We were flabbergasted!

We had to make the decision to pull the plug, he was on life support. Dad had designated Bertha as his Power of Attorney, she was the one to decide when it was time to pull the plug. Dad did not want to be resuscitated, particularly not in this condition. We called Sandi to let her know about her birth father's condition. She would not come, although she asked to be kept informed.

Dad hung on for three days while we all absorbed what was happening. I was overly optimistic and still had hope of Dad waking up and recovering. His eyes flew open on a couple of occasions and he looked right at me. I looked deep into his eyes trying to see if he was "there" and said with enthusiasm, "Hi Dad! It's me, Tania! Hi Dad! I love you!" I held his gaze until his eyes shut and he fell back into his coma. When Mom died, as I held her hand and caressed her ever so gently, Dad said, "I know Mom would appreciate all the love you are giving her. I hope you do the same for me." And that I did, I held his hand and I caressed his arm as he used to do to Michelle and me when he wanted to soothe us.

It was March 17, 2005; Saint Patrick's Day, but I was unaware, I didn't care, my world was spinning. The machine hooked up to Dad, keeping him breathing, had been turned off. Within minutes, we watched Dad take his last breath. The first worst day of my life was when I lost my mother, the second worst day of my life was this day. Watching your loved ones take their last breath is a life altering event.

He was gone. I threw my head back as a scream escaped my lips. I then threw my head into my hands and began sobbing heavily. Bertha rushed over to me, grabbed me by the shoulders and said, "Hush! You are going to scare your father. Now shut up!"

Really lady? My Dad just fucking died, and you are going to tell me to shut up because I am scaring him? I am going to scare my dead Dad? I gently pulled away from Bertha and she released me from her grip.

We called Sandi and let her know, but since Dad had already passed away, she chose not to come.

St. Patrick's Day, this was a day that Dad would be proud of. I believe this day was handpicked for him. Michelle and I were in a fog. We had no idea what day it was. We also had no choice in this matter, it was his time. Dad was always bragging about his full Irish heritage, it soothed me knowing in my heart, that this day now belonged to him, forever.

I now understand what Mom was trying to tell me. I now understand that she was trying to warn me that Dad was coming to be with her in the heavens. Mom had passed eight years ago, it was time for Dad to join her. I like to think that while Dad was in surgery, he saw Mom in the light and ran as fast as he could into her open arms. This is what heals me, knowing Dad can now again be with the love of his life, Mom, again and for eternity.

After Dad passed away, we went back to Bertha's home, she had a guest house we were staying in. I sat alone outside the guest house for a brief moment to collect my thoughts. As I sat on the bench, a white butterfly came up to my face and fluttered around me for a few seconds, holding my deepest attention. I whispered, "Dad?"

Dad sent me a butterfly to soothe my soul, just as mom had sent me a hummingbird. He knew how much I loved butterflies. White is what my Dad always called the color of his hair. He would say, "My hair is not gray, it is white", so in my mind the "white" butterfly was logical. To this day, when a hummingbird zips down from the tree and over my shoulder, I am reminded of my mother. When the white butterfly gently flutters by, I am reminded of my father and I am always grateful for these signs. Coinsidence maybe? But then again, maybe not.

It was time to leave Arizona and go back to reality. As we were packing up our belongings, Michelle brought up some deep seeded anger towards me. She snapped, "We missed Mom's death because of you! Because you are ALWAYS late! You are rude, Tania! It is all your fault that we didn't make it to the hospital in time!" Michelle didn't know any other way at the time to express herself, so she yelled at me instead. Brennan and Amanda stood awekwardly as we argued.

I responded in anger, "In time for what? In time to watch Mom die? Maybe Mom didn't want us to watch her die. She moved all the way to Arizona so we wouldn't have to watch her die! It is quite possible that she waited until she was all alone with Dad to let go. And why are you trying to make me feel guilty about something I can't change?" Michelle lost it, she was having a melt down, and I now understand why. We are now alone in this world, no more parents to guide us. No more picking up the phone to call them and ask a question or just to hear their voice and say, "I love you." It was all over, they were gone. We dropped the argument and continued packing in silence.

We finished packing and made breakfast at Bertha's before we had to leave for the airport. Bertha made coffee and offered some to me. I accepted. I would need a coffe mug. I walked over to the cabinet and opened it. The offee mugs were on the top shelf. As I reached for a mug, I noticed my mom's mug, it was right there on the top shelf facing me. I loved that mug of Mom's, it was a large black mug with two colorful cats on the front. Mom had had that mug since we were teenagers. I was excited to see it again! I smiled and reached up to grab the mug. Yes, this is the mug I will have my coffee in this morning.

I poured myself a cup of coffee and proceeded to go into the other room to drink it. Before I made it to the other room, I noticed Bertha was in toe. She was directly behind me and a little too close for comfort. As I turned my head to look at her, she grabbed me. Bertha grabbed my arm at the elbow and held tight. It was the same arm that was holding the coffee mug.

She looked at me sternly narrowing her eyes, still squeezing my arm and spat out angrily, "Where did you get that?"

I said, "Get what?"

"Where did you get that mug?" she yelled.

I said a bit alarmed and a bit perturbed all rolled into one, "I got it from the cupbord."

She said, "How DARE you go rummaging through my cabinets!"

"Rummaging? It was right in the front. Plus, it's my mother's mug." I replied.

She squeezed my arm a little tighter and angrily held my gaze.

I looked at her just as sternly and said, "Get your hands off of me."

She glared at me and squeezed my arm a little tighter.

I held her gaze and said, "Get the fuck off of me Bertha!"

She continued to squeeze. What was happening here? A 66-yea- old lady is trying to physically intimidate me? Michelle and Brennan heard the commotion and ran into the room to mediate the situation. As Bertha stood and squeezed my arm tightly, Michelle and Brennan tried to reason with her.

I said one last time nice and slow, in case she was having a hard time understanding what I meant, "Get the fuck off of me!"

She let go and walked away.

Michelle and I, once again, had to go back to Arizona for the memorial service that Bertha had planned for Dad. It was a very nice service, there were more than a hundred people who attended, Dad would have been proud to know that he was loved by so many. When it was over, Bertha walked over to give eveyone hugs. She came to me last as I sat in my seat, I would not budge. She leaned in to attempt to hug me. I stood rigid. Wow, this is awekward, what would make her think that I would be receptive to this? That I would forget the way she treated me the last time I saw her, is that what she thought? She thought wrong.

She must have felt my tension because she backed off immediately and said, "Oh. Too soon?"

"Yes", I said as I turned to lock eyes with her, "Too soon."

Michelle and Bren were to be married in two months. Not only would our mother not be attending, but now our father; we were devastated. At the wedding, there would now be two empty chairs, one for each of them. A rose on Mom;s chair and one of Dad's hankie's on his. Although we are adults, we now felt like orphans.

I searched the internet to track down Philip to inform him of Dad's passing. I was not surprised, I found him back in prison.

Prior to this, Philip had been out of prison for a few years and was doing well. He had a friend who got him a job in construction, building scaffolding making $23.00 an hour.

In 2001, Philip's mom, Mary, had developed Acute Mycotic Leukemia. Philip was having dinner with his girlfriend, Helen, when he received a call from his mother. Mary thought she was having a heart attack. Philip ran out of the restaurant and rushed to take his mother to the hospital in Elmhurst, where she had worked for many years. When the Leukemia was diagnosed, the hospital transferred Mary to Mount Sinai in Manhattan for chemo-therapy. Mary had one round of the chemo and was ready for her second when her heart gave out. Mary passed away from a heart attack.

Philip did not know how to handle his emotions, his anger. Not only had he already lost two women that he loved dearly, he would now lose a third, his mother. Philip would soon dive right back into smoking crack. There were a couple of prostitutes around his apartment complex who had no "protection." Philip offered his apartment and his protection, he became their pimp. Philip would be arrested again, though not for the pimping, but for dealing. He was found with 13 bags of crack in his possession. Philip would do another year in prison and get out in 2003.

When he was released in 2003, he had no one, he was homeless. He was in and out of shelters, he was hungry and he was desperate. Philip had no money and could not find work. It is quite a challenge when you are an ex-convict finding anyone who will hire you. Philip was desperate, so he robbed a bank. Yes, he robbed a bank and he was armed. He was caught a couple of days later and went back to prison, yet again.

I was able to call the prison when dad passed away and was able to leave a message for my brother. Due to the special circumstances of his father's passing, they would allow the message to go through. The next day, the priest from the prison called me to discuss with me personally, the passing of our father. He informed me that if his father's service was local, he could arrange for Philip to attend. I let the Father know that the service would be in Arizona. The priest said he would relay the message to Philip.

Philip called me collect the next day and I was able to personally deliver the news to him. Philip did not cry and I can understand. Was he sad about his dad dying? I am sure that he was, but even more distraught that his "father" was never really a father to him and the chance for that to happen was no longer an option. Philip would be in prison until the year 2007. After his release, he met a petite woman named Lisa in rehab; the two married shortly thereafter. Philip has managed to keep himself out of prison since 2007. He has someone to share his life with now and that makes life worth living.

Michelle and I had rekindled a relationship, of sorts, with Sandi, however that began to fade quickly for me because she was in the middle of Bertha and us. Bertha was desperately trying to hold on to someone who was related to Dad and Sandi was the one she chose, easy enough to understand, because Michelle and I were done with her and she knew it. Sandi had never even met Bertha.

Dad, like Mom, would be cremated. Bertha, Michelle and I would all meet at the crematorium. For some reason, Bertha was convinced Dad's ashes were going home with her. Michelle and I were beside ourselves. Why is this woman so difficult? She had been his girlfriend, not his wife! By now, we could barely stand to be around this woman.

We were guided to a private room inside the crematorium. Michelle and I sat together on one side of the table. Bertha took a seat at the head of the table. The woman attending to us took the seat between Bertha and Michelle and I. The woman began to speak directly to Michelle and I about the cremation process.

Bertha did not like it and firmly stated, "Richard's remains will be going with me!"

The woman asked, "And who are you? Are you his widow?"

"No." I am his girlfriend." Bertha said.

The woman said, "I am sorry, but the remains will go to the next of kin."

Bertha shouted, "But I have the Power of Attorney!"

The woman stated very calmly, "Power of Attorney is only valid while the person is alive. Once the person dies, that Power of Attorney is null and void. The remains will go to the next of kin." When the woman completed this sentence, she turned her back to Bertha and completed the meeting with Michelle and I. Bertha sat there seething. She had lost control and she was furious.

Ostensibly, Bertha needed to gain back control, she attempted to keep all of our father's belongings. Michelle and I had to fight Bertha to get his belongings, as well as the things that Dad still had of our mother's. We had to threaten her with lawyers. She finally let her son arrange it with us, to pick up what rightfully belonged to us.

Michelle and I flew out there, rented a U-haul and drove to Bertha's house. She had everything in the garage. But was it "everything?" No. Bertha would not let us enter her house. Bertha took it upon herself to decide who received what. Meaning between Michelle and I and Sandi. Sandi did not even like our father nor did she even know Bertha, they had met only once. Why was she getting involved? Why is Bertha the one who gets to decide who gets what? This is insane! Michelle and I should have the right to distribute Dad's things and decide who gets what. I told Bertha that she was welcome to keep any painting that our dad created while he was with her, and he had plenty.

Dad's paintings and Mom's Hummel collection, that is all I cared about. Bertha had only a handful of paintings in the garage, four to be exact. Michelle would keep two and I would keep two. We were fortunate to each have one of Dad's paintings already in our homes. Where were all the other paintings?

Michelle later received a package in the mail from Bertha. There was no note, just a cut ponytail of Dad's hair. Michelle lost it and dropped the piece of Dad's hair on the floor. She was horrified.

She called Bertha and asked her to explain herself, she said simply, "I thought you would want it." Michelle said, "A warning and a note would have been appreciated."

I was furious with Sandi for being involved with Bertha, a woman she did not know. Did Sandi want a relationship with Bertha because she knew she was a muli-millionaire? I wondered, because I found it very interesting that she was so eager to have a relationship with Bertha, when she did not ever really want a relationship with her "birth father". While I chose to walk away from Sandi, Michelle chose to continue a relationship with her, she didn't want to stop talking to her just because I had.

Sandi had invited Michelle and Brennan to her daughter Samantha's birthday party. Michelle and Brennan walked through the door of the party when he abruptly stopped Michelle dead in her tracks.

Brennan said, "Do not be alarmed, and do no look now, but Bertha is here."

Michelle's heart sank, "What?" What do you mean Bertha is here?"

Brennan, "I am just telling you what I see, and I see that Bertha is here."

Michelle was civil but sick to her stomach. Why didn't Sandi give Michelle the courtesy of telling her that she was intending to invite Bertha?

Without our knowledge at the time, Bertha brought Sandi seven of Richard's paintings and several of Phyllis' Hummels. Sandi would accept these items not because she wanted to hold the items close to her heart, she wanted the items out of spite for Michelle and me. These items would be stashed in Sandi's garage never to be seen again or appreciated by those that loved and admired him. The items rightfully belonged to Michelle and me, legally and morally.

Michelle, Amanda and I now had to do the dreaded task of spreading our Dad's ashes, of course he would be placed under the same rock as our mother. These were amongst the saddest days of my life. First my mother and now my father. I longed for the experience to grow old with them. There are so many questions I have that will be left unanswered for eternity.

We spread Dad's ashes to reunite with the earth and most importantly with our mother. Who knew it would be more than ten years until we would return to this memorial site.

# CHAPTER 22

# THE ROAD TO SABINO

I chose to contact Sandi and try this "sister" thing again. I could not live with myself if anything ever happened to her and I had not made amends. I could not get through to her by email for some reason, so I found her on *Facebook* and sent her a message. I would resume a relationship again, and this time around I chose to treat her as my sister. I know this is what she truly longed for.

Sandi still had bitterness towards Dad and continued to blame him for her adoption. It was not until I began my research for this book that she finally understood, or at least she said she did. It was our mother's body and ultimately her choice. I had the chance to record a conversation with Auntie Lolly regarding the circumstances of her and Mom's pregnancies. Auntie Lolly explained that in that day and age, one did not disrespect their parents by becoming pregnant prior to marriage, no matter what their age, as I played the recording for Sandi. I think it sunk in, hearing someone else say it. She now hopefully understands the dilemma over her adoption. I do understand that Sandi may feel that she missed out on growing up with her biological family, but I am not sure she has ever once thought about how Michelle and I have been affected by this deep dark secret, it completely altered our entire perception. Sandi knew her entire existence that she was adopted, Michelle and I had no idea that we had a sister who was given up.

Amanda and I were living in an apartment. I asked my mother several times, "Is Dad was with you?" I talked to my mother often when I was alone in the car. I knew she communicated with me through music. I interpret her messages through song lyrics, but where is Dad?

"Are you together Mom? Is Dad with you because I don't feel him. Can you tell Dad to send me a sign to let me know he is there?"

I asked repeatedly until one afternoon, I was sitting in my family room watching television. The drapes were closed behind the TV. Something on the curtain caught my eye, I stood up to get a closer look, there were letters spelling out "d-a-d" and there was a shape of an arrow below the letters which pointed down. I gasped as tears immediately ran down my cheeks. Dad is down there? In horror I asked my mother, "Mom! Is Dad in hell? What does this mean?" I was distraught.

The next morning I went to teach a Pilates class at the gym. I couldn't wait to talk to my friend, Wendy Kern, who was so faithful to me and my classes and was there just as I expected. I wanted to discuss my recent experience with her, she was a spiritual human being and understood me as a person. I trusted that she would not make fun of the way I felt about my mom and dads presence, as some people had done in the past. I knew she would help me to understand my message from Heaven. After Pilates class, I explained to Wendy what I read on the curtain.

I asked her, "Is my dad in hell?"

She said, "No, Tania. Your Dad is here. You asked your Mom where your Dad was, and she answered, your dad is here."

A few months later, Amanda and I laid our heads down to sleep for the night. At some time in the middle of the night, Amanda came running into my room and jumped into bed with me.

"Mom, something happened."

"What happened?" I asked groggily.

"I think Poppa was here."

My eyes popped wide open, "Poppa? What do you mean?"

Amanda explained, "I was laying there with my eyes closed and I felt someone touch my forehead. Right after someone touched my forehead, I heard a voice say, 'YEAH'".

"It's Poppa! (Amanda called her grandarent's Mimi and Poppa). He was able to connect with you! He probably kissed you on the forehead and when you felt it, he exclaimed, 'YEAH!'" A tear rolled out of my eye. I can picture it now, thumbs up like *Fonze*, as he spoke that single word, proud that he was able to communicate with Amanda and that she responded to his touch. Happy Day's was a family favorite and often Dad would immitate Fonze's mannerism's back in the day.

Amanda said, "Mom, can I please sleep with you tonight?"

"Of course you can. I am sure he did not mean to scare you."

"I know Mom, but I still want to sleep in here with you."

✳ ✳ ✳

Amanda, by 23 years of age, had had enough of the California life and decided to move to North Carolina. She was proud to learn through her geneology projects of the Hoyt's and the Iritano's, that her Mimi (her grandmother, my mother) had also made her trek across the country at age 23. Why North Carolina? Amanda's Dad, Scott, was there with his family, his wife Angela and their five children whom Amanda wanted to spend time with and watch them all grow up. After she received her Bachelor's Degree in Psychology from Channel Islands University, in California, in honor of her grandparents, she packed it up and moved. Not more than two years later, she accomplished one of her goals, which was to purchase a home by the time she was 25 years old. She purchased a three bedroom home on ¾ of an acre of land. I could not be more proud of her! Due to the fact that our lives may not have been so stable at all times and all of the moving around we did, I am sure she wanted stability.

Amanda was six years old when her Mimi passed away. I recalled a conversation I had with my mother prior to her passing. I said, "Amanda, Mimi was worried that you would not remember her."

Amanda confessed, "Mom, I don't remember her, but with all the stories you tell and all the pictures surrounding us, I feel that I do know her." I made sure to kept their spirits alive by speaking their names and telling their stories often. I was proud to know that her Mimi and Poppa were still an influence in her life, although they were not in the physical world.

By the time I was 41 years old, I met my future husband, John Jensen. I knew John in high school, he was a senior and I was a sophmore. We didn't hang out in high school but I would always see him at those infamous backyard parties back in the day. We ran into each other at an unfortunate place, a memorial service for a fellow classmate of his, Mike Budding. Out of Mike's unfortunate death came the love of two people, we would marry on May 11, 2013.

Sandi, Samantha, Amanda and I decided to take a trip to Boston. Not only see my mother's side of the family, but to introduce them all to Sandi and Samantha. Sandi and Samantha had only previosuly met Auntie Tootsie and Uncle Sam at Michelle's wedding many years ago.

Michelle did not accompany us on this trip. Michelle and Brennan had two small children, it was costly for a family of four. Amanda flew in from North Carolina and the rest of us flew together. We hadn't been to Boston to visit in about 12 years when Dad, Michelle, Amanda and I all flew out for the christening of cousin Bob and Karen's new born twins.

I know Mom would want us to keep a connection with her family in Boston and I felt she would want us to introduce Sandi to the entire family. Auntie Katie was 91 years old, Auntie Tootise was 89, Auntie Dottie 87, and Auntie Lolly 85. Prior to our visit and on September 1, 2011, cousin Bob passed away from cancer which came back with a vengance and riddled his body once again, he was only 51 years old. Within the next year Uncle Sam, Bob's father, would stop eating and drinking. He would develop kidney failure and die in October of 2012, possibly from a broken heart. I can only imagine that losing your "child" no matter what their age, is the most difficult time in one's life, it is not the way it is "supposed" to happen.

It was a joy being in the presence of family! Nevermind that I had very few interactions with them over time, when I am in their presence, I am home. Cousin Karen's house (Auntie Katie's daughter), was filled with wild, crazy, loud, fun loving Italians! I was always told growing up, that Italians were known to be loud and crazy, and that's where I got my loud and crazy side. I had a hard time understanding this because Mom was not your typical "Italian." She was quiet and reserved. I rarely ever heard her raise her voice or lose control of her demeanor. Dad, on the other hand, was a boisterous Irish man, and that is who I believed I was most like. Michelle is quiet and reserved, like Mom, and so is my daughter, Amanda.

Being an adult around my loud, Italian family made me realize I am a blend of both the Italian crazy and the Irish rowdy. Regardless of my comfort level, I believe all four of us felt at home during our visit back east. We had inadvertently planned this visit to Boston in March, it was still winter there. Winter? It was already spring in California. We didn't realize winter was a time that everyone stayed indoors. We all had a blast being able to experience a real winter and Boston snow. They however, were most likely not thrilled with us for visiting during snow season, but were happy we were there nonetheless.

Amanda, Samantha, Sandi and I were outside playing in the snow at our Cousin Karen's making a snow-man. We dressed it with a scarf around its neck, gave it eyes with pebbles and arms made out of sticks, we even put "buttons" down the front of the snowman. We all walked back to be inside for a pot luck of amazing Italian food. As we ate, I played Mom's music that Dad had converted from reel-to-reel to CD for my Auntie's. I had uploaded Mom and Dad's music to my iPhone. When the last song ended, I turned off the music and closed the application and placed the phone on the table while we finished eathing.

When we peeked outside at our snowman, it had fallen over. I grabbed my phone while Sandi and I rushed outside and placed a beer bottle near it as if it were a drunken snowman. We laughed, took pictures and went back inside. The next time we walked by the window, we noticed the snowman had been put back together! Our sweet cousin Jimmy, Karen's son, brought the snowman back to life for us.

Sandi and I bundled up and went back outside in the cold snow to replace the beer bottle with a coffee mug, we were having fun. As we kneeled down to fix up Mr. Snowman with his coffee mug, music started playing, it was muffled. Sandi and I looked at each other a little baffled and asked each other where the music was coming from. We stood up, the music continued playing. As we stood ever so quietly to listen, I realized it was coming from my pocket, it was coming from my phone. I retrieved the phone from my pocket and looked at the screen, it was my mother, her picture staring up at me. The song that was playing was, "Say it Isn't So", a song she had recorded. Neither of us said a word. I burst into tears. I understand that somehow, the play button could have been pushed when I bent down, but I closed the program. How did the program open? I also had my phone password protected after two minutes of idle time. How did my phone get unlocked? I was sure Mom was there with us. Sandi and I looked at each other in amazment, I then burst into tears as Sandi embraced me. We would go back inside and share our story with Cousin Karen, she was a believer, she lost her father several years back and believes that he too comes down from the heavens and visits her.

The four of us took a side trip to New York from Boston. While we were in New York, I searched for my brother. I had not spoken with him since Dad died in 2005. I searched for him on the internet, I searched for him on Facebook, I searched for him in the white pages. Who knew there were so many people in New York with the name Philip Hoyt? I even checked the prison systems and was unable to locate him. I was happy not to find him in prison this time!

Not long afterwards, I received a Facebook friend request from a Philip Hoyt. I sent a message and asked, "Is this my long lost brother?" He replied that indeed it was. Facebook is one of the coolest things ever, my brother and I were now reconnected!

Since reuniting with my brother, he and I have been in constant contact. One afternoon we were talking on the phone, he asked me, "Why did Dad leave me? Was it something I did?"

I could not even pretend that I was not crying because when I began to speak, I found it challenging. My voice was hoarse and shaky.

I regained my composure and said, "My brother, Dad was a wreck for a long time. I am sorry he ran away, but it wasn't anything you did. It was not because of you. It was him. He was fucked up for a long time and was afraid he would be the kind of father to you, as his father was to him."

*If I could turn back time.*

I long to be able to talk to Dad and ask him why. Why did you have no participation in your son's life until the New York court system sent him to live with us in hopes that you could "fix" him. When you wrote that you battered Philip when he was a mere 3 weeks old, what does that mean? What did you do to him?

I long to talk to Mom and ask her how she felt when Michelle burned her arm when she was three years old. How did she feel as she handed her first born over to someone else? I want to know the entire story of her first pregnancy.

Why didn't I ask these questions while they were still alive?

Next stop, Arizona, to visit the site where our parents were reunited with the earth, Sabino Canyon. Michelle, Amanda and I hadn't been there for 10 years and Sandi had never been there. The last trip we made was to spread Dad's ashes with Mom's, to reunite the two of them forever and reincarnate them with Mother Earth. This is when I finally begin to understand Dad's facination with Buddah. Buddah's main goal is to find the end of suffering where suffering once existed. Dad found the end of his suffering until Mom died and he will suffer no longer now that has joined her. We dropped off Dad so long ago, to be with Mom and had not returned since. Michelle and I wanted to introduce Sandi to Mom and Dad's "resting" place. Amanda flew out from North Carolina and we all caravanned to Arizona. Michelle, Brennan and their two children, Perry and Evyn, in their car, while Sandi, Amanda and I were in another car. It was a long drive down to Tuscon, AZ.

Eight and a half hours later, we arrived at our shady looking hotel that was located in the middle of a parking lot next to a Big Lots. It would have to do. We were here for one reason and one reason only, to visit our parents up in Sabino Canyon.

In December of 2015, I decided that I would get my first tattoo. I had been contemplating this since I was 40 years old. I finally went down to a place in Simi Valley called the *The Tattoo Room* just after I turned 46. My tattoo was a hummingbird and a white butterfly, surrounded by colorful flowers.

When we were in line to purchase our tram tickets at Sabino Canyon, just in case we decide while on the trail that we no longer wanted to walk, a park employee noticed my tattoo. She said, "What a beautiful tattoo you have."

Being the chatterbox that I am, I shared the story behind the tattoo and that Sabino is dear to our hearts. The woman informed me, "Interesting that you should say that. Sabino Canyon is known for its plentiful presence of butterflies and hummingbirds." I could not help myself, tears snuck out of my eyes and rolled down my cheeks, although I maintained a smile on my face. The woman cried with me, we then hugged and parted ways.

I was a little nervous about whether or not we would remember where the site was. I brushed it off, of course we would remember. How could we forget?

It turns out that in the past ten years things can change, a lot of erosion had taken place. It did not look the same as the last time we ventured out here. We could not locate the spot where we spread their ashes. We continued climbing higher and higher up the mountain searching for a familiar sign. I briefly paused at a certain location, shook my head, and continued on. Michelle and the kids, Perry and Evyn, were way ahead of us. Michelle was on a mission to find their resting spot. I do not recall being this far up the mountain. I asked Brennan what he thought. He agreed, we had gone too far. We called to Michelle and the kids to come back down. I started to panic. As we descended back down the mountain, Amanda comforted me and assured me that everything was going to be alright and that we would find their resting place.

As tears silently streamed down my cheeks, I begged and pleaded with my angels to lead me to their site. To allow me to recognize where they were reunited with the earth. I strained my brain as I searched out the land looking for something that would tell me where they were. Almost in sync, Brennan and I halted and starred at the very same location that I had noticed on the way up. This was it!

The trees and bushes were so overgrown, the side of the mountain seemed to have eroded away, but as I stepped through the bushes I knew we were where we were supposed to be.

After we all settled into the area, Michelle and I found the rocks that we felt may have been THE rocks that we spread their ashes under oh so long ago. We each grabbed under a rock and lifted them to display the raw earth the picture that Dad had put there was not there, I am sure it decomposed by now because that was eighteen years ago. Each of us then wrote a note to Mom and Dad, Mimi and Poppa, Phyllis and Richard. Once we all finsihed, we would each fold our notes and place them in a pile on the earth where the rocks had previously been displaced. We then replaced the rocks to their original positions, covering our notes. We stopped for a moment of silence and in loving memory of our mother and father.

Ten years had gone by since we visited their resting place. I knew Mom and Dad live in our hearts and in our minds, however I felt a bit of guilt for not visiting sooner.

I wiped my tears away as I whispered, "I love you Mom and Dad, and I miss you so."

We all pulled ourselves together and began our journey back down the mountain. We hiked more than three miles up and now three miles back down. Why does it always seem like a longer trip back? We vowed to come back here more often, to not let so much time slip away. This was a time for all of us to bond together as a family unit, something our parents would have been proud to witness. It felt good to be there, and at the same time it was also a very sad place to be. My parents will forever be a part of Sabino Canyon.

I always find "goodbye" to be the hardest word to say. Therefore, I will not say "goodbye", instead I said to Mom and Dad as we left Sabino Canyon, "Until we meet again, on the *Other Side of the Tracks*".

Shortly after our visit to Sabino, I awoke from a dream. I had been asking for many years, but was still unsure, I wanted to know if Mom and Dad were together. On February 19, 2017, I received my answer. In my dream, Mom and Dad were sitting down, on what I have no idea, I remember a bright white light surrounding them. They sat together and held hands as they smiled down upon me. I particularly remember the way Dad looked, he was grinning ear to ear.

His smile said to me, "I am with your mother, and we are here for you."

A song was ringing in my ears, a message from my mother, "Your love is lifting me higher, higher than I have ever been lifted before....I'll be by your side forever more." Rita Hayworth, or the original form Jackie Wilson in

1967, I knew the song, but it was not a song I ever listened to.

The next song that was strong in my head was George Michael's, *Freedom*, "I won't let you down. I will not give you up. Gotta have some faith in the sound. It's the one good thing that I've got.", a message from my daddy.

I was with my dear friend, Chris Barrett, planning for our 30 year high school reunion. I shared my dream with her. I explained that I felt it must be me singing to my mother, "Your love is lifting me higher."

Chris said, "Oh no dear Tania, your mother is singing that song to you. Your love is lifting HER higher." Higher into the heavens.

I long to have my parents near. I wish Dad would run out the front door now to hug me. I surely would not roll my eyes, but turn around and embrace him. I wish I never told my mother I hated her when I was an unruly teenager, and until my very own daughter said those words to me, I held on to guilt. I knew my daughter did not hate me, at the moment yes, but as a whole, no. As I have experienced it myself and now have the knowledge and assurance to know that my mother understood, I never hated her.

When I hear Frank Sinatra singing, "*I did it my way*", I think of Dad, it's the story of his life, "*I've lived a life that's full. I've traveled each and every highway. And more, much more than this, I did it my way.*" And that he did.

Dad is *At Last* with Mom. Etta James sang, "At last, *my love has come along, my lonely days are over, and life is like a song….and here we are in heaven, and you are mine…AT LAST.*" I know they are together again, *At Last.*

"Life is a choice, you know. Have whatever kind of day you want to have." This was my fathers outgoing message on his answering machine for at least 20 years. Dad is correct, life is a choice. I must respect the choices he made in his life. I am proud of all that my father overcame in his life's journey and am proud to say…

that's my daddy!

# ABOUT THE AUTHOR

*Photographer: David Muller*

Tania Hoyt Jensen has been a dance instructor and choreographer in southern California for the past 20 years, instructing many genres, both children through adult. Tania filmed two fitness videos: *Body Transforming Pilates by Tania* and *Pilates for Dancers,* of which can be found on YouTube. For 15 years, Tania was the adjunct Professor of Dance Aerobics at California Lutheran University, designing her course to encompass a variety of genres including Pilates Mat, Yoga and Ballet Fitness. As a master teacher of Pilates Mat, Tania has instructed Pilates for many dance studios, focusing on technique specific to their trade. She is owner of BeFit with Tania, instructing a variety of fitness classes, inclusive with mini-trampoline fitness, tap & dance fitness, Pilates Mat, Yoga for Sport and Flow Yoga. Tania was also a Group Fitness instructor for one of the largest chain gyms in southern California for 10 years, amongst many other gyms. Tania recently retired from the dance and fitness industries to focus on the composition this book. This is Tania's first publication as an author, in hopes of the opportunity for many more.